The Cover Illustration

There have been many inquires about the cover illustration of this book. For anyone that is interested, here is the story behind the cover...

The illustration is a representation of Adam and Eve in the Garden of Eden about to engage in marital intimacy. The snakes represent the demons of sexual perversion approaching to pervert human intimacy. The larger snake on Eve's leg is satan, attempting to enter into Eve before Adam does. The bitten fruit on the ground is there to show that perversion contaminated human intimacy after man had initially disobeyed The Creator. The fire represents the demons coming up out of hell, but also represents The LORD's consuming fire and His plan to destroy evil and to purify humankind once again.

Every aspect of this book was inspired by The LORD. When I asked Him for the cover, what you have seen is the vision that He showed me. I really struggled when I first saw the completed illustration. I knew that many "church folk" would have a problem with it. I tried in every way that I could to have the artist conceal the shocking nudity of the beautiful bodies of Adam and Eve, **without** compromising the vision. It was not possible. The Father finally gave me peace when He helped me to understand that the cover not only has a message in it, but it also appeals to those who are struggling with the very issues that this book addresses.

I did purposefully blur the illustration on the front cover to tone down the sensuality of it at least some, but truthfully, those who really want to be helped and those who want to help others are not bothered by the provocativeness of the cover. They understand the reality of sexual perversion and the necessity to try to hide no longer, our need for deliverance. If how this issue has been handled in the church in the past were effective, wouldn't we be getting better results?

Perhaps it is time to give the platform to real people, with real testimonies, for a real deliverance to help educate the Body of Christ on a topic that most Pastors are obviously too uncomfortable, or are not properly equipped, to deal with. Consider those who have fallen recently; look at the epidemic of sexual perversion in the church; look at the divorce rate; look at how ineffective we have been in influencing sexual purity in government and society. *It is time that we awake from our slumber...*

THE SPIRITS OF SEXUAL PERVERSION
Reference Book
2013 Edition

By Prophetess

Laneen "Dr. Intimacy" Haniah

Creative Solutions R BEST

The Spirits of Sexual Perversion Reference Book, 2013 Edition
Copyright © 2004, 2011, 2013 by Laneen A. Haniah
Library of Congress Control Number: 2013900865
ISBN: 978-0-9794210-6-8
Creative Solutions R BEST, LLC. www.creativesolutionsrbest.com

Unless otherwise indicated, all Scripture quotations are taken from the Holy Bible, New Living Translation *(NLT)*, copyright © 1996. Used by permission of Tyndale House Publishers, Inc., Wheaton, Illinois 60189. All rights reserved.

"Scripture quotations marked *(AMP)* are taken from the Amplified® Bible, Copyright © 1954, 1958, 1962, 1964, 1965, 1987 by The Lockman Foundation. Used by permission. (www.Lockman.org)"

Scripture quotations marked *(KJV)* are taken from the Holy Bible, Kings James Version. The KJV is part of the United States public domain and may be copied and quoted without restriction.

Scripture quotations marked *(MSG)* are taken from The Message, copyright © 1993, 1994, 1995, 1996, 2000, 2001, 2002. Used by permission of NavPress Publishing Group. All rights reserved.

All Hebrew and Greek Definitions have been taken from Crosswalk.com, Bible Study Tools Page. ©Copyright 1995-2004, Crosswalk.com. All rights reserved. The definitions used are part of the United States Public domain and may be copied and quoted without restriction.

MERRIAM-WEBSTERCOLLEGIATE.COM has been used to retrieve all definition quotations. (www.Merriam-WebsterCollegiate.com) copyright © 2004 by Merriam-Webster, Incorporated. Included within Collegiate.com is the version quoted within the text: Merriam-Webster's Collegiate Dictionary, Eleventh Edition copyright © 2003 by Merriam-Webster, Incorporated.

Any definition that is not placed within quotations is an originally coined definition by the author, Laneen A. Haniah. Such definitions are considered derived from her personal knowledge as a literary intellectual; Yahweh's wisdom given to her as a gift.

Disclaimer: The title "Dr. Intimacy" is a spiritual nick-name and is not intended to suggest that Prophetess Laneen Haniah has a doctorate or medical degree of any kind. Her credentials have been earned in The Kingdom of YHWH GOD, as opposed to an educational institution. However, an educational degree is currently pending.

All rights reserved under international copyright law. No part of this publication may be reproduced, stored in a retrieval system, or transmitted in any form or by any means – for example, electronic, photocopy, recording – without the prior written permission of the author. The only exception to this rule would be the use of brief quotations for the purpose of printed reviews, or for ministerial or personal use.

Acknowledgements

I thank **my first husband Emmanuel Haniah** for being a friend to me and a good father to our children. You helped me push greatness out, and I could not have written my first book without you. I will always be grateful to you in spite of the course on which we ended up.

I thank **my children** Ja'Keim, Nebiyah, Benjamin, Judah, Zechariah, Mi'Kara and Anayvah for patiently enduring while I poured myself into this ministry. I will make it up to you, but more importantly, Yahweh will reward you!

I thank **my Mom, Gail Wilson**. You gave me my love for writing and helped me to develop this anointing. Thanks Mom, I love you.

To **my big sister Karmina Dai**, who calls me the older sister (*smile*). You have encouraged and supported me all my life long so consistently and without fail. You have been more than just a sister; you are a true friend.

To **my little sister Jamila Wilson**, Sergeant Hungry: I thank you for all your support and the laughter you bring into my life. See you in two weeks kid!

To **Dainelle Brown,** who never stopped until she found me and with her own resources sowed this book into the lives of those in need.

To **Prophetess Ginger "Trouble Maker" Taylor**, who made trouble for the devil when she drew my assignment out of hibernation.

Also to some **leaders that have inspired me** either with their testimony or their support: The Late Bishop Moylan Jackson and his widow Valerie Jackson, Prophet Andre Cook, Prophetess Juanita Bynum, Pastor Donnie McClurkin, Prophet Todd Hall, Apostle Diane Clark, Minister Nadira Lewis, Evangelist Marilyn Swanigan, Pastors Brenda and Tommy Todd, Elder Garry Cooper, Pastors Terrance and April Kenan, Prophetess Ginger Taylor and most of all Elder Gail T. Wilson, my Mom.

Lastly, to **my dearest friend Mr. Otis Tucker, Sr.** Yahweh sent you to protect me when I no longer cared to protect myself. Your friendship has remained faithful in my darkest moments. Thank you so much. *All things work together for the good of those that Love the Lord and are the called according to His purpose.*

Foreword

It is not by coincidence that God has picked someone like Prophetess Laneen Haniah to bring deliverance through, **"The Spirits of Sexual Perversion Reference Book"** in an area that has become a hidden struggle in so many lives. We have become professionals at hiding; we are not realistic in our approach when dealing with sexual perversion. We've allowed the enemy to use us to judge the heart of others, not searching our own hearts and allowing God to reveal the blind deception fostering our own struggle(s).

After reading this book, you will soon realize that God loves you very much and that He sees what no one else can see. He wants to provide a way of escape for you, if you are seeking deliverance from being trapped in a circle of thoughts that form patterns of sinful behavior. I think it's important to know that satan is not limited by your title, prestige, knowledge or education. Without the wisdom of God's Word, you can continue to live your life with a veil over your eyes – thinking that these spirits of sexual perversion have no real effect on you or the people around you.

"Dr. Intimacy" has done an excellent job demonstrating that you can be both voluntarily and involuntarily exposed to these spirits. She reveals to you the understanding that each of these spirits has a specific assignment and that they seek to destroy you and your relationship with God. Once you have this understanding, it will awaken you from a false sense of hope, as you say to yourself, *"I am OK."; "This is just how I am."*

It is sad to say that although there are many people in need of deliverance from these spirits, they are afraid to confront or even admit the problem that they have. Through sharing her experiences, Prophetess Haniah opens up a dark and painful part of her life that allows you to see the entrances used by these spirits, and how they can follow you from generation to generation. Once you understand how these spirits affect your worship, you will never be the same. It will make you see yourself as you really are *"in desperate need of a Savior!"*

I cannot express how much I have personally been transformed by the truth in the revelations that God has given my friend, Prophetess Laneen Haniah, appropriately called "Dr. Intimacy". I pray that she will continue to allow God to use her to expose the powers of darkness so that many more lives will be transformed and saved through her obedience.

Minister Nadira A. Lewis
CEO/Founder of Inner Beauty Girlz
www.innerbeautygirlz.info

Table of Contents

Autograph Page	i
Cover Illustration	ii
Title Page	iv
Publication Information	v
Acknowledgements	vi
Foreword by Nadira Lewis	vii
Table of Contents	viii
Dedication	x
Preface – The Challenge Writing This Book	xi
Introduction: A Note from the Doctor	**1**
Chapter 1: I Understand What You're Going Through	6
Poem: What Do You See When You Look At Me?	**18**
Chapter 2: Why Did God Create Sexual Intimacy?	19
Break Free In Intimacy	**31**
Chapter 3: How Did Sexual Intimacy Become So Perverse?	33
The Devil Wants to Steal Your Worship!	**39**
Chapter 4: A Special Word for Married and Engaged Couples	43
Guidelines for Marital Sexual Purity	**49**
Have the Best Sex of Your Life!	**61**
Chapter 5: A Warning to Believers and the 'So-Called Sanctified'	64
Are You A Virgin or Did You Marry As One?	**69**
Chapter 6: Defining Sexual Perversion	71
A Prayer of Victory for You!	**80**
Chapter 7: Fornication	81
The Myth of "Premarital Sex"	**91**
Chapter 8: Masturbation	101
Do Chemical Reactions in the Body Play a Part in Sexual Sin?	**115**
Chapter 9: Adultery	117

Table of Contents *continued*

Christian Women and Adultery	**127**
Chapter 10: Incest	131
The Spirit of Incest in Organizations	**140**
Chapter 11: Homosexuality	143
Intersexuality	**159**
Chapter 12: Prostitution	165
The Prostitute and Her Redeemer	**175**
Chapter 13: Pornography (Sexual Fantasy)	179
Reclaiming Your Spiritual Vision	**190**
Chapter 14: Rape (Sexual Abuse)	197
The Unsung Victims of Sexual Abuse	**214**
Chapter 15: Bestiality	219
The Desensitization of Society	**225**
Chapter 16: Promiscuity	228
The Number One Cause of Divorce is Marriage	**238**
Chapter 17: Sexual Lust (Lasciviousness)	244
Three Steps to Disempowering Lust in Your Life!	**256**
Chapter 18: Incubus and Succubus – Sex Demons of the Night	263
Divorce the Devil – Get Away from Your Abuser!	**276**
Chapter 19: The Conclusion of the Matter	279
A Final Prayer	**302**
Epilogue: Start a New Life Today!	303
Your Personal Notes *(blank pages)*	306
STDs: Sexually Transmitted Demons	311
Poem: I Am Victoriously Free!	**312**
Contact Information	313

Dedicated To

This book is dedicated to My Confidant, My Counselor, My Comforter, My Hero, My Lover, My Healer, My Mentor, My Covering, My King, My Partner, My Best Friend and My True Lover – **Yeshua (Jesus Christ) My Lord and Savior, My Savior and Lord**. I have finally learned that there is none like You and no one else can touch my heart like You do. Your love is the greatest love. You Adonai chose and ordained me, although I'd been rejected by man. You are my Everything Lord. Thank You for writing this book through my hands and redeeming my life.

Preface - The Challenge Writing This Book

I completed the first version of this book in February of 2004 entitled, ***"The Spirits of Sexual Perversion Handbook"***. I can remember how I felt when I received the call from The Spirit to write it. I had always wanted to write and publish a book. That has been my goal since I was a little girl, but my notion was to write imaginative novels. I did not intend to lay my life bare; all of my most shameful sins; from the most painful seasons of my life; in a platform that was open to a great deal of scrutiny. Not to mention, it was a very trying time of my life. I was six months pregnant with my fifth child at the time, and all of my children were very young.

Now I look back on the difficulty of that first calling to write the book and almost long for it. Those circumstances seem ideal compared to the ones that I faced when receiving the call to re-write the book for the version that you now hold in your hand. During the first undertaking, I was married, and although my husband and I had a very troubled marriage, I can say most assuredly that he was supportive when it came to my writing that book. His direct support in writing it, and the comfort of having a husband to cover me when I showed the world my scars, was invaluable. I am certain that I would not have written the book, had I not been married.

In April of 2009, my life began a dramatic, downward spiral when I became aware that one of my children had been sexually violated by a family member. My marriage was hanging on by a thread already, and that thread snapped quickly as the trauma we faced with our child revealed the **"utter nothingness"** of our relationship. After pouring my life out for the deliverance of others in the area of sexual perversion, The LORD had refused to answer my one greatest prayer. *"Father, please protect my children from ever being sexually violated..."* I prayed it almost every day for 10 years consistently, and when my prayer was not answered, I soon stopped praying.

At the deterioration of my marriage and family and having been emotionally cut off from the source of my strength – the intense prayer life that had become non-existent – I found myself in a place that I never, ever thought I would be in. I found myself doing things that I never, ever thought the *Born-Again-Sanctified-Preaching-Me* would do. My husband

and I would have previously tackled such issues *together* in prayer, but he too was in a fallen place at the time. I had no church home, no solidified ministry covering, no close friends and no great relationship with extended family. The devil had me right where he wanted me: wounded and isolated in a dark place, without weapons, protection or even a voice to cry for help.

After 11 years of victory over the life that I had formerly lived, I had fallen into the pit of sexual sin once again. The devastation of falling was exceedingly more burdensome to me than the trauma to my child or even my divorce, which took place about a year after our family's tragedy. I hated myself for falling. I was tormented by the letters and testimonies that were still coming in regularly. *"Dear Prophetess Haniah, you changed my life..." "Dear Dr. Intimacy, after reading your book I can say I am finally FREE..." "Dear Laneen, before you came to preach at my church I was bound..."* I wanted to die, and I mean that literally – I was suicidal at times. The hand of The Father kept me from being completely consumed by the darkness that had overcome me.

When I wrote the first book, I had so many experiences to share. Before I became a leader in The Body of Christ, I had dibbed and dabbed in nearly every form of sexual vice concocted. I was "experienced" to say the least. But that was ALL IN MY PAST. I was SO PROUD that I could talk about those things as what *I used to do*. I had so much compassion for people caught up in the circumstances that *I used to face before I was sanctified*. I was an icon of hope and restoration – seemingly the perfect marriage, the perfect family and the perfect testimony, with a perfect record!

As I meditated on the destruction of ME and the desecration of the story that had captivated so many people, that is when it hit me – I had made the ministry all about **MY STORY**. I was such a perfect icon of deliverance that my story was out-shining **GOD'S GLORY**! And while I basked in my boasting that those were all things that *I used to do*, I failed to realize that I could not even relate to the people that The LORD had really called me to. I am a leader that is called to leaders. I am not called to the streets where *I used to do* those things. I am called to The Church, to the Body of Christ where *people are currently doing* those things!

We are all commissioned to preach The Gospel to the world and be living epistles. However, my specific calling is to cleanse and deliver those that are lost within the church. As a Prophet, I am called to my co-laborers in The Body of Christ and to those that lead them. Yet, I looked down my nose at so many of those struggling saints and leaders. It was OK to struggle as an unbeliever, backslider or babe in Christ. But for the mature Christian and church leader, I had an almost **zero tolerance policy**. *How could you preach with such gifting and fire, then turn around and get a congregant pregnant? How could you preach against homosexuality when you practice it? How could you be getting high before service and drunk afterward? How could you, how dare you! How dare you have that church! How dare you stand in that pulpit! God is going to judge you!!!*

And so went on my angry, self-righteous ranting of judgment, until one day – *I was one of them.* It took quite some time for me to come to grips with the fact that pride sent me crashing down into my own vomit. Not having the revelation of *'why'* I had fallen; I stopped ministering and withdrew into defeat. I was like Jonah and said out of my own mouth, *"I don't ever want to preach again."* And, I so sincerely meant it when I said it. I became one of those people that violated my own zero tolerance policy and therefore declared myself unworthy for the work of ministry; especially in the area of sexual perversion.

As you can imagine, under such bondage and condemnation, writing a book entitled, ***"The Spirits of Sexual Perversion Reference Book"*** is the last thing that I wanted to do. It was done under duress; out of sheer obedience to The Spirit of The Most High. However, I can honestly say that it was not until I started re-writing this book that I finally began to understand what had happened to me and the reason for it. I can now say that I am better than I was before. Since I am better, this book is better. It is not only about ME or MY STORY any longer. It is compassionate toward everyone and not just those "I deem worthy" of compassion. It is straightforward and challenging to those that don't believe and to those that do; to those that are babes and those that are seemingly mature.

When I first started writing this book, I thought I would just be going through the original *(old)* book and editing out my story while adding a few updates. But as I wrote, it became apparent to me that I could not put new wine into old wineskins. Nothing about me, my life or my understanding of my assignment is the same. I am new, and this book is new too. It has a new name, a new theme, a new cover design, many new chapters and rich new revelations, but the foundation of The LORD's truth about intimacy in worship and sexual perversion is still the same.

As in the case with King David, many that saw my shameful behavior have scorned and mocked me. Many have already judged me doomed for hell. My ugly scars are apparent. The devastation of my former land of milk and honey is laid bare for everyone to marvel at. I have no more story, no more perfect family, no more perfect marriage and no more perfect record. But I do have something that I did not have before; something that makes me exceedingly better than I ever could have been when I was so "perfect". I have a revelation of YAHWEH'S **PERFECT** LOVE.

His perfect Love is completely unconditional. It is not affected by anything I could ever do. It is powerful enough to cover all of my sins and only grows stronger when I am weak. Prior to this season of my life, I could not share the love that I had never learned how to receive. But in learning to embrace His "in spite of", Perfect Love; what I now have is the ability to love you, like never before. And now I hear the voice of the Savior saying to me,

"Laneen Haniah, do you love Me more than these?"
"Yes, Lord," I reply, *"You know I love You."*
"Then feed My lambs," Yeshua tells me.
Yeshua repeats the question. *"Laneen Haniah, do you love Me?"*
"Yes, Lord," I say, *"You know I love You."*
"Then take care of My sheep," Yeshua says.
A third time He asks me, *"Laneen Haniah, known as Dr. Intimacy, do you love Me?"*
I am hurt that He asks me the question a third time. I say to Him, *"Lord, You know everything. You know that I love You."*
And so He says to me, *"Then feed My sheep."* (John 21:15-17)

In the Power of His Love,
Prophetess Laneen A. Haniah
Known to the world as "Dr. Intimacy"

Introduction

A Note from the Doctor

PLEASE READ, VERY IMPORTANT GROUND LAYING INFORMATION FOR YOUR SUCCESSFUL COMPLETION OF THIS BOOK!

Why Did I Write This Book?

I am a person who is not ashamed to share the 'test' in my 'TESTimony'. For this reason, The LORD has given me a mandate to expose the spirits of sexual perversion in the earth and help lead His people to deliverance. My number one heart's desire for this book is to see people restored back to true relationship with, and intimate worship of, YAHWEH, the True and Living God. My second greatest desire concerning this work is to see people totally set free from sexual addictions and perversion. My third greatest desire concerning this work is that it would create an opportunity for the total destruction of the shroud of secrecy concerning sexual sin and addictions that exist in the world and in the church. It is this secrecy that has empowered satan so greatly in this area and has kept people in bondage for so long.

I never fathomed the wealth of wisdom and revelation that the Holy Spirit was going to pour into me concerning this topic. I have discovered during the writing of this book that there is much deception concerning sexual perversion. Most people have not attained a precise understanding of exactly what sexual perversion is and are subsequently bound to continue in a defeated life full of failure in this area. There are numerous people, sinners and saints alike, that struggle desperately with sexual perversion. In most instances, those bound by sexual perversion feel powerless, lost and trapped.

There is no need to feel powerless anymore though because many questions concerning sexual perversion are answered in this book. If you are a person that is now struggling or has ever struggled with sexual sin; if you were exposed to sexual sin as a child or as an adult whether voluntarily or involuntarily; if you have ever been raped, molested or sexually abused; if you have a spouse that has been unfaithful to you or has an addiction; if you live a life of promiscuity that you just cannot seem to break free of; this book is for you!

Did you know that you can still be bound by spirits of sexual perversion even if you are a sanctified, Spirit-filled Christian, a married person and/or a person who is not actually *performing acts* of sexual sin? Learning this was one of the most eye-opening elements of this book for me. Please listen to me, no matter how faithful your Christian walk; you NEED to read this book. It contains wisdom imparted directly from the mind of The LORD and is a vital resource for **EVERY BELIEVER**.

I see this book as a fundamental necessity for every person that will ever have to confront the spirits of sexual perversion on any level. Understanding The LORD's true purpose for sexual intimacy and satan's true purpose for sexual perversion are the foundational truths that have eluded so many of us for so long, but now these truths have been disclosed. I believe that every essential revelation has been provided or presented in this manuscript for anyone that is truly serious about developing deeper intimacy with The Father and those who want to help others to do so.

The LORD has impressed upon my spirit the urgency of getting this information into the minds of His children. The Body of Christ and this nation of the United States are under attack. Our greatest enemy is not terrorism; our greatest enemy is sexual perversion. Sexual perversion can destroy as no other enemy can. Therefore, we must arm ourselves and declare the perverting of our nation and the perverting of The Church as an act of war! This book contains the war plan that will help lead us to victory!

As you read on, you will see for yourself that this book is very intimate and for mature audiences only. I openly expose the former works of sin in my life because I want you to be able to identify with The Father's grace and deliverance in my life. The Bible clearly states that we overcome satan by the Blood of the Lamb and the word of our testimony *(Rev 12:11)!* **I choose to be an overcomer** and want to help others transform into overcomers, as well. Yahweh God has my full cooperation to use me as a living witness. As I stated earlier, my goal is that many be delivered from sexual sin and addiction and develop an understanding of true intimacy.

How to Get the Most Out of This Book

In this book, we are going to learn a lot about how and when sexual perversion entered the earth, the spirits of sexual perversion and how they operate. I tried to write this book as an easy read but at the same time cover all of the necessary elements. Depending on your level of Bible knowledge, this book may be a little more difficult to understand at times, but I implore you not to skim through it or skip ahead. It is critically important that we understand satan's strategy, in order to successfully move forward in the deliverance process. We must build a solid foundation of knowledge.

To help you successfully read through this book, I suggest that you read slowly, somewhere that there are little to no distractions, at a time that you are very alert. Read through certain sections repeatedly, as needed, for a full understanding. Furthermore, always, ALWAYS pray beforehand for understanding **every time you pick up this book**. This is an effective prayer to say before reading, and I encourage you to print it out and use it: *"Father God, please anoint me to read, comprehend, write and retain for full understanding and application of all that is in this book. In Yeshua's (Jesus') name, Amen."*

It would also be a great idea to read this book with a partner, sponsor or as part of a group study. If you are suffering from a serious stronghold, allow yourself to be held accountable by one of the above. A ***sponsor*** should be someone that has no current sexual strongholds in their life and a person that has read or will commit to reading this book to help you apply the principles in it. A ***partner*** can be anyone that currently has an issue in this area and will read the book with you and commit to understanding and applying the knowledge found within it. A ***study group*** would be a group of people that will read the book together on a committed schedule and meet once or twice weekly to discuss what they've read, share their experiences, pray and encourage one another. A group leader is helpful but not necessary as the Holy Spirit will gladly handle the leadership role by rising up in an available vessel at each meeting.

Someone that you are currently or have recently engaged in sexual sin with should not be your partner. Even if it is your best friend, you need to choose someone else to partner with. The exception to this would be married couples, those engaged to be married or you and the person both being a part of a larger group study. Spouses and engaged couples should always partner with one another when possible. It is very important that each partner has a personal copy of this book and that they read it during the same time period! I strongly urge married couples to agree together to abstain from sexual activity during the course of studying this book. *(The reason for this will be covered in chapter four.)*

If you are a married or engaged couple that has been involved in sexual sin, try to partner together as connected to a larger **_couples study group_** for added strength and accountability. If there is no group study near you – start one! Perhaps a local book club or the singles, married or recovery ministry at your church would enjoy doing a group study of this book once you bring it to their attention. If none of these resources are available, asking some of your peers to purchase the book and read it with you is an option, as well. Whichever route you choose, be sure to test the fruit of the partnership. If the partnership is producing good fruit, and you are both making progress, then continue in it. But if the partnership is producing bad fruit, it may be necessary to partner with someone else or read the book alone – *even if you are part of a couple.* Remember that you always have the Holy Spirit as your ultimate Partner and Teacher!

Throughout the reading of this book keep a journal with you. As you read, write down things that you want to remember or any revelations the Holy Spirit may give you concerning your own life. There are a few blank pages beginning on page 306 to get you started, but try to keep a dedicated journal with you at all times when reading this book. You should also purchase and keep with you the coinciding **"The Spirits of Sexual Perversion Workbook"**. *(Coming soon, watch out for it on my website!)*

As you read the book, you are going to notice that some scriptures are quoted and some are only referenced. Scriptures that are referenced but not quoted are referenced only for validation and extra study. I did not quote them because they are not essential to the revelations in this book. I, therefore, suggest that you do not look these scriptures up while you are reading the text because it may cause you to lose the train of thought that is being portrayed. If you want to study these extra scriptures, it would be more advantageous for you to look them up at the end of each section or chapter, instead of during the reading of the body of the text.

For the most part, I only use Jesus' originally given Hebrew name, which is Yeshua[1] (yeh-o-shoo-ah). I also use The <u>Name</u> of the Father God Almighty, which according to Exodus 6:3[2], in the first and original King James Version of the Bible, is Yahweh/Yah (YHWH). He is also known by Elohim, El Shaddai, Adonai, El Elyon and many other wonderful names. Yah says that we ought to exalt **His Name**, and this is why I use His Name Yahweh many times throughout the book. Also, I have purposefully spelled satan's name with a lowercase 's' throughout the book. I will even break literary rules to defame him. He gets no honor in my life! *This is just FYI (smile).*

OK... So, I know this book is lengthy, and that might be intimidating for those of you that are short on time or not avid readers. However, the truth is that reading just 10 pages per day will take you through the meat of the book in about 30 days. DO NOT let satan – as he surely will try – stop you from completing this book. It cannot help you just lying around somewhere! So let's get started!

IT IS TIME TO GO DEEPER IN INTIMACY WITH YAHWEH GOD, YOUR FATHER AND CREATOR, AND FINALLY WALK IN PURPOSE!!!

---

[1] Jesus' originally given Hebraic name has a variety of different spellings. This is my preferred spelling of those that I found listed in my research. The same is true for the name of the True God Yahweh.
[2] Also Ps 83:18, Isa 12:2 & 26:4

Chapter 1

I Understand What You're Going Through

I want you to know that I am writing this book because I have been there, and I understand what you are going through.

My Story Begins[3]

Someone recently asked me, *in a rather smug way I might add*, why I am qualified to do what I do in ministry. I just laughed, as I rehearsed in my mind the things you are about to read in this chapter. I am so glad that you are holding this book in your hand right now. I know that it is by divine appointment that you are doing so. We are about to take a journey together through the wisdom and insight of God the Father, into a place where deliverance lives. We will have to travel through some dense forests and some dark caves, but there shall lay a well-lit path before us at all times that will lead us into the open fields of victory that are awaiting our arrival.

As you read this book, I want you to feel as if you are sitting down and talking with a trusted confidant. I am here to take you by the hand and escort you where you have been longing to go. I am here to encourage and to guide you. I pray that the love that I have for you reach you wherever you are, as I personally mentor you in learning to hear and follow the guidance of the Holy Spirit. Instead of just reading a book, may you have a total life-transforming experience of deliverance, with someone whom you will come to call a friend.

---

[3] Before continuing, I'm going to ask that if you have not already done so, please go back and read the *Preface* and *Doctor's Note*. This is very important.

First, let me share with you some of the experiences that began my preparation for the *Insights from Dr. Intimacy Ministries*. I was once bound by numerous spirits of sexual perversion. Sexual perversion has been a part of my life for as long as I can remember. Before I was even conceived, sexual perversion was already the lot assigned me by the devil through the sins of my forefathers. Sexual sin is a generational curse that can be traced back in my ancestry as far back as my great-great grandparents, although I am sure it reaches back much further.

Any person who has ancestors that have been corrupted by sexual perversion, will almost always, at a very young age, be exposed to and contaminated by sexual perversion as well. This is how the devil attempts to secure his place in a person's family bloodline. I was no exception to this rule. My parents struggled terribly with spirits of sexual perversion, as did the rest of all of the family members that were in my life. Sexually perverse acts were commonplace in my life and surroundings. Beginning at the age of two, I was regularly molested by a lesbian babysitter. Then shortly afterward, I was raped by one of my male relatives. I suppose that I could have overcome these incidents with the right support system. Unfortunately though, all of the adults in my life were too busy getting high, drunk and indulging in their own sexual fetishes to even notice what was happening to me. These two incidents of molestation and my living environment were a jumpstart into a life full of sexual perversion.

My childhood memories include watching pornography; seeing people have sex in front of me; lying in bed next to people who were masturbating and being instructed on how to do it to myself; playing with sex toys and being casually and haphazardly touched in my intimate places, by male and female relatives, just as a matter of habit. I certainly became a product of the environment in which I grew up. I started masturbating, developed a fond interest in pornography, took on a homosexual nature and attempted to have intercourse all starting at the age of five. If you can believe it or not, my greatest desire at the age of five was to see a male's private parts! I was absolutely obsessed with seeing a man's "pee-pee" and tenaciously pursued my goal.

Two of the greatest factors in fostering sexual addictions are rejection and insecurity. I suffered greatly from both. I can remember even at the age of four when I was in preschool that the other children did not like me. I don't know what it was about me that caused them to dislike me so much, but I was a misfit and an outcast before I even knew how to spell my own name. From the time I was six, other girls were calling me "lesbo" and "dyke". Even more detrimental than these two factors though, there is a third – A NEGATIVE SELF-PERCEPTION. Life taught me this lesson well starting at a very young age.

When I was about six, my Mom tried to clean up her life. She decided to get married, but the same demons of perversion, rejection and insecurity followed us right into our new lives. She did try to choose carefully, but Mom always had a natural inclination toward picking the wrong men. She chose someone that she believed to be a God-fearing, family man. However, he turned out to be yet another one of sexual perversion's helpless victims. Consequently, by his hands, sexual perversion, abuse and molestation continued on in my household behind closed doors. *(You can read more about this in the "Insights from Dr. Intimacy" article at the end of chapter 14.)*

It was during that period of time, when I was at the age of eight, that I was struck with a terminal illness; an illness that doctors stated had no known cause other than the body's reaction to extreme stress. The illness crippled my body, and the medication that I was taking caused my face to look funny. Due to these physical deformities, bad matters only got worse. I had already been suffering from rejection and bullying, but from that point forward, I was viewed as an absolute freak by my peers.

The doctors eventually were successful in bringing the disease that I had under control, but the medications had ravaged my body and greatly damaged my reproductive system. I was crushed when I was told at the age of 10 that I would not be able to have children. Getting married and having a beautiful family one day had been my biggest dream. I wanted to make the type of family that I did not have, and it seemed that opportunity was robbed from me.

The list of influences and abuses could go on and on, but I mention these incidents only to point out that spirits of sexual perversion had their place in my life at a very early age. By the time I hit my teen-age years, I was **out of control**. I graduated from fondling myself; to inserting things into my body; to having unprotected sex with real, live men. I didn't care about my life or health at that point. I was looking for love and acceptance in all the wrong places, and I was determined to prove those doctors wrong – I wanted to have a baby!

At first I thought sex fun, but not long after, I was sick and tired of being a slave to sex. Sexual perversion had completely taken over my life, and it did not take long for me to begin to feel as if I would never be free. I believe the depth of my sexual sins is why The LORD has chosen me to write this book, and although this book is Bible-based and written from a Christian perspective, it is not just for Christians. This book is not only biblical, it is also practical and real and is therefore for anyone who just like I was, is sick and tired of being a slave to sexual perversion. Even before I was a Born Again Believer, I deeply desired to change my way of living.

Many people, like me back then – Believers and unbelievers alike – despise the sexually perverse acts that they commit. They despise themselves for continually indulging in these acts knowing how they will feel afterward. There are some sexually perverse people that do greatly enjoy their sins for a moment, but there are others that do not even get momentary pleasure out of the acts. There is no pleasure in it for them at all. Most people just feel *driven* to do the things that they do and seem unable to stop. *Why do people do what they do not want to do?*

That is what it was like for me...
- ✓ I hated my life. I hated the way I lived. I hated what I represented. I had been raped on three different occasions because of my reputation and the way I carried myself.
- ✓ I knew that I was destroying myself. I knew that I was assisting to destroy others as well. I knew that there would be no happiness or peace for me if I continued on the way that I was living. Yet, I just felt helpless to stop.

- ✓ I knew about the risk of unwanted pregnancy. After finally realizing my dream of having a child, I got pregnant several times not wanting the baby and had an abortion on one of these occasions.
- ✓ I knew about sexually transmitted diseases. I had contracted them more than once. I knew about HIV/AIDS. I had been tested many times and had even once been scared to death after being raped by a man who carried the disease.
- ✓ I knew about the likelihood of never being loved by a man because of my lifestyle...

Yet, none of these grim facts successfully deterred me from my destructive behavior. Sexual perversion was all that I knew; I just *did not **know** how to be any other way. (Read more about my young adult life in my book, "STDs: Sexually Transmitted Demons". It is a great book for young people, new Believers and those involved with youth.)*

New Life and Renewed Hope, But...

After I gave my life to Yeshua, I thought things would change for me. I was seriously in love with my Savior and understood the unrighteousness of sexual perversion. I was sure that since I went to church and shouted and danced and spoke in tongues that I would give up my old lifestyle. Oh, how wrong I was though! I was ready to give up the devil, but the devil was not ready to give up me. I came to church and fell on the floor and left the church and fell right back into the bed of sin. After truly giving my best to The LORD and still not being able to break free of sexual perversion, the devil had convinced me that even the power of the Almighty God Himself could not change me.

I felt so hopeless. I wanted so desperately to serve my Lord, but every time I fell into sexual sin, I was so laden with guilt that it hindered me from seeking Him. I was convinced that He wanted nothing to do with me. There is no other sin tantamount to sexual perversion in its ability to make a person feel so utterly filthy. I thought I was too dirty to come into the presence of my Most Holy God, and thus my relationship with Him was like a roller coaster. ***Every time I*** *messed up, I would backslide into the world; and every time the world messed me up, I would slide back into the church.*

I wanted help, but people in the church either judged and despised me or wanted to lay with me! I did not get any help from the preacher either. Those that have never really struggled with sexual sin will never understand what a prison it truly is, and they therefore, tend to lack compassion. I got so tired of those indignant preachers standing behind the pulpit condemning to hell everyone that commits sexual vice, ignorantly declaring, *"You would stop if you wanted to!"* Only Jesus and I really knew how many nights I had begged and cried out for a change in my ways, but I was just so bound that I could not get out that easily. I thought I would be trapped forever. *Does this remind you of yourself or maybe someone you know?*

I really feel blessed to be able to write this book because the truth of the matter is sexual perversion is rampant not only among unbelievers but among churchgoers, as well. You would be surprised at how many of those little ol' "sanctified" mothers, dressed in all white, with skirts on down to the floor go home and masturbate; how many fire preaching bishops are cheating on their wives; how many prissy pastor's wives have gay sex partners; how many diligent deacons are having sex with their young daughters. I used to be naive about sexual perversion in the church, but similar spirits are attracted to one another. Because I went to church not yet delivered from these spirits, other Believers that carried these same spirits were drawn to me. I, therefore, experienced as much perversion in the church as I did in the world!

As a matter of fact, I encountered sexual perversion at the very first ministry that I came in contact with after giving my life to Christ. Coming into Christianity, I thought that Christian men would be different from worldly men, so my guard was down. There was a particular minister who was one of the leaders of the ministry that I had been fellowshipping with, and he was supposedly "mentoring" me at the time.

I developed a serious crush on this man. **Against God's counsel to me**, I let the guy know how I felt about him. His response to me was that he had another young lady that he was interested in but that he liked me more. The other young lady lived a good distance away in another state, and they had just begun their relationship. It thus seemed like a simple enough solution to me – break it off with her and get with me! I even suggested that he date us both. In pride, I thought for sure I could win his affections over "some chic" that was hundreds of miles away.

You have to understand that I was fresh out of the womb at that time, in my walk with The LORD. My umbilical cord had not even healed yet and let me tell you, I played right into the devils hands. **Rev'ren Playa** liked the idea of dating us both. He took me out on a date, led me on and played all kinds of mind games with me. What was interesting is that because I perceived him to be such a "Holy man of God", I had never once had any type of sexual thought about him at that time. I felt that to think of him in such a way would be disrespectful because he seemed to be so serious about The LORD. However, the night that he told me that I looked like I had kissable lips, everything changed. The sexual temptation alarm went off in my spirit, and it was on!

After a while of communicating with both me and the other girl, he decided that since he was *having such a hard time choosing* between the two of us, he was going to allow us to compete for him at a win-all-or-go-home dinner. (He was the true inventor of the TV show "*The Bachelor*"!) The plan was that he, I and "the competitor" would all dine together. Then he would make his decision based on... *Who knows?* This was to be done at a Passover dinner nonetheless!

I was a very competitive person, so I was definitely up for the game. He had told me prior that he did not believe in dating. His belief was that you should meet a person, know that they are your future spouse and get engaged for marriage immediately. So I was very excited about the competition because winning meant an automatic husband for me. This is the craziness that was going through my mind anyway (*laugh*).

I spent the only, little bit of money that I had from my fixed income to buy clothes and accessories for the evening. I practiced my feminine charms more every day as the event drew near, preparing for my "one night with the king". However, my hopes were suddenly thwarted. I believe the reality of what he was doing finally hit Rev'ren Playa as the day was approaching. You see as I was to find out later, the other young lady had no idea as to what had been going on. She was not aware of me or any competition.

He had been lying to us both, so he bailed out by calling me from work one day to tell me that he had good news. *"I have chosen my wife. I'm going to marry Diana."* He aloofly said to me. My heart dropped to the floor and shattered into a million pieces. I had just come out of an abusive, two-year relationship with a married alcoholic, and I had set my heart on marrying this *so-called* man of God that I was pursuing. I just wanted to have a happy life for a change. I wanted my dreams of having a family to come true. How dare he get my hopes up just to crush me?!

As he waited silently on the other end of the phone, after his announcement; I mustered up a few nice words to say, as I choked back the tears, but in my mind all I could think about was fighting back. I was so angry – angry at him, angry at me, angry at God. I had been walking with Yeshua for nearly seven months at that time and had been upright before Him in almost every way, but that day I just wanted to be **bad**. I pulled my *hoochie gear* out of the closet – clothes that I had not put on since the day I first called Jesus' name – then I got all sexy and went to the mall. I wanted some attention and affirmation. I wanted someone to whistle at me, call me 'Shorty', ask for my number, anything... **"Please, just let me know that I still got that appeal 'cuz' I don't think this Holiness thing is working!!!"** This is what I was thinking.

I am sure you have heard of 'God's timing', but did you know that the devil has timing too? I could not believe it when I ran into Rev Playa's daughter at the mall. She lived with him, and we were close in age. She asked me to come visit her at the house that night and have dinner with them. She had no idea what had happened, but I can't imagine that she could not see the evil in my eyes as I accepted her invitation. I'm sure she would have seen the horns atop my head if she had looked twice!

Anyway, to make a long story short, I went to their house and Rev Playa and I ended up alone that night. The daughter left the house and that was the worst thing that could have happened. I still had revenge on my mind, and the only thing I could think of to do to him at that time was to tease him. I knew that men hate to be teased sexually, and so I sat on the couch next to him in my sexy clothes – clothes that he had never seen me in before – and I laid the seduction on thick. It was not long before he was huffing and puffing and grunting and eagerly trying to finish what I had started.

Suddenly the realization of what I was doing hit me like a mac truck going 150 miles per hour on a highway. The way he was acting was the same way that all the men had acted. I was being set up by the devil, and suddenly I realized it! I had been sexually pure for four months. That was a huge accomplishment for me. I did not want to lose Jesus because we had grown so close. I did not want to cause this minister to be in sin. I just wanted to get out of there. I was so sorry for what I had started. I told him that I had to go. I kept trying to leave, but he was pulling me back. I told him that I did not want to do it, but he was like a possessed man at that point.

It was as if he did not even hear me or see me. I didn't know what to do. I knew that it was my fault that I was there, and I did not want to make a scene because his daughter had returned home by then and was in her room close by. I begged him to stop, but there was no daunting him. His body was set to do what he had in mind to do. So I just did what I had gotten accustomed to doing for the seven years that I had been sexually active. I turned over on my belly so I would not have to see his face; laid there numb and limp; withdrew all resistance; let him pleasure himself at my expense, and began the torment of self-hatred. I felt the guilt of a million sins all at once in that moment. I did not know how I could ever be restored after that.

We had actually been there on the couch for the entire night by that time, probably about six hours. When _he_ finally finished having sex, *(I truly was not a part of it)* the sun was cracking the sky. With the break of day, a new hope dawned in my soul. I remembered that Rev Playa had told me that if he ever had sex with a woman he would marry her. I think deep in my sub-conscious that had been on my mind all along, and at that memory my eyes widened with expectation. *Would he be my husband after all? Would he redeem me from the degradation of sexual perversion?*

I lay silently as he pushed himself off of me. I rolled onto the floor from the couch, carefully avoiding his eyes. I remained quiet. Drum rolls beat in my heart, as I waited for him to comment, but what came out of his mouth, I never expected. You see even though we were not going to have our "competition dinner" anymore, Diana was still on her way into town in just a few days. He had let me know a few times prior that Diana was a virgin, and that is what "gave her the advantage" over me. He wanted a virgin girl; not some used up single mother *(even though he had been married four times already)*! Yet still, I had hoped against hope that he would **choose me**. However, when he made the comment that I'm about to reveal, I understood just what he meant.

Finally gaining the courage to look at him, I watched him lean back on the couch and rub his belly in the same way that people recline in their chair after eating a big, delicious meal. Looking rather satisfied, obviously not experiencing any of the torment of guilt that I was, he sighed deeply, looked me in the eyes and said with a gentle smile, *"Now when Diana comes, I'll be alright."* And with those words, I knew most certainly that even as a Christian, I was still that same ol' slut that I had always been – there would never be deliverance for me. I got up and quietly readied myself to leave. He walked me to the bus, and I just wanted him to go away. *Couldn't he at least allow me to mourn my wounded pride and broken dreams privately?*

What I Never Learned in Church

After this incident occurred, I tried to get help. I went to the head of the ministry and talked the matter over with him. Not out of spite; I was just so scared. I did not want to lose my True Lover. Yeshua had been so good to me. How could I do this to Him? I cried and cried but avoided talking to The Father. I thought the ministry leader would help me be restored, but instead he blamed and rebuked me. He accused me of causing Rev Playa to fall, and I was eventually ostracized from the ministry – not even allowed to come back and fellowship with them anymore. By his assessment, I was trouble and not worth the hope of redemption. That simply said to me that The LORD did not want me anymore, and so I stopped pursuing Him all together.

Going full speed back into the world, my life was worse and more sexually perverse than it had ever been. The devil had me back in his camp and did not intend to let me get away ever again *(or so he thought.)* I remained wayward for eight months, and every time I tried to come back to the church, I encountered that same sexually perverse spirit in different church leaders. Single or married, young or old, pastor, elder, or minister; it did not matter who they were. I wanted counsel, and they wanted sex. It was like being trapped in a maze; I knew that there was a way out, but I just could not see it. Fortunately, I never stopped wanting The LORD back in my life, and He never stopped wanting me and so eventually, He Himself restored me. I thank Yeshua that His Spirit living in me was greater than the spirit that is in the world and that The Father will never leave nor forsake His children *(1 John 4:4, Heb 13:5)*!

I learned two important lessons though. First of all, I learned that there is a terrible veil of deception about sexual perversion in the church; and secondly, I learned that the church can be the worse place to go for counseling concerning sexual struggles! Very few people in the church want to be honest and just admit that they have been delivered or that they are struggling and need deliverance. The few daring souls that do "come out of the closet" are so persecuted that they often times become worse off than they were before they sought out help. Others that are in bondage observe this and opt to keep up the *appearance* of deliverance, instead of putting their necks on the line for the real deal.

When I would seek counsel concerning the sexual sins in my life, all I found was judgment, more perversion or uncomfortable stares with a quick offer to pray and change the subject. The wisdom in this book is the counsel that I was seeking back then. Though I had no man to teach me, the Holy Spirit Himself taught me what I longed to know, and now I am going to share with you what He taught me! Hallelujah!

As you continue to read on, you will discover the answer to the questions of why sex was created; how and why it was perverted; and what the danger is to those who may think they do not have a problem in this area. You will also learn a comprehensive definition for sexual perversion and how to assess each of its major demons. **Read every word** because it is very important that you understand the basic truths concerning sex and sexual perversion, in order to be totally delivered.

Throughout the book, I try to take nothing for granted. I do hope to appeal to Believers and non-believers as well. Therefore, the book is written with the 'total unbeliever', as well as the 'very spiritually mature, sanctified Believer' in mind. Having prior biblical knowledge will help, but no matter which level you are on, you can gain powerful insights and understanding from this book. This book is easy to follow, and I am confident that you will learn something that you did not know before that will cause you to think with a new perspective concerning sexual perversion and true intimacy.

Now you can get the help that you need without being persecuted. What you could not learn in church, you will learn in this book. This book is not full of judgment and wrath. I will truthfully say that it is full of some bitter and hard truths to swallow, but it is also full of compassion and understanding and some real **powerful information** and **practical answers** that can lead you to victory. I come to you as one who has been there. I know the way in, and now I know the way out. My heart's desire is for you to experience freedom, peace and the joy of deliverance from spirits of sexual perversion. Yeshua's deliverance power can set you **totally free** from sexual perversion and even erase the stain that gets left behind!

What Do You See When You Look at Me?

What do you see when you look at me?
A nasty girl, a freak – spending my life making men peak?
But you don't see the words that made my heart weak.
You don't see the hatred that made my life bleak.
Look more closely and please let me speak.

What do you see when you look at me?
A harlot and a whore? A slut who wants more?
But you don't see the abuse behind the closed door.
You don't see the child that none would adore.
Look more deeply, please I implore.

What do you see when you look at me?
A fool? A lust-filled cesspool, using every sex tool?
But you don't see my upbringing,
The teachings of my generational school.
You don't see the influences by which devised I this self-rule.
Take a second look cuz your judgment's not cool.

What do you see when you look at me?
A home-wrecker? A family divider?
A treacherous b%#tch, a black widow spider?
But you don't see the deceit,
The slick words of those lying tongue gliders.
You don't see the innocence,
The youth that was stolen by the many rough riders.
You might try to look again, but you're still an outsider.

What do you see when you look at me?
A hopeless case, irreconcilable defection?
A dangerous enemy devoid of direction?
But you don't see the rejection,
You don't know my loneliness or the lack of affection.

But thanks be to Yah that by Yeshua's resurrection,
I'm still His selection; by His Blood I have protection.
Despite your deflection, I will still receive perfection;
Because when all is said and done, I am yet His election!

What do I see when I look at me?
I see restoration, and I see victory!
What does Yah see when He looks at me,
That is all that matters, and He sees His glory!

Chapter 2

Why Did God Create Sexual Intimacy?

We will deal with this question first because the answer to this question will lay the foundation that we need for a deeper understanding of the entire matter.

I believe that the three greatest weaknesses of humanity, in the flesh, are: **1) The need to eat; 2) The need to sleep;** and **3) The urge to have sex.** I note these three needs to emphasize how the spirits of sexual perversion work. They take advantage of one of the greatest weaknesses of the flesh – our built-in desire to have sex.

Yahweh told man and woman in the book of Genesis to, *"...Be fruitful and multiply and replenish the earth... (Gen 1:28)"* There is of course spiritual significance to what He said to them on that day, but there is also natural, practical significance. In laymen's terms, The LORD was basically saying, *"I command you to have sex and lots of it!"* This may be a little hard to swallow because of our perception of sex. We generally think of sex as something forbidden, naughty or perverse. Let us consider it practically though.

In order for them to multiply *(in its most literal sense meaning to have children)* they would have to engage in intercourse to afford conception an opportunity. Then in order to **replenish** the earth, which is a tall order to fill, they would have to engage in intercourse often so that they might improve the likelihood of frequent conception. Another point to consider is the fact that when Yah gave this command people did not wear clothing. All of us, who are or once were sexually active, would probably agree that the absence of clothing often times stirs sexual desire. This is especially true if you are in a relationship with someone that you are highly attracted to and in love with. There is no reason to believe there were any exceptions to this basic instinct at the dawn of creation. Yahweh is a very deliberate God, and all of this was by no means a coincidence! Thus, the truth of the matter is that The LORD created us to frequently engage in and enjoy sexual intimacy.

What we have to realize is that because man was created in the image and likeness of The Lord God Almighty *(Gen 1:26)*, humanity was created in Holy Perfection. Everything about man *(and woman)* was good and pure at the time of creation, including the act of sex. But once sin entered into the earth, it perverted everything He had created on the earth.

You may be asking the question: How did sin enter into all of creation on earth considering that humanity alone committed sin? This is because all of creation on earth was under man's dominion. Once humanity became corrupt, all that we had dominion over became corrupt along with us. Sin had entered into man and corrupted us in our entirety. The corruption of sin caused us to be separated from Elohim the Creator and without that connection to I AM, all of creation and everything about it became subject to perversity and evil. That is one of the reasons why David says in the book of Psalms, *"I was shapen in iniquity, and in sin did my mother conceive me. (Ps 51:5, KJV)"* The act of sex is just another part of what was perverted by sin at the fall of humanity.

So now we understand that Yahweh actually ordained sexual intimacy and that **<u>sex is not bad</u>**, but we still need to understand why He implemented sexual intimacy as a part of the normal routine of humanity. First off, it is important to understand that everything that exists in the natural world, exists first in the spiritual world. The Bible teaches us that God is a Spirit and indicates that His Kingdom is a spiritual one *(John 4:24; 14:17; Mat 12:28, 16:26)*. The earth and all it entails, was created to be a natural and physical emulation of Yahweh's Spiritual Kingdom. That is why nature was made with such splendor and glorious detail, such precision and perfection. He has given us everything in the natural to help us understand something about His

Kingdom and the spirit realm, which is the realm of eternity and is also where the true existence of each and every one of us lives. As a part of this natural representation of Him and His Kingdom, Yah implemented sexual intimacy and marriage between man and woman to teach humanity something about the spirit realm. More specifically as far as sex and marriage is concerned, it is to teach us about our relationship with Him.

Through study and revelation of the scriptures, we learn that sexual intimacy in the natural is a parallel to worship in the spirit. We can see this by looking at some scriptures in the third chapter of Jeremiah. *(Keep in mind that 'Israel' and 'Judah' were used as names for the collective chosen nation of (Yahweh/God in the Old Testament).* "*⁶...Have you seen what fickle Israel does?* **_Like a wife who commits adultery_**, *Israel has* **_worshiped other gods_**... *⁷...And though her faithless sister Judah saw this, ⁸she paid no attention. She saw that* **_I had divorced faithless Israel_** *and sent her away. But now Judah, too,* **_has left me and given herself to prostitution._**"

Scriptures similar to these, referring to idol worship as adultery or some other type of illicit sexual act, can be found all throughout the books of the prophets. In both the Old and New Testament of the Bible, the people of The Kingdom are commonly referred to as "wife" or "bride" *(Isa 62:5, Jer 2:2, 2 Cor 11:2, Eph 5:23)*. Marriage is clearly a symbolic picture of our relationship with Yahweh, and the Bible makes a strong and clear comparison between sex and worship. Therefore, there is no question that sexual intimacy in the natural is a parallel to worship in the spirit, or "spiritual intimacy".

In certain scriptures, we can even see a strong parallel between Adam's relationship to Eve and our relationship to The Creator, before sin entered in. In Genesis 2:22-24 it reads, "*²²Then the LORD God made a woman from the rib he had taken out of the man, and he brought her to the man. ²³The man said, "This is now bone of my bones and flesh of my flesh; she shall be called 'woman,' for she was taken out of man. ²⁴That is why a man leaves his father and mother and is united to his wife, and they become one flesh. (NLT)*" Then if we take a look at Ephesians 1:4 it reads, *⁴Even as [in His love] He chose us [actually picked us out for Himself as His own]* **<u>in Christ</u>** *before the foundation of the world, that we should be holy (consecrated and* **<u>set apart for Him</u>**) *and blameless in His sight, even above reproach, before Him in love. (AMP)"*

While restraining myself from starting an entirely new book expounding upon the depth of revelation hidden in these two scriptures, I just want to point out a couple of nuggets. The woman – the wife – was **taken out of** the man. We – the bride of Christ – were **taken out of** Christ. The woman was **made in the man's own likeness**. We were **made in the likeness of Yahweh**. The woman was **made just for the man** and set apart just for him. In the same way, we were **made just for Yahweh** and set apart just for Him. Lastly, **the man leaves his mother and father to unite with his wife and become one flesh with her**. Likewise **Yeshua (Jesus) left His Father to unite with us, His bride, and he became flesh with us**!

PLEASE DO NOT SLEEP on the importance and weighty significance of these symbolisms and parallels. If you fail to fully grasp the revelations in this chapter, the rest of this book will hold little meaning to you. That being said, if you don't understand something, read it again and again until it becomes a living word in your soul. Read slowly and with full alertness, and take plenty of notes to help you retain this knowledge. Your level of true deliverance will depend heavily on your understanding of this chapter. Now, let us continue to build on what has been revealed so far, by exploring exactly what it is that we are to learn in all of this.

There are four things about the spirit realm – Yah's Kingdom and our relationship with Him that we can learn through marital relations and sexual intimacy.

1. Worship Only One God - YHWH the Living God

The first, and I believe the **most important**, purpose of sexual intimacy is to help us understand that we are to worship only *one* God – Yahweh, the True and Living God that created us. We learn in the scriptures from the previous section that just as a married person is to have sex only with their one spouse, we are to worship only our one Lord. The LORD implemented sexual intimacy as an act to be performed between one man and one woman only. This is obvious because He took only one rib from Adam's body to create only one woman *(Gen 2:21-22)*. There was no other man on earth that Adam had to share his wife with!

Every other activity that spouses do together can be done with someone else as well. **Sex is the only act** that a spouse cannot do *(lawfully in the sight of the True God)* with any other human being. Understanding that sexual intimacy is a parallel to worship, we can easily see that this is true in our relationship with Yah as well. We can interact with others in many of the same ways in which we interact with Him. We talk to The LORD – we can talk to people; we seek The LORD – we can seek things; we praise The LORD – we can praise accomplishments; we desire The LORD – and we can desire people too.

Performing any of these acts toward people or other pursuits is perfectly lawful in The LORD's sight. Worship is the one thing that He tells us we are to do to Him and *Him alone,* as is stated in Exodus 34:14, *"You must worship no other gods, for the Lord, whose very name is Jealous, is a God who is jealous about his relationship with you."* So you can see how sexual intimacy between husband and wife in the natural, is symbolic of spiritual intimacy (worship) between Yahweh and humanity in the spirit. Just think of how jealous and hurt a man or woman is when they know that their spouse has been unfaithful to them. Our Lord feels the same way when we worship any other god *(a god can be an object, person, pursuit or activity)* beside Him.

2. Establishing and Strengthening the Blood Covenant

The second, and I believe the **most powerful**, lesson that we can learn from the act of sexual intercourse is the great importance of worshiping Yahweh for the establishing and maintaining of our blood covenant with Him. The most critical purpose of sexual intimacy between a husband and wife is to strengthen and re-establish the covenant bond and partnership between them. Friendships may come a dime a dozen, but covenant relationships are rare. That is part of what makes the marital relationship so special, it is a covenant relationship that is established in blood.

Let's examine this. It is medically known that the first time a woman has intercourse, she sheds blood. This can happen at times other than the first as well though. It is actually an increase in blood flow to the woman's genital area that enables arousal and lubrication before and during sex, allowing blood to escape through the skin of the genital area anytime there is sexual activity. Blood is also the driving force behind the erection and ejaculation of a man. A man's penis is actually made up of tiny vessels that fill with blood during arousal, and swell to cause an erection. This blood stimulates all of the sensitive nerve endings in his genital area, helping him to maintain the erection until the pleasure build up causes him to release his seed. When it comes right down to it – **SEX IS ALL ABOUT BLOOD FLOW**!

You may be wondering what the significance of this is. Well, in the Bible we learn that the most powerful covenant that can be made is one that is established in blood *(Ex 24:8, Zech 9:11, Mat 26:28, Heb 9:18-22)*. Taking into consideration the blood flow involved in ALL sexual acts, please understand that a blood covenant is created between every man and woman the first time they engage in sexual activity – REGARDLESS OF VIRGINITY OR LACK THEREOF.

Through sexual intimacy, a husband and wife become partners to one another <u>for life</u>. A blood covenant, once created, can only be broken by death or by the establishing of a new blood covenant, which cancels out or ratifies the old one *(1 Cor 7:39, Luke 22:20)*. Thus every time a couple connects their bodies and blood through sexual activity, they are strengthening the established bond and covenant between them. We too are in a blood covenant (through the Blood of Yeshua) with The Father. Just as is the case with a husband and wife, each time we worship Him, we re-establish and strengthen our bond and spiritual covenant with Him.

We see a picture of this parallel even in the practice of communion, where we partake of the <u>Body</u> and <u>Blood</u> of The Messiah. "^{24}and when He had given thanks, He broke it and said, "Take, eat; this *is My body which is broken for you; do this in remembrance of Me."* [25]*In the same manner He also took the cup after supper, saying, "This cup is the new covenant in My blood. This do, as often as you drink it, in remembrance of Me."* [26]*For as often as you eat this bread and drink this cup, you proclaim the Lord's death till He comes. (1 Cor 11:24-26, NKJV)"* This scripture tells us we are to participate in The Lord's Supper "in remembrance" of Yeshua, who brought us the New **Covenant**. In other words, the only purpose of the practice of communion is to remind us of our blood covenant with Him, and strengthen our commitment to that covenant. **You practice spiritual intimacy every time you take communion; and you take communion every time you engage in physical intimacy!**

Let us examine this truth. During sex a couple takes in one another's bodies, becoming a part of each other. In the same way, as we eat the bread and ingest it, we symbolically take in the Body of The Messiah and become one with Him. A couple also drinks one another's blood during sexual intimacy, by the exchange of fluids that occur during open-mouthed kissing *(there are blood cells in saliva)*. In the same way, as we drink the wine, we symbolically drink The Blood of The Messiah. This partaking of body and blood through sexual intimacy was designed by Yahweh only to happen within the confines of marriage, because it should be done in honor of one's commitment to a sacred marital covenant. This is why couples still need sexual intimacy, even when procreation is not desired. Likewise, the communion meal was designed only to be participated in by those of us who acknowledge and honor our commitment to our sacred covenant with Yahweh, as the bride of Christ. That is why we are encouraged in scripture to do it often.

This is also a hint as to why there is a natural drive for sexual intercourse after an argument. Discord weakens the bond that holds the marital covenant together; sexual intercourse re-establishes that broken bond. Couples NEED to share intercourse frequently, and we likewise NEED to worship The LORD frequently. If you were to observe a couple that has poor and infrequent sexual relations, you would find that couple does not understand the concepts of partnership, loyalty and commitment in marriage. *(There are always exceptions due to illness, distance, age, etcetera – but any close, intimate couple had frequent and enjoyable intercourse at some point in their marriage.)* Unsatisfactory sexual intimacy is the number one cause for infidelity. This is not because the physical aspect of the sex is so important, but is instead because without the intimacy that sex represents, there is a disconnect in all other aspects of the relationship.

It is so important for a married couple to have mutually enjoyable sexual intimacy often. Each time they lay together and partake of one another's bodies and blood, they should do so in remembrance of the covenant they made to one another as husband and wife. This bond is strengthened as time and tribulations reveal their commitment to one another. It is equally as important for us to experience mutually enjoyable worship with Our Heavenly Lover. Even in the midst of trials and tribulations, our acts of intimate worship help us remember our Blood covenant with The Messiah, and help us remain faithful to Him.

3. The Intimacy of Worship in Spirit

The third, and I believe the **most rewarding**, lesson that we learn through human sexual relations is about the *intimacy* of worshiping The Great I AM. A man and woman that are truly in love enjoy the act of sexual intimacy immensely. They consent that their bodies belong to one another *(1 Cor 7:4)* and they use every part of those bodies, and all five of their senses, to express their love and desire. They touch, smell, taste, hear and see their lover during sexual intimacy. Not out of a lustful desire, but instead out of their love for one another, they are easily aroused sexually.

Unashamed, true lovers embrace in nakedness to explore one another in body, soul and spirit. Through intercourse they become one in all three realms, as they completely give themselves over to each other. Likewise, Yahweh wants to own us and wants us to give Him ALL of ourselves in worship. He wants us to be easily aroused – ready to worship Him at any moment. He does not want us to come to Him ashamed and covered, but instead He wants us in spiritual nakedness to allow Him to freely explore and touch every part of our spirits. He desires to freely and fully give Himself to us as well. He wants to reveal Himself to us. He desires oneness with us His creation, but we have to be willing to embrace Him. Who, beside an abuser, really enjoys sex when their partner is resisting them?

For scriptural proof that the intimacy of worship is <u>essential</u> to The LORD's heart, we can look at John 4:23, *"...true worshipers shall worship the Father in spirit and in truth: **<u>for the Father seeketh such to worship Him</u>**."* How important must worship be, if The God Who Is Sovereign and owns everything, is actually *seeking* true worshipers? Wow!

To worship Yah in spirit means to give Him everything in you, as you worship Him not from the head or even from the flesh, but from your heart. In the natural there is a difference between "making love" and merely "having sex". Having sex is a pleasurable physical experience but is empty of heart and soul. When a couple that is in love has sex, they do it with their entire beings. It is not just a physical act, but instead is the Ultimate Physical Expression of a deep abiding love that comes from the spirit. True worshipers are those that worship The LORD in spirit, in the same way a husband and wife who are truly in love share sexual intimacy in the natural. We worship with our hearts and not just our bodies.

To worship Yah in truth means to come humbly but boldly to Him, in the sincerity of all that you are; knowing that He will accept you because of the great love shared between you and Him. Have you ever wondered how a very attractive woman ends up with a "hard on the eyes" man? Her love covers all of his faults; in her eyes he is beautiful just as he is. This kind of love reveals to us the meaning of Adam and Eve being before the Lord *"naked and not ashamed"* (Gen 2:25). A loving couple has no problem standing completely nude before one another even in bright, revealing lights, regardless of the condition of their bodies.

Can you imagine the shock of a man thinking that a woman has naturally long hair, and then during sex he accidently pulls off her wig?

(Laugh). It sounds funny I know, but this is how we usually present ourselves to Our Heavenly Lover! Of course, He is not shocked when "our wigs come off"; He is just disappointed that we thought we needed them. When a woman knows that she is truly loved, she doesn't have to go to bed with make-up on, or wear wigs and fancy sex outfits to try and present an image that she thinks is more acceptable than the truth of who she truly is. This is how Yahweh wants us to come to Him, in truth, allowing His love to cover all of our faults. We are beautiful in His eyes just the way we are.

To find this kind of worship is rare, and that is why Yahweh is actually *seeking* those that will worship Him this way. Worshipers of this kind are actually restoring back to Him what He lost in the garden at the fall. *Yes, God Almighty lost something too...* What He lost are vessels that will stand before Him naked and unashamed; allowing Him to enjoy the perfect design that He created us with; not marring our beauty with fig leaves – which are nothing more than dead trees. We prevent authentic intimacy with Him by wrapping ourselves in the death of shame and self-condemnation, instead of allowing Him to cover us with His Purifying, Unconditional Love!

You show me a couple that lack sexual intimacy in their relationship, and I will show you a couple that is disconnected mentally and emotionally; one that does not know each other well as friends, does not enjoy spending time with one another and misrepresents one another in the presence of others. It is the exact same way for Believers that do not worship Yahweh intimately. Given that we are His vessels and representation here on earth, you can understand how crucial it is that we stay connected to The Vine *(John 15:5)* through worship. However, what is even more beautiful is the reward that we personally reap from this kind of intimacy with The Creator!

4. The Creative Power of Worship

The fourth and I believe the **most beneficial**, thing that sexual intimacy in the natural teaches us about worshiping Yahweh is that we have creative power when we join together with The Creator intimately in worship. Sexual intercourse in marriage not only demands monogamy, establishes covenant and promotes intimacy, but it also gives a couple creative power. The sexual expression of love between a husband and wife can cause a baby to be born here on earth.

The power to create a baby does not come merely from sperm and egg. Something more powerful must first exist that will bring the man and woman together, in order to afford conception an opportunity. In other words, before a sperm and egg can meet to form an embryo, something has to motivate the-would-be-parents to engage in sexual intercourse. Sexual intimacy, in a marriage ordained by Yahweh, is fueled by the love that exists between the man and the woman. It is the power of that love that brings the couple together.

Let us consider that for a moment. In essence, the love between a husband and wife cannot be seen, heard, touched, tasted or smelled. To us that live in a seen and tangible world, love is more of a "concept" than an actual "thing". Something is only *real* in this realm when we can interact with it using our five senses. Yet, the intangible and unseen concept of love can be manifested, or made *real* here on earth when the sexual intimacy that is fostered by that love causes a living, breathing human being to be conceived and born.

Before the baby is ever born, it already exists inside of the bodies of its parents. The love that the parents share already exists too. But neither the baby nor the love can be seen with the naked eye or actually *brought into manifestation,* until the couple comes together in sexual intimacy and the husband deposits what is inside of him into his wife. It is as if once the baby is born you can actually "see" the love, by seeing what the physical expression of that love (sexual intimacy) has produced. Even though the existence of the love and the baby was always certain in eternity, a physical vessel was needed to create something that could be considered real here in the earth realm. Thus, the unseen love and the unseen baby, is manifested using our seen, physical vessels.

In just the same way, Yah's unseen Kingdom is brought into manifestation here on earth through our seen, physical vessels. We know that Yahweh is the Creator of all things, and that in the beginning

He created everything that we now see through that which could not be seen – the power of Christ *(Gen chap 1, Heb 11:3)*. But after creating all *things*, He ordained the laws of nature, and He now adheres to those laws that He Himself set in order. Therefore, in order for Yah to manifest *things* that exists in the spirit realm (the unseen world) here in the earthly realm (the seen world); He will always use physical vessels.

Everything that ever has, does now or ever will exist here on this earth has always eternally existed in Yahweh's Spiritual Kingdom. Yet by His own sovereignty, The Father chose to use us as a way to get it from "there" to "here". When we join together intimately with Him in worship, we have the same creative power spiritually that an earthly husband and wife do naturally, when they join together intimately with one another in sex. When we worship Him, He makes a deposit in us. His Spirit, His power and all that He is, is implanted into us. We conceive and give birth to His Kingdom and His will and cause it to be done here on earth, just as it is in heaven *(Mat 6:10)*.

Why is it necessary though for us to have this creative power spiritually? Just because The Sovereign LORD ordained it so! It cannot be done any other way. Outside of modern medical technology, the way Yah originally designed it is that without sexual intercourse, a couple cannot conceive a baby – they have no natural, creative power. Without us worshiping The Almighty intimately, we cannot conceive His Kingdom – we have no spiritual, creative power! The same way that babies exist in the bodies of their parents even before they are ever born, Yah created in us seeds of greatness. Seeds of the power, majesty, splendor, greatness and glory of His Kingdom already exist within each of us, but He must first enter into us and fertilize those seeds in order for them to ever become anything more – anything **real**. He can only fertilize what is in us when we come together with Him intimately in worship, and then we together with the Almighty Creator, can be used as vessels to manifest His creative power.

Just think about it. Yahweh could have multiplied the earth in any way that He chose. Every so often a human being could have just popped up out of the soil like a plant. So why did He chose to do it through the process of sexual intercourse and procreation? He designed it this way because He wanted us to understand our creative power when one with Him! How wonderful is our LORD to share with us the benefit of His awesome power to create. HalleluYAH!

Insights from Dr. Intimacy

Break Free In Intimacy

People often ask me questions about how to experience true deliverance. Sometimes deliverance can seem like an elusive mystery or unattainable goal. Yet, I have learned on my own quest for deliverance that the shortest distance from where I am to the deliverance that I need, is the measure of distance between my face and the floor! There is no surer and more thorough way to receive an authentic breakthrough than to break free in intimacy with the LORD.

Worship is intimacy with The Father – it is pure, mind-blowing, flesh-numbing, over-powering, over-flowing, gushing, explosive intimacy. Real intimacy with your Creator is what brings about true deliverance. Prayer changes things, but intimacy **transforms** you. When something changes, it can always change back. Change is only temporary, but transformation is everlasting!

Your true deliverance is in the intimacy of worship, in the intimate oneness of time in His presence where there is *transformation*. Once He transforms you, you can never go back to being what you once were. You cannot stay bound; you cannot stay chained. You cannot remain the same when you are really touched by Yahweh God in your intimate places! It is like a virgin that will never be the same once touched; it is impossible to be what you used to be after The Lover of Your Soul touches you.

When you finally become intimate with Him and allow Him to penetrate your spirit and impregnate you, **YOU WILL NOT BE THE SAME.** This very truth that I am stating is why chapter 2, lesson three, *"The Intimacy of Worship in Spirit"*, is <u>MY FAVORITE</u> section of this book. If I were you, I would read it over and over and over again. I would print it out and post it around me. I would post it on my social media networks and even write a daily decree based on this revelation of intimacy with Yahweh.

Why do I say this? Why do I feel so strongly about it? Because the moment you forget it, defeat sets in. The moment you allow yourself to believe that true deliverance can come by any other means, is the moment the enemy has a backdoor entrance to steal, kill and destroy your purpose in life. I know this all too well and too personally. I had been "away" for a while, off the scene where no one could find me. And to be totally honest with you, I disappeared because I just didn't feel worthy of this call on my life.

I had been fighting a battle for a long time, questioning my worth to The Body of Christ and even as a human being. The more I pressed in to be a blessing to the people Yahweh has assigned me to, the further away I seemed to get from actually fulfilling my purpose. But The Word of The Lord came to me one night *as I worshiped*, and by His Word I was made clean... I was made whole... I was made aware once again that the battle is not mine, it is The LORD's! But the only way to turn the battle over to Him and stop trying to fight it myself was through the oneness of intimate worship.

I know why the enemy wants my hands to stay still from typing and my mouth shut from speaking, but I declare that I will not be still, nor will I be silent! My assignment is not to teach people about sex or to deal with people's sexual issues. The topics that are addressed in this ministry platform are necessary discussions but only because such issues often steal from us the privilege to worship Our Creator freely. *So go for yours!* Go after your total deliverance in His intimate presence. That is what I did. I worshiped in pure intimacy and broke free. BREAK FREE in His presence!

Your deliverance is in Intimacy with God. True and lasting deliverance is in the ***transformation*** that happens when you BEAK FREE in intimacy, ***pure worship intimacy...***

Chapter 3

How Did Sexual Intimacy Become So Perverse?

Understanding the origin of sexual perversion and the devil's true purpose for it is the next layer of our foundation.

Now that we have a better understanding of God's _purpose_ for sexual intimacy, it will be easier for us to understand how the spirits of sexual perversion operate, and why. As we have now learned, The Father is actually seeking those who will worship Him in spirit and in truth *(John 4:23)*. Just like sexual intimacy is important in marriage, worship is extremely important in our relationship with Yahweh God. The devil understands the importance of worship. We must be mindful of the fact that he once dwelled in the very presence of The Almighty *(Isa 14:12, Luke 10:18)*. He probably understands better than most Christians how important worship is to The Creator and our relationship with Him.

Satan's aim in introducing sexual perversion into the earth was to distort our understanding of this worship. If satan can successfully pervert our ability to be sexually intimate on earth with our true mate, then he can pervert our ability to be worshipfully intimate in spirit with our True God. Our thinking about satan is much too finite. His purposes always stretch far beyond just the act of sin in the flesh. You have to remember that he too is a spirit and operates not only in the earth, but in the spirit realm as well. His ultimate goal is that we be destroyed in the spirit realm, not the earth realm. Our flesh is just the physical vessel that he seeks to use to fulfill his true intentions.

Once mankind was created, the devil did not waste any time introducing sexual perversion to the earth. Let's trace it back in the Bible to Genesis chapter 4 and verse 19, where it tells us that Lamech married two women. Lamech was born five generations down in the bloodline of Cain *(the first child born to Eve, whom killed his brother Abel)*. The Bible does not talk much about Cain after his judgment *(Genesis 4:14, 16)*. He was no longer remembered because he was cast out of The Creator's presence and the presence of Adam and Eve. He thus lost all of his rights as a son. Subsequently, the generations of Cain are barely discussed. As far as Adam's genealogy is concerned, Cain never even existed.

Yet, I noticed in the studying of the text that the bloodline of Cain is discussed briefly up until Lamech. None of Cain's other descendants born before Lamech are mentioned at all, beside their names and their sons' names. Lamech is discussed in a bit more detail though. The only distinction that I noted with Lamech is the fact that he had two wives. He was the first man recorded in the Bible to have more than one wife. This was obviously very significant for the Bible to make note of it. After Lamech and his children are written about in Genesis chapter 4, none of Cain's other descendants are named. When the descendants of Adam are listed in detail in chapter 5, neither Cain's name, nor the names of any of his descendants are mentioned at all! This once again makes it plain that there was a distinction with Lamech, and that distinction was the fact that he had two wives.

"Lamech married two women – Adah and Zillah. (Genesis 4:19)" What was so significant about Lamech having two wives, and why was he the first man to do this? Lamech having two wives was significant because this was the first recorded and clearly successful attempt of satan to pervert the sexual relations between human beings. The covenant and commitment that Lamech was intended to have with only one woman, he divided between two women. We all know that the more commitments we have, the less dedicated we are to each of them. Since marriage and sexual relations were implemented to help people understand our commitment to and relationship with Yahweh, Lamech having more than one wife was used to pervert humanity's understanding. It introduced the idea that if a man could have sex with more than one woman, then he could also worship more than one god. It was a subtle way for satan to pervert our relationship with The Father by distorting our perception of the proper use of sexual intimacy.

Cain and his descendants were likely candidates to be first used by satan to pervert sexual intimacy. This is because the Bible lets us know in Genesis 4:14 and 4:16 that Cain was literally *cast out* of Yahweh God's presence. He was no longer in the presence of The Creator and therefore, no longer able to serve or worship Him. In the book of Ecclesiastes it tells us that the whole duty of man is to fear Yahweh and to keep His commandments *(12:13)*. Once Cain was cast out of Yah's presence and could no longer serve and worship Him, he ceased to have a purpose for existing. His entire understanding of life on earth and his relationship with his Creator was distorted. He passed this purposelessness and lack of understanding down to his descendants. Bearing in mind also that Yahweh is love *(1 John 4:8)*, and without a connection to Him we are incapable of loving **unconditionally**, sex was merely a physical act in the lives of Cain and his descendants. For Lamech and his bloodline, sex served no purpose other than its use for pleasure and procreation.

Then let us consider even more in depth, Lamech's detachment from Yah. We learn in the Bible that all that is in the world is the lust of flesh, the lust of the eyes and the pride of life *(1 John 2:16)*. The more *detached* we become from The Father, the more *attached* we become to the world. Lust then begins to **consume** us. As was stated earlier, Lamech was a fifth generation descendant of Cain who had been cast out of Yah's presence. Thus Lamech was also part of the sixth generation of cursed humanity on earth. Theologically, six is the number of mankind. Therefore Lamech's bloodline and his generation – as descendants of the outcast – symbolized humanity in all of its wickedness and lustfulness, completely detached from The Holy One. Because of this symbolism, I believe that Lamech was deliberately targeted by satan to be the first man to willfully pervert sexual intimacy. **We are purely evil when completely detached from the Source of Love!**

I found it interesting also that the Bible gives the names of Lamech's two wives. It does not give the name of the wife of Cain or any of Cain's other descendant's wives. Lamech's first wife's name was Adah, which translates "Ornament". She was his gift, his ornament, his beauty and his true helpmeet. She accentuated his strength and complimented his manhood. His second wife's name was Zillah, which translates "Shade". It was simply lust of the flesh that caused him to marry a second wife when he had already been joined together with his ornament. His second wife Zillah was just a shade of the glory of his first wife Adah. It is just like us who already have Yahweh, the Lord God Almighty, as our very own and then seek out another god. Any other god is just a shade of His glory and pales in comparison!

Now let's go on to the next instance of sexual perversion recorded in the Bible, which can be found in Genesis 6. In the first four verses of this chapter it is discussed how the "sons of God" made wives of the "daughters of the men". *"¹And it came to pass, when men began to multiply on the face of the earth, and daughters were born unto them, ²That the sons of God saw the daughters of men that they were fair; and they took them wives of all which they chose."* I know that there are a lot of questions about this scripture and the use of the term "the sons of God". Who are the sons of God? Well when Jesus was on the earth He often referred to Himself as the "Son of Man" *(Mat 8:20, Mark 2:10)*. This was to indicate that He had been _born of the flesh_.

In the text that we just read, the scripture differentiates between the "sons _of God (who is of spirit)_" and the "daughters _of men (who are of flesh)_". This is recorded to help us differentiate between *spiritual beings* and *earthly beings*. So in this text the term "sons of God" could just as easily have been translated as "spiritual beings", and the term "daughters of men" could have been translated as "earthly women". I believe that these spiritual beings were a part of the fallen angels that satan had deceived while still in Heaven *(Jude 1:6, Rev 12:4)*. Yah's Holy angels are just that – **HOLY**. They are ministering servants that help to further The LORD's purposes and not to hinder them.

At any rate, when the Bible says, *"they took them wives"*, that means in laymen's terms that they had sex with them. To break it down into simplest form, demon spirits had sex with human women. The devil was not satisfied with the subtle influence that he had on humanity through Lamech and the distortion of marriage. He wanted to literally <u>enter</u> into human beings and take total control of us. He accomplished this by assigning demons to have sex with and impregnate human women. To further prove this point we can look at verse 4 of the same chapter, which says, *"[4]In those days, and even afterward, giants lived on the earth,* **for whenever the sons of God had intercourse with human women,** *they gave birth to children who became the heroes mentioned in legends of old."*

When you think *legend*, when you think *superhero* – what sort of image pops into your head? Perhaps Superman, Spiderman or the Incredible Hulk is what comes to mind. What causes those characters mentioned above to be characterized as superheroes? The fact that they all have superhuman strength is what causes them to be categorized as superheroes. These characters all operated with a supernatural power; the type of power that is not available to average human beings. These characters that I mentioned are all fictional, but my point is still proven that when the Bible says that these women *"gave birth to children who became the heroes mentioned in legends of old"*, it is a clear indication that they gave birth to children who possessed supernatural powers. Why did these children possess supernatural powers? These children were conceived with a supernatural seed. They possessed supernatural powers because they themselves were possessed with demons – conceived through the seed of demon spirits.[4] Thus, these demons of sexual perversion literally entered into and possessed mankind.

If you read on in chapter 6 of Genesis and verse 5, which is the very next verse after demons and humans having sex is mentioned, it says, *"[5]Now The Lord observed the extent of the people's wickedness,*

---

[4] See chapter 18 for a more in-depth study on demons that have sex with humans.

and he saw that all their thoughts were consistently and totally evil." It is not by coincidence that Yahweh makes this observation after sexual perversion becomes rampant on the earth. Satan knew just what he was doing when he perverted sexual intimacy on the earth. He distorted humanity's ability to understand their relationship with Yahweh and their ability to be intimate in worship with Him. As a result, because of the lack of worship and relationship with Yah, humanity became totally consumed with the evil nature of the flesh and the world. The only other sin mentioned up until this point in the Bible is murder *(a manifestation of a detachment from love and intimacy)*. Both Cain and Lamech murdered. Other than murder, sexual perversion is the only sin that is distinctly mentioned. **Hatred destroys intimacy and perversion breeds hatred...**

How offensive must sexual sin be to Yah for it to cause Him to go on to say in the following verse, *"⁶So The Lord was sorry he had ever made them. It broke his heart. ⁷And God said, 'I will completely wipe out this human race that I have created'..."*? *(This scripture was referring to the coming flood that would destroy all life on earth except Noah and those in the ark.)* Yet, I do not believe that it was the physical acts of sexual perversion that grieved The Father so much, but instead what they symbolized concerning humanity and its relationship with Him. Not only did mankind turn away from intimacy with the True God, but they also turned to intimacy with the devil himself! Instead of receiving into them the Spirit of the King, they worshiped satan and received his spirit. *"...for whenever the sons of God had intercourse with human women, they gave birth to children who became the heroes mentioned in legends of old."* They received, conceived and gave birth to evil. Yahweh's precious wife gave herself to His enemy and bore His enemy's children, and it *"broke his heart"*.

The devil truly is a deceiver and a liar. Just imagine what it must have been like back in those days. People were just discovering the momentary pleasures of sexual perversion, not realizing that their souls were being destroyed in the process. Then satan just sat back and watched with pleasure as they were all destroyed. It is the same today as well! So just to ensure that I leave no room for him to deceive you any longer: **THE DEVIL'S AGENDA IS TO STEAL YOUR WORSHIP** away from Yahweh God and impregnate you with his evil will, leading to your ultimate destruction. What you lose through sexual perversion is so much more than just your "good morals". You lose your very connection with your purpose for being alive and your ability to experience the fullness of love and intimacy as Yahweh's creation. *You become like Cain…*

Insights from Dr. Intimacy

The Devil Wants to Steal Your Worship!

The two foundational and most critical revelations in this book are:

1) Yahweh wants to share spiritual intimacy with us in the same way He designed for couples to experience physical intimacy in marriage.

2) The devil's only agenda in sexual perversion is to steal your worship!

If you get a firm and insightful understanding of these two important truths, your battle with sexual perversion is already half over. So let's explore the real reason satan is so after your worship, by taking a look at some scriptures in Job.

⁸"Then the Lord said to Satan, "Have you considered My servant Job, that there is none like him on the earth, a blameless and upright man, one who fears God and shuns evil?" ⁹Satan answered the Lord and said, "Does Job fear God for nothing? ¹⁰Have You not made a hedge around him, around his household, and around all that he has on every side? You have blessed the work of his hands, and his possessions have increased in the land. ¹¹But now, stretch out Your hand and touch all that he has, and he will surely curse You to Your face!" (Job 1:8-11, NKJV)"

I have heard this text preached many times and in many ways, but I never heard it presented the way the Holy Spirit showed it to me one day, as I was preparing for a conference. He opened up the eyes of my understanding so I could see that this entire story is really about worship. The way the text is translated makes it appear as if The LORD invited satan to attack Job, but this was actually not the case. The context clues of Job chapter 1 make it apparent that the LORD and satan were engaged in a dialogue about satan's activity on the earth. As satan was being true to his nature, probably bringing heinous accusations against the earth and boasting about the legal right he had to cause destruction due to people's sins; Yahweh responded by defending His creation through the example of Job and pointed out to the accuser that His Righteousness was still exalted on the earth. *It seems that the conversation probably was something to this effect.*

So looking at verse 8 where it reads, *"have you considered"*, in a different translation of the Hebrew, that phrase could mean *"have you violently laid a hand upon"*. Then when you look at the word *"fear"* in that same verse that word can also be translated *"worship"*. So if we read the text again with these different translated meanings, it would read as follows: *"'Then the Lord said to satan 'have you violently laid a hand upon my servant job, there is none like him on the earth, a blameless and upright man, one who worships me and shuns evil?'"* This was a taunting dialogue for the enemy because the point that The LORD was making, which is made clear through examining satan's response, is that Job was under divine protection due to his lifestyle of consistent worship and Righteousness.

In chapter 1, The Father lifts His divine protection from Job's life and gives the enemy liberty to afflict all that he owns. Satan destroys everything in Job's life, but is not permitted to afflict Job's physical body. Satan then returns to converse with The Most High and this is what is said in chapter 2:3-5 *(using revealed translation)* ³*Then the Lord said to Satan, "Have you violently laid a hand upon My servant Job, there is none like him on the earth, a blameless and upright man, one who worships God and shuns evil? And still he holds fast to his integrity, although you incited Me against him, to destroy him without cause."* ⁴*So Satan answered the Lord and said, "Skin for skin! Yes, all that a man* *has he will give for his life. ⁵But stretch out Your hand now, and touch his bone and his flesh, and he will surely curse You to Your face!"*

For many years the book of Job disturbed me because of this phrase in verse 3, *"although you incited Me against him, to destroy him without cause"*. I asked myself, *"Why would Yahweh deliberately stir up satan's wrath against a blameless and upright man?"* It was in searching for an answer to this question that the revelation was made clear. What The God of All Wisdom was really saying is, **"You dared me to challenge the worship of Job, my servant. You challenged me to prove to you satan that his intimacy with me means more than all that he has! You provoked me to prove to you that I can allow you to take away all that I have given him and he will still worship me!"**

When the Holy Spirit showed me this, I was blown away. Job had experienced the richness of worship and intimacy with The Creator and because of that nothing else mattered to him. Although his possessions were valuable, His WORSHIP WAS PRICELESS. That is why even when his wife came against him, he still would not curse God; when Job's marital intimacy stopped, he still had his worship intimacy with Yahweh. What satan was really after was not Job's possessions. Satan has access to every earthly possession and wealth imaginable. What he wanted was Job's worship. He despised, with green envy, the intimacy between Job and the LORD.

Look at all that the enemy did to Job, and yet Job never cursed – or attempted to break his covenant – with The Father. The devil knows this to be the nature of the heart of all TRUE worshippers. Once satan loses you to intimacy with Your Creator, it is unlikely that he will ever retrieve you! He doesn't care if you have a gift; work in ministry; sow large offerings; fast and pray for long periods in pursuit of selfish ambitions, but he never wants you to experience the fullness of worship and intimacy!

This is why he so desperately wants to keep you locked into sexual perversion. If you win the battle over sexual sin, you will be transformed into a beautiful and holy vessel of pure worship. And the enemy knows that in that kind of pure worship, there is the release of everything else that Yahweh has for you. Everything is hidden in your intimacy with Him. Satan wants to steal your worship. He wants to steal your blessing; he wants to steal your destiny. In Job 29 we see an even clearer picture of what Job's worship gave birth to in his life:

^{2}"Oh, that I were as in months past, As in the days when God watched over me; ^{3}When His lamp shone upon my head, And when by His light I walked through darkness; ^{4}Just as I was in the days of my prime, When the friendly counsel of God was over my tent; ^{5}When the Almighty was yet with me, When my children were around me; ^{6}When my steps were bathed with cream, **And the rock poured out rivers of oil for me!**"

In these verses, as Job reminisces on the way life was before his affliction, notice that he does not mention his possessions. He paints a picture of divine **protection**, divine **favor**, divine **guidance**, divine **prosperity**, divine **wisdom**, divine **fellowship**, divine **multiplication**, divine **ease of living**, and a consistent flow of **The Anointing**! Wow, WOW, W-O-W!!!

There is so much more than just your sexual purity that the enemy wants to take away from you when he sets himself to afflict you with sexual perversion. What he is really after is your worship because all of the blessings that Job enjoyed are connected to your worship. Furthermore, worship is required for The Anointing to *flow* in your life. So the very next time you are tempted to masturbate, have illicit sex, watch porn, cheat on your spouse, lay with the same gender, be sexually inappropriate with a relative, sell your body for sex, violate a child, molest an animal or lust in your heart – please hear these words ringing loudly in your spirit: **THE DEVIL WANTS TO STEAL YOUR WORSHIP!** As a matter of fact, say it out loud to yourself three times as loud as you can:

THE DEVIL WANTS TO STEAL MY WORSHIP!

THE DEVIL WANTS TO STEAL MY WORSHIP!

THE DEVIL WANTS TO STEAL MY WORSHIP!

And then, DON'T LET HIM!!!

Chapter 4

A Special Word for Married and Engaged Couples

There are some specific concerns and issues that arise concerning sex, when dealing with couples. This chapter will help couples understand how to get the most out of their marriage.

Understanding Perversion in Marriage

I do not want to neglect to address couples more specifically. When I say *couple*, I am referring to those who are officially married or engaged. When I say *engaged*, I am referring to those that have committed to marriage in the near future, with a ring to prove it and/or an estimated wedding date. If you are not officially married or engaged, you are just "playing house" and giving yourself the excuse that you need to continue to live in sexual sin.

Dr. Intimacy's #1 rule on dating: "If you don't feel ready to get married, you have no business dating!" That's my take on it. Therefore, if you do not technically fall into the category of "couple", you have my permission to skip this chapter and go on to the next one – *if you want to*. Just be sure to read it once you are ready to make that move.

Having said that, let's get back to the topic at hand. The veil of matrimony can conceal quite a bit of confusion and deception where sex is concerned. However, spirits of sexual perversion can still be at work in our lives even when we are married. I was married for eleven years to a devout Christian man. He and I both loved The LORD as much as we had knowledge to. But as the scripture says, *"My people are destroyed for lack of knowledge. (Hos 4:6)"* It is never what we know that kills us. It is always what we don't know that trips us up!

I and my ex-husband both came from very sexually perverse backgrounds. When we got married, I thought a marriage license was also a license to go buck wild in the bedroom *(or any room for that matter – laugh)*. I thought that having 'legal' sex with my husband would be more gratifying and intimate than sex with other men had been. I was disappointed to find myself not feeling much different than I had, when formerly engaging in sinful sex. As I took my concerns to Yahweh, He began to reveal to me how much perversity was still operative in my husband and me. Although we were married, the same spirits of sexual perversion were still influencing us.

I would have all types of perverse images of my past while trying to be intimate with my husband. At times, I felt like I was still being raped. Other times, I felt like a prostitute or lesbian. Sometimes he would ask me to do something, and I would feel like a sinner all over again. I literally cried afterward on more than one occasion. It was really quite disturbing, and my husband was experiencing similar difficulties. I began to really fast and pray about this issue. I did not know what was wrong, but I did know that something *was wrong*. I knew that Holy matrimony and the undefiled marriage bed *(Heb 13:4)* had to be about more than what I was experiencing.

The more I prayed it out, fasted, consecrated and studied concerning our sex-life, the more the Holy Spirit was able to reveal to me that spirits of sexual perversion still had us bound. At first, it did not make much sense to me, and when I tried to seek counsel concerning this issue, the advice went from one extreme to the next. I either heard some *undercover Christian freak* say something like: *"Marriage is honorable and the bed undefiled. You can do whatever you want (followed by a devilish laugh and a wink of the eye)."* Or, I would hear from some deranged sex-hater, who thought that everything sexual is dirty, married or not, and that a couple should only have sex to make babies: *"No touching, no kissing, no nothin'. Just stick it in, plant the seed and get outta there as quickly as you can. Then go pray, so God can cleanse ya!"* OK, I know that sounds funny, but this is really what some legalistic, religious folks believe.

The sad thing about it is that both groups of advisers had either never been married, were bitterly divorced or were in the midst of a miserable marriage. I was really turned aside by their opinionated lack of true wisdom concerning the matter. The LORD does know how to get you to go directly to Him; *I'll tell you that much!* The breakthrough began as the Holy Spirit revealed to me the ignorance surrounding the scripture, *"Marriage is honorable in all, and the bed undefiled. (Hebrews 13:4, KJV)"* If you look at the same scripture in the Amplified version of the Bible, you gain understanding of the message that the author was truly trying to convey.

"Let marriage be held in honor (esteemed worthy, precious, of great price, and especially dear) in all things. And thus let the marriage bed be undefiled (kept undishonored); for God will judge and punish the unchaste [all guilty of sexual vice] and adulterous."

Insight into this scripture brought me to understand that although the marriage bed itself is truly undefiled because The LORD has ordained it Holy, the persons who lay down in it may not be. In the Old Testament of the Bible, it was made plain that if anything *clean* came in contact with something that was *unclean*, the clean thing became unclean through that contact *(Lev chap 15)*. When defiled people come in contact with an undefiled marriage bed, they can easily cause the bed to become defiled. And let us make no mistake here – when the scripture says *"bed"*, it is expressly referring to the sexual relations of husbands and wives.

Being able to break past the language barriers of the King James Version of the Bible, we can clearly see that it is possible to be guilty of sexual perversion even within the confines of marriage. I am sorry to bust the bubble of those of you who thought you could get off *scot-free*, doing *whatever, whenever* and *however* once you get married. That is just not the case. I do agree that what you do in privacy, as a married couple, is between you and your God. However, I will implore you married, Christian couples to come out from under the veil of deception that has you thinking that any and everything sexual is acceptable in the sight of your Heavenly Father once you are married.

Everything sexual is not acceptable in His sight and much of it can still be demonically influenced. Neither becoming a Born Again Believer, nor getting married, is an automatic eviction notice for demons of sexual perversion that have already taken residence with us. It can happen that way, and for some people it does, but that is not a given and is **a very dangerous assumption to make**. We have to – with deliberate effort – allow The LORD to close the specific doors and tear down the specific strongholds that gave those spirits of sexual perversion access to us in the first place.

In order to know the truth about the defilement of our marriage beds, we must explore our motives behind doing something. Yahweh is always looking at the motives of our hearts, and that is what He judges us based upon. Take for instance a position other than "missionary". If a man watched pornography, made a mental note of a position that looked pleasurable and then said to himself, *"Yeah, I wanna give it to my wife like that!"* Once he carries out that act in his marriage bed, he is certainly being driven by a spirit of sexual perversion to engage in that particular position. Now let's say his wife is pregnant and is uncomfortable in the "missionary" position. If he uses that same position that was perverse when motivated by memories of a porn flick, out of tender love for his wife and his desire to protect her instead, then that particular position is pure and intimate. No position is necessarily "good" or "evil" in and of itself; it is what a person thinks in his or her heart concerning a position that makes it either.

It was not until I understood this revelation about motives that I finally began to recognize the cause of the problems in my sexual relations with my husband. There were some sexual acts that I engaged in during the earlier part of my marriage that after fasting, praying and seeking The LORD, I realized were being influenced by sexually perverse spirits from my past. Some of the acts, I stopped all together. Others, after being delivered from the spirits, I engaged in again with a new perspective and being motivated by intimacy instead of perversion and lust.

The key factor in this is – *understanding the intent of your heart*. *Your* motives might permit you to engage in certain sexual practices that *my* motives may not permit me, and vice versa. That is why I can only give you "guidelines" as far as how you can have sex as a married couple, as opposed to a list of "hard and fast rules". This is because even if you are in a plain, missionary position, doing nothing extraordinary, you might still be practicing perversion. At the same time, you could be doing something unconventional and seemingly wild and yet be totally pure in your heart. It is not so much about what you are doing in the flesh, as much as it is about what is going on in your heart while you are doing it, and what spirit is influencing or controlling you. The question is:

"Where did you learn that and why are you doing it?"

Is your only goal to get a *good feeling*? Anyone – your spouse or anybody else, even yourself – can give you a *good feeling*. So if this is your **only** motivation for having sex with your spouse, then you fail to understand what Yahweh's true purpose for intimacy in marriage is. Due to the fact that sex is the physical equivalent of worshiping Him, it should be exceedingly intimate. When we as Believers truly understand intimacy and perform it the way that The Creator intended for us to, it invokes worship in our spirits. Once you and your spouse understand this, you will enjoy your marital sex immensely. Implementing Yahweh's Holiness into your love-making will transform it from a mere flesh-gratifying experience, into a supernatural experience of Holiness and worship.

You may reject the very idea of sex and Holiness as synonymous and/or parallel terms. But how can you emphatically deny what is being stated here, if you have never actively pursued to experience this type of marital sexual exchange? This type of "worship experience" in marital sex does exist, you can achieve it, and you should pursue it – *believe me, you really, really should (reminiscent smile and sigh)...* Yet in order to get there, you will have to deal with truth, trust The Father and make sacrifices.

Personal Note: Why the Guidelines?

I had no written guidelines when striving to reach sexual purity in my marriage. The Holy Spirit did lead me through a great deal of deliverance, but the process was long and messy and unfortunately concluded with a divorce that was directly related to sexual sin. I feel strongly about preachers "meddling" in married couples sexual business, and for that reason, I refrained from sharing these guidelines when I first wrote this book. However, after my own experience of failure, which was brought on directly through sexual perversion in my marriage, I am now inclined to include the following section, detailing the appropriate guidelines for perversion-free sex in marriage.

I just feel that if two people who prayed and studied as frequently as me and my ex did; if two people who fasted until bones poked through and so carefully offered up their lives to right living; if two people like us could still get it wrong after 11 years, I am not willing to leave it to chance for anyone else. Not everyone hears The Spirit clearly. Not everyone has a mature prayer life. *"Exploring the naked truth about sex, intimacy and worship"* is the tagline for my web blog, and I must live up to that tag. My name is known as *Dr. Intimacy*, and I have an obligation to share the revelations that I have received on this topic and the experiences that I have had or know of.

So for anyone who feels I have no business giving sexual guidelines to couples, you don't have to read them. Even for those who choose to continue to read this next section, I still implore you to prayerfully consider adhering to these guides. They may, or may not, be applicable to you and your spouse. However, for those of you who feel as clueless as I did when I got married; for those of you who actually desire someone to give biblical guidelines that at least give you a starting point to build from, I am glad to oblige.

Having said that, I must issue this WARNING: It may be advisable for you to refrain from reading the remainder of this chapter, including the *Insights from Dr. Intimacy* article at the end, unless you are married or engaged, with a scheduled wedding date within the next 90 days. For single leaders and counselors, I would say be prayerful about it because you may need to read it for your followers' sakes. However, if you are currently struggling with an issue of perversion, then I would say definitely DO NOT read it – leader or not.

The following section and article will share some explicit words and topics that could produce strong images, inciting sexual desire. If you are not married or engaged, or assigned by Yahweh God to minister in this area, there may be no need for you to expose yourself to the possible temptation. Of course, if you are sexually pure and FREE of all spiritual perversion, it should not pose a threat for you. Then again, most people, whether they know it or not, picked up this book because they have an issue with sexual perversion. I doubt you are the exception. So that is my warning, proceed at your own risk!

Guidelines for Marital Sexual Purity

Many people say that marital sex can *legally* be whatever a couple agrees to. However I hold to this belief, as quoted in 1 Corinthians 6:12 in the Amplified Bible, *"Everything is permissible (allowable and lawful) for me; but not all things are helpful (good for me to do, expedient and profitable when considered with other things). Everything is lawful for me, but I will not become the slave of anything or be brought under its power."* Or as it is even more plainly stated in The Message Bible,

"Just because something is technically legal doesn't mean that it's spiritually appropriate. If I went around doing whatever I thought I could get by with, I'd be a slave to my whims."

I am so grieved by some of the "so-called Christian" sex articles and books that I have seen: they are just pure perversion iced over with Hebrews 13:4; *"...the marriage bed is undefiled"*. I recall a particular website sharing graphic details on how to perform erotic sexual acts, even encouraging couples to watch "Christian pornography" together.

OK, really? If the devil's agents are willing to that boldly mislead people in the name of love and marriage, then how much bolder should I be about properly guiding those who want Holy matrimony?

There are some acts that, although arguably lawful within the confines of marriage, are unquestionably spiritually unhealthy. These acts open doors for perversion to occur, inside and outside of the martial bedroom. So let's deal with some truth concerning marital sex, as I outline a list of acts that we should seriously consider omitting from our marriage beds. As you read through them, please remember that I am basing these guidelines on the *impure motives* that drive people to practice these acts, as opposed to looking for a scripture that says, *"Thou shalt not..."* If you and your spouse perform these acts and want to continue them, the next time you are engaged in such, I encourage you to ask yourself these questions: **"What is my motive for doing this?" "Where did I learn this?" "Does this act incite feelings of intimacy toward my spouse, or feelings of lust for my spouse?"**

You can never lose sight of the fact that sexual intimacy between a husband and wife was given to us as a physical representation of our spiritual worship to The Creator. Sexual intimacy is a form of worship. The marriage bed is an altar, and the acts you perform on it are acts of worship. Now which God you choose to worship on that altar is up to you. Is it a worship to the most Holy God or to the god of this world? Read the following, and then be led by the Holy Spirit in determining the answer to that question!

Vulgar Language - The Bible tells us in Ephesians 4:29, *"Let no foul or polluting language, nor evil word nor unwholesome or worthless talk [ever] come out of your mouth, but only such [speech] as is good and beneficial to the spiritual progress of others, as is fitting to the need and the occasion, that it may be a blessing and give grace (God's favor) to those who hear it. (AMP)"* How then can the marital bedroom be an appropriate place to use vulgar language? God forbid! Dirty bedroom talk in no way promotes this mandate given to us in Ephesians 4:29. It does nothing to encourage and edify your spouse and certainly does not depict our worship to The LORD. Yeshua says that out of the abundance of the heart, the mouth speaks *(Mat 12:34)*. All dirty bedroom talk really proves is that your heart is still perverted and your sexuality corrupted! **This is an open door for lust.**

Anal Sex – Yahweh put a great deal of care into instructing the Israelites on how to dispose of feces, and violation of these practices could result in one being cut off from the community *(Deut 23:12-13, NLT)*. The rectum is a filthy, bacteria carrying part of the body. No matter how much you wash the outside (the anus), you cannot get rid of the stench on the inside (the rectal canal). Anal sex is by nature a filthy and unhealthy act for both the male and the female involved, introducing bacteria and possible infection to the body.

What would be your motive for choosing the anus over the vagina? The rectum is specifically designed to transport toxic waste out of the body. It is an *exit*, not an *entrance*. When you release your seed into the rectum, you are saying that the seed inside of you is waste. If your seed is toxic waste, then so are you because you can only reproduce what you are! *"You shall make a distinction and recognize a difference between the holy and the common or unholy, and between the unclean and the clean. (Lev 10:10, AMP)"* **This is an open door for homosexuality and lasciviousness, in both men and women.**

Sadomasochism (S & M) - This is the use of bondage and/or physical abuse, as a part of sexual activity. It usually includes whips, chains, handcuffs *(and other such vices)*, as well as certain types of outfits. This is a common practice in satanic rituals and in rape. In the book of Ephesians 5:28-29 it reads, *"²⁸In the same way, husbands ought to love their wives as they love their own bodies. For a man who loves his wife actually shows love for himself. ²⁹No one hates his own body but feeds and cares for it, just as Christ cares for the church. (NLT)"* What would be the motive behind this practice for a loving, married couple? How does it exemplify the above scripture? Is our worship to The Father a forced, violent experience? This is not to say that sex has to be *virgin soft and gentle* all the time. Yet to engage in intentionally rough sex, and deliberately inflict pain on your spouse, does not depict pure intimacy or worship. **This is an open door for violence, rape and**

pedophilia (child molestation) and at times leads to accidental death or internal damage in the female.

Public Sex – *Hello...* it's illegal! You can be arrested for performing sex acts in public. This is not to say that marital sex has to be confined to a bed or even a bedroom for that matter. However, the Bible teaches us, *"¹Everyone must submit to governing authorities. For all authority comes from God, and those in positions of authority have been placed there by God. ²So anyone who rebels against authority is rebelling against what God has instituted, and they will be punished. (Rom 13:1-2, NLT)"* Certainly Yahweh does not intend for marital intimacy to break the law.

Sexual intimacy between a husband and wife should be cherished and guarded as sacred, with ultimate privacy. Even in the same way that the Holy of Holies, where the deepest acts of worship to Yahweh took place, was cherished and guarded as sacred, protected behind a thick impenetrable veil in the heart of the temple; should not our sexual intimacy be given the same regard? No one should see it, hear it or be told about it after the fact! After all, is this a Holy lovemaking experience or a pornography show? **This is an open door for adultery and pornography.**

Role Playing – *"²...[for your husband; you are to feel for him all that reverence includes: to respect, defer to, revere him--to honor, esteem, appreciate, prize, and, in the human sense, to adore him, that is, to admire, praise, be devoted to, deeply love, and enjoy your husband]. "⁷In the same way you married men should live considerately with [your wives], with an intelligent recognition [of the marriage relation]... (1 Pet 3:2b, 7a, AMP)"* Why would you want your spouse to pretend to be someone else, or why would you pretend to be someone else for your spouse? How can role playing truly fulfill the honor and endearment depicted in the above scriptures or enact your worship to God?

As quoted in chapter two, *"To worship Yah in truth means to come humbly but boldly to Him, in the sincerity of all that YOU ARE; knowing that He will accept you because of the great love shared between you and Him..."* If you still think that this practice is OK, you need to read chapter two again. You are supposed to love and be content with **your** spouse. Role playing is an extension of adultery. And it goes without saying that if role-playing is adultery, then swapping partners with another couple, what is commonly called "swinging", is completely out of the question! **This is an open door for discontentment, adultery, pornography, sexual fantasy and DIVORCE.**

Strip Teasing and Lingerie - Remember, sex is a depiction of our worship to The LORD. Yah is a Spirit. We cannot SEE Him, we only FEEL Him! *"Those that worship Him, must worship Him in spirit and in truth. (John 4:23)"* This is not to say that a woman should be walking around in a moo-moo or afraid to let her husband look at her, nor is it wrong to put on a "bedroom only" outfit. However, that should be a romantic **option**, as opposed to a necessary visual stimulant. I know this is probably a shocker, but think about it; most men are visual. When a woman puts lingerie on, just remember that her husband is likely to see that same outfit on a supermodel in the media. Who do you think it will look better on? Most wives cannot compete!

The more deadly factor in this practice though is that it further trains a man to be sexually stimulated by what he sees, which is why so many husbands become discontent with their wives as they age. With the unfavorable changes to the wife's body, a man is no longer attracted to what he sees. At the same time, he still sees the sexy bed clothes that his wife used to wear, on a supermodel somewhere and is longing to recapture that visual stimulation. Husbands and wives please do not train yourselves this way! Men, learn to be attracted to your wife because of the connection you have with her – and this will cause her to always look beautiful to you.

A loving couple has no problem standing completely nude before one another even in bright, revealing lights, regardless of the condition of their bodies. And let us not forget that at the time of creation, man and woman stood completely nude before one another. A man can see a number of different women when he sees you in lingerie, but he can only see YOU, when he sees you naked! **This act is** an open door for pornography, adultery and unexpected divorce after many years of marriage.

Masturbation – This is not a healthy marital sex practice. Remember that in marriage your bodies belong to each other. *"²But since sexual immorality is occurring, each man should have sexual relations with his own wife, and each woman with her own husband. ³The husband should fulfill his marital duty to his wife, and likewise the wife to her husband. ⁴The wife does not have authority over her own body but yields it to her husband. In the same way, the husband does not have authority over his own body but yields it to his wife. (1 Cor 7:2-5)"* The goal is for the husband to pleasure the wife and the wife to pleasure the husband. How does masturbation accomplish this? What would be the pure motive for performing this act in marriage?

Furthermore, whether done alone or with your spouse, masturbation can desensitize your genitals. This can make it difficult for a woman to achieve orgasm with her husband or for a man to maintain an erection for a long period of time. Most dangerous of all is that it will cause you to crave that feeling of your own touch when you are not with your spouse, setting a trap for a masturbation addiction, which will completely destroy your marital sex life! **Masturbation can cause many problems in your marriage and your personal life. It is an open door for all forms of sexual perversion.**

Positioning - Did you ever notice that humans are the only created beings that are physically wired to have sex face-to-face? When facing each other, we can be truly intimate, looking into each other's eyes; feeling one another's breath; pressing our torsos together, which contain our hearts and being able to join our mouths together to kiss. Animals do not have this privilege. Having sex in rear-entry, animal-like positions, all the time, robs a couple of more meaningful intimacy. I know of no specific scripture to support this belief, but throughout scripture reference is made to "lying prostrate" in worship. Besides, it takes only common sense to understand the point that is being made about the distinction in the face-to-face sexual capability of human beings that animals cannot participate in.

This is not to suggest that you be in a missionary position all the time, with the woman on her back and the man on top. There are many positions that can produce intimacy. It is just to remind you that marital lovemaking should be an intimate depiction of worship, and there is just some bedroom activity that cannot accomplish this. Be careful about your positioning during sex with your spouse. If a position doesn't feel right in your heart, don't force it because there is probably demonic influence from your pass attached to it. Let the passion to be ONE with your spouse always be your motive for coming together sexually, and then whatever position you end up in, it will be pure. **This can be an open door for all forms of sexual perversion, including bestiality and lasciviousness.**

Lotions, Potions, Pills & Thrills – There are a number of sexual aids available, for use by couples, that supposedly enhance the sexual experience. There is no specific scriptural reference for the use of such aids, and thus I will share advice from my own wisdom concerning this matter. Firstly, concerning male enhancement or erectile dysfunction issues and female libido concerns, you should never take a <u>drug</u> that is not prescribed by a doctor. That is just dangerous and desperate and... *illegal*. I am a strong advocate for the use of herbs and natural supplements for the body, whether it be for sexual performance, more energy or better sleep. Therefore, if your performance is lacking or your libido is low, find the right supplements to rectify the issue – whether a pill, potion or lotion! *(Contact me for recommendations.)*

Secondly, concerning sex toys: I find this unfit, especially any foreign object being inserted into the body. Remember that the beauty of pure sex is the exchange of blood that happens with intercourse and the entire beautiful process of physical intimacy and touch, leading up to penetration. There are some toys that are designed to help with libido or stamina, and such devices may be okay to use *temporarily* for therapeutic purposes, if you are having difficulty with sex. But I wouldn't suggest long term use of such devices and would use them only as a last resort. There are lust demons attached to many such devices, and addictions could easily be developed from the use of them.

Lastly, some couples use pornography to create arousal. Pornography is a sinful act – point blank, hands down, without any exceptions. This includes *homemade pornography*; in other words, it is not fitting for you to make sex tapes or photos with your spouse. This media could end up in the wrong hands, violating the sacredness of your intimacy. But more importantly than that, each sexual experience should be a fresh, new intimate encounter; not a stale copy. **The need for any external simulation to become aroused and enjoy sex with your spouse, is a sign of very serious trouble in your marriage.** You can take that statement to the bank!

I am sure that there are a number of additional topics that I could cover in this section, but it is impossible to address every specific manifestation of lust. The basic rule of thumb is this: Keep it pure, stay focused on oneness and creating a worship experience. True intimacy is about sharing the "authentic you" without anything added or taken away. Sex is thrilling, but it's not about getting a *thrill*; it's about getting a *fill* – a fill of the essence of the one you are in covenant with!

<u>**Oral Sex**</u> – I know this is a "sensitive" topic for the world of churchgoers, so I want to take my time with this one. People have strong beliefs, both for and against oral sex as a practice in marriage. I hold to the belief that oral sex is clearly depicted in The Song of Solomon as a beautiful part of marital intimacy. However, the devil has greatly perverted oral sex through homosexuality, pornography and prostitution. For some couples with certain backgrounds, oral sex may not be an expedient practice. People that previously practiced homosexuality; those that were or are addicted to pornography; those with promiscuous backgrounds; former participants in prostitution and those brought up being taught that oral sex is a sin – would all fall into the category of those that should probably omit oral sex as a practice. This would be advisable, at least, until you have gone through a <u>**thorough and definitive cleansing process**</u>.

Aside from these precautions, it is a matter of your own conviction, whether or not you practice oral sex as a pure act of intimacy in your marriage. If you desire this act and your spouse is opposed to it, submit to your spouse. And likewise, if you are opposed to this act and your spouse desires it, submit to your spouse. You do well either way, bearing in mind that in marriage, you should always be aiming to please your spouse in sexual relations – not pushing your own agenda. Although the act seems purely lustful to many people, the motive for oral sex can go beyond just a desire for a good feeling. For some people, it is a selfless act of service, in which they surrender their own pleasure, in order to satisfy their spouse. For some, it symbolizes a deeper more intimate connection with the person they love. Furthermore, there are many analogies made in the Bible, in reference to eating and drinking, in terms of our relationship with The LORD. Eating was an act of worship amongst the Levitical priesthood *(Lev 5:14-6:7, one of many references)*. Even David tells us to taste and see that The Lord is good *(Ps 34:8)*.

It is wrong for people to try to nullify the validity of the intimacy of oral sex, within the confines of marriage, just because they may have had a negative past experience with it, or because society has tried to claim this act exclusively for perversion. Just imagine if the church began to preach against the use of rainbows because gays now use the rainbow as their symbol of freedom to choose the gay lifestyle! I am not going to ban the use of a rainbow image, just because society has attempted to claim it as a symbol of perversion, and Christian couples should not be banned from practicing oral sex, even though society has attempted to claim it as a symbol of perversion.

There is NO biblical validity for preaching against oral sex in marriage, NONE. Every teaching I have ever seen or heard on it is based on scriptures being used out of context or are based on the world's perverted depiction of the act. So please, let this be a choice made between you and your spouse. If you enjoy it, don't feel condemned or guilty. If you don't feel comfortable with it then don't do it, but don't try to make a doctrine out of it to limit the freedom of other couples. Just always remember – motives! Listen to the voice of the Holy Spirit inside of you, and don't force it if it does not feel clean.

"^{12}[Young Man] You are my private garden, my treasure, my bride, a secluded spring, a hidden fountain. ^{13}Your thighs shelter a paradise of pomegranates with rare spices— henna with nard, ^{14}nard

and saffron, fragrant calamus and cinnamon, with all the trees of frankincense, myrrh, and aloes, and every other lovely spice. ^{15}You are a garden fountain, a well of fresh water streaming down from Lebanon's mountains. ^{16}[Young Woman] Awake, north wind! Rise up, south wind! Blow on my garden and spread its fragrance all around. Come into your garden, my love; taste its finest fruits. (Song of Solomon 4:12-16)"

Help, My Marriage Bed is Dirty!

Reading this chapter may have been quite an eye opener for you. You may now realize that even if you have been married for many years, you never truly understood the purpose of marital sex. Perhaps you have never experienced lovemaking as a worshipful experience that glorifies The Most High God. It may have hit you like a ton of bricks that spirits of sexual perversion are operative in your life. Maybe every single act on the "omit list" is on your "favorites list"! Be encouraged though, awareness is the first key to effecting change in our lives.

Please do not be disheartened or feel overwhelmed, and by no means should you fear what you might have to sacrifice sexually in your marriage, in order to get delivered. There will be sacrifices, and some of your current "favorites" might have to go – for a while, or even forever. However, be assured that whatever you sacrifice will be exceedingly outweighed by what the Holy Spirit gives you in return! You will not think of, nor even slightly miss, anything you give up that does not glorify Him.

I mentioned in the *Introduction* that married couples should read this book as partners. I want to expound upon that. It is important to understand that as a married couple, **YOU SHOULD GO THROUGH THE DELIVERANCE PROCESS TOGETHER**. Deliverance is discussed later in the book, but understand that studying this book will be the foundation of your deliverance from sexual perversion. If you and your spouse study it together, you will both have the same foundational understanding and truth to build upon. If you study it as part of a couples group, as was suggested in the introduction that will empower the two of you even more greatly.

You are going to learn in the upcoming chapters that demons are transferable. Therefore, if both you and your spouse are not cleansed simultaneously, these demons will be passed back and forth between the two of you like an STD. This is, sadly, a truth that I did not understand for quite some time when I was married. Even after much fasting and prayer individually, demons of sexual perversion still had access to me and my husband through our contact with one another. Ultimately, even though my ex-husband and I were both devout followers of Christ during our marriage, our failure to understand this truth and get delivered together as a couple eventually destroyed our marriage. That is why I encourage husbands and wives to read this book together and partner with one another in deliverance.

It is strongly advisable that you agree together to abstain from sexual activity during the course of studying this book *(with a set time of no greater than 40 days)*. However, if you have an unbelieving spouse; if your spouse is not willing or perhaps is unable to go through this process with you, please do not feel that it is hopeless. It will be more challenging if you have to work on it without their assistance, but once you acknowledge the problem; there are some effective steps that you can take by yourself.

For <u>step one</u>, anoint yourself, your bed and your spouse *(while they are sleeping)*. As <u>step two</u>, you should bind in the name of Yeshua (Jesus) any demons of sexual perversion, before and after intercourse, to prevent them from affecting you. Bind the spirits vocally, BUT VERY **DISCREETLY AND NOT IN YOUR SPOUSE'S HEARING**. *(That would be a definite turn-off, smile.)* In <u>step three</u>, continually pray for your spouse, standing in the gap for him or her. And most importantly, as <u>step four</u>; you must live uprightly before your spouse!

Either way you study this book, rather together with your spouse or together with just you and the Holy Spirit – please read chapter two again, in order to understand what your sexual intimacy with your spouse should be like. I have written many pieces over the years; however, the four points written in chapter two about what The Spirit teaches us through sexual intimacy, is the most beautiful thing I have ever written. Surely that is because I did not write it but the Holy

Spirit did. Read that chapter again and again for the rest of your life, and **never forget what your married sex represents**!

In my understanding, pure, intimate, loving sex is the most beautiful thing The Creator created and the greatest gift that He gave mankind. And truly it has to be because that is how beautiful intimate worship in spirit is to Him. Loving sex is a representation of His Unconditional Love, the very essence of Who HE Is. HE is LOVE; Love is the greatest gift, and He reveals a facet of this to us through the beauty and passion of physical intimacy between a husband and wife.

The first time this revelation really becomes **ALIVE** in you, and you actually act it out in your marriage bed, you will probably find yourself on your face prostrate before The LORD. You will have finally shared the **Ultimate Physical Expression of Love and Intimacy** with your spouse! Operating in the fullness of this revelation is so powerful that you can even sanctify an unclean and unbelieving spouse through lovemaking, once you really understand the power of marital sex. This is the hidden revelation of 1 Corinthians 7:14,

"For the unbelieving husband has been sanctified through his wife, and the unbelieving wife has been sanctified through her believing husband. Otherwise your children would be unclean, but as it is, they are holy."

Yes! I am saying that through sex with your spouse, you can actually bring deliverance to them! Once you have a firm understanding of the power of sexual intimacy and the exchange of spiritual energy that takes place, you can take **COMPLETE AUTHORITY** over every spirit of sexual perversion that is operative in your spouse's life. So it doesn't matter if they are in agreement with you or not. **LOVE IS THE GREATEST POWER IN THE UNIVERSE**, and you can use the power of love and intimacy to transfer a desire for Righteousness to them and drive out demonic powers. *Greater is HE that is in you, than he that is in the world (1 John 4:4)!* When you are submitted to The God of Love, you can overpower the god of this world operating in your spouse. It may take some time to learn how to walk in this revelation, but in the meantime, just enjoy practicing – **a lot** *(smile)*!

Insights from Dr. Intimacy

Have the Best Sex of Your Life!

Everything that I have shared thus far concerning marital sex has addressed primarily the spiritual dynamics, but sex is a physical act and so I would be remiss not to address some practical aspects as well. Sex is, in essence, much more spiritual than it is physical, and therefore what we have learned about the spiritual parallel between sex and worship is the most important ingredient in improving your sex life. At the same time, we ultimately relate to sex more physically than we do spiritually. Therefore, the physical dynamics of how we approach sexuality in marriage are very important as well.

I choose not to go into a great deal of detail about how to "do sex the right way". That could be another book all by itself – and could get a little pornographic *(lol)*. In all honesty though, I just truly believe that surrendering your body to your spouse, and flowing with the liberty of the Holy Spirit, will give you the strategy for enjoying your marital sex life. Furthermore, the ability to creatively enjoy sex is innate – a built-in instinct that will guide you, once you learn to move past the mental and emotional blockages that have hindered you in the past.

However, there are some issues that are just a matter of common sense and practicality. And while it seems that these are things that people should *"just know"*, my best friend always says to me, *"What's common about sense"!* So let's go over some bullet points that will help you improve your marital sex life. These are the ones that I believe are most prevalent.

- **Spontaneity** is very important. The same position, time of day, place and demeanor can become mechanical. Be open to creative ideas and giving into sudden urges.
- **Good hygiene** can make or break a marital bed. Keep your body clean – especially your breath and genital area – at all times possible. This helps with spontaneity as well.

- **Grooming** and appearance can really be a turn on or a turn off. Even when around the house, make a habit of keeping your appearance as attractive as you can.
- **Unpleasant health challenges** such as gas, snoring, sinus drip or otherwise, should be taken care of – use herbs, change your diet, visit a doctor. Do what you have to do and in the meantime, try to keep it out of the bedroom. *(i.e. don't cut the cheese in the bedroom or blow your nose in the bed when you know you are about to have an intimate moment!)*
- **Your natural sex drive** may be too low. If you have difficulty maintaining an erection (for males) or climaxing (for females), don't just ignore the problem. It is not likely to get better! Do your due diligence to improve the situation. *(Please contact me for some great herbal products to help with your libido.)*
- **Overweight or badly aging** bodies should not be accepted as a normal part of getting older – *getting* older does not have to mean *growing* older. Do your part to remain fit and healthy. Going on health challenges together, as a couple, can be fun. Abstinence can be your discipline and sex your reward for reaching certain goals!
- **Talk about your sex life**. You don't understand what sex is like for your spouse because you are the opposite SEX, so... TALK ABOUT IT! Have open, honest conversations about your sex life. Discuss what you like, what you don't like and ideas for improvement. Watch scientific documentaries together about the human body and sexuality. Take learning about each other's bodies very seriously, but make it fun, even giving each other quizzes and rewards.
- **Get counseling** if you have experienced sexual abuse, adultery, addictive sexual perversion behaviors or other traumatic issues in the past! These kinds of scars can fester for a lifetime without proper attention.
- **Create ambience** in your home. Keep your house clean. Cleanliness is, believe it or not, very sexy. A bouquet of a dozen roses just looks more romantic on a clean polished dresser, than on the floor competing against a stack of unfiled junk mail and a pile of dirty laundry!

- **Have frequent *play* dates**. Even if you can't afford something fancy, do anything together that will make you laugh. Laughter releases the hormones that stir sexual desire.
- **Tongue Kissing** releases hormones in both the male and the female. Kiss passionately before, during and after sex. Sexual desire tends to build momentum – the more you enjoy it, the more your body craves it and adapts to performing it well. So keep those engines burning by kissing often!
- **Foreplay** means to "play around before" penetration. Foreplay can be instrumental in experiencing more intense ecstasy during intercourse. Foreplay can be happening all day long, not just in the bed. How you interact with your spouse throughout the day can be a precursor to an awesome sexual explosion later on. For example, helping her in the kitchen can be very sexy to a wife; enjoying a sports program with him, can really be a turn on to a husband!

There is so much more but these are some basic, common sense pointers that should be highly regarded when it comes to having a dynamic sex life. If there is one thing that I believe strongly about marital sex, it is that IT SHOULD KNOCK SINFUL SEX OUT OF THE BALLPARK! Marital sex should be mind-blowing, explosive, passionate and unforgettable. **UNFORGETTABLE** – meaning when the temptation of adultery presents itself to you, you can't forget the last mind-blowing orgasm that you had with your spouse! **UNFORGETTABLE** – meaning when divorce crosses your mind, you quickly remember your desire to continue sharing explosive ecstasy with your spouse forever and go to counseling instead! **UNFORGETTABLE** – meaning that you just can't go to sleep angry because as soon as you lie down in your bed, your genitals burn with desire, as you remember the night before, and you are compelled to "make up"! Yes **UNFORGETTABLE** – like never forget; you are mine; I am yours, and... *that's the way, uh-huh, uh-huh we like it, uh-huh, uh-huh!* LOL

Implement everything that you have learned in this chapter, and you will experience **THE BEST SEX OF YOUR LIFE**!!!

Chapter 5

A Warning to Believers And the "So-Called Sanctified"!

Even as Believers, we live in a world full of sexual perversion. Are we really liberated? After reading this, you may think twice!

I really feel pressed in my spirit to more specifically address us church-going brothers and sisters, in Christ, on this issue before we continue – all of us who think we are "OK". As we will learn in the next chapter, each act of sexual perversion is titled after a demonic spirit that causes that act to take place. With this understanding in mind, it cannot be stressed enough the importance of understanding that the chief assignment of every spirit of sexual perversion is to <u>**distort your intimate relationship with your Savior.**</u>

The act of sexual sin in the flesh itself is only a means to an end; that end being a distorted intimate relationship with Yahweh God. If the spirit of sexual perversion that has been assigned to operate in your life can get to that end by a different means, it will do so because distorting your relationship with The LORD is the greater goal and the task that is most important to that spirit. As a matter of fact, this book could have actually been named, ***"The Spirits of <u>Worship</u> Perversion"***! What I am trying to get you to understand is that you may have spirits of sexual perversion operating in your life, even if you no longer *physically* commit acts of sexual sin or even if you **never** did!!!

Let us consider at a practical example to illustrate this point. A man who is infected with the HIV virus for instance, may not have any *physical* symptoms. Yet, the virus is active in his blood. Although he may *seem* healthy, he is infected and is in turn able to infect others. Sometimes we as Believers think that we are spiritually healthy just because we do not see any *physical* manifestation of the spirits that have us bound. In other words, if we do not commit **the act of sin in the flesh** then we believe that we are free of that particular sin or spirit. However, this is not at all, always the case. Taking into consideration once again that the act of sexual sin occurring physically, is just a method that is used by spirits of sexual perversion to achieve the greater goal of distorting our intimate relationship with Yahweh – let's consider the following parable, for further illustration.

Staying Focused on the Ultimate Goal

There was a young man whose ultimate life goal was to own a multi-million dollar corporation. He mapped out a plan of action to achieve this goal. His action plan included going to college to get his PhD, starting a small business, and finally growing that small business into a multi-million dollar corporation. The young man implemented his action plan by beginning college. However, in the midst of his studies, his wealthy uncle died and willed to the young man, an already established, multi-million dollar corporation.

The man would have to leave college in order to run this corporation, or he would lose it. The young student pondered over whether or not he should leave his studies to take his place as owner of the corporation. He began to re-evaluate his ultimate goal. His ultimate goal was to own a multi-million dollar corporation. His goal was never to go to college, it was to own a corporation. Going to college was only a method or a means that he was using to get to the greater goal at the end. He easily realized that his goal had been accomplished and that he would be a fool to turn down the greater for the lesser!

The young man left college, resolving in his mind that he may at some point in time return to school to get that degree, if it became necessary to help him maintain his corporation or maybe even just for the sake of gaining additional knowledge. Yet, he knew that if he was never able to go back to college and was still able to maintain or increase the status of his multi-million dollar corporation, he would *certainly die content and satisfied with that part of his life. He had already achieved his ultimate life goal!*

This analogy helps us understand the intent and strategy of *spirits of worship perversion*. Their goal is not necessarily to get us to physically commit acts of sexual sin. Their ultimate goal is to distort our intimate relationship with The Father. Physical acts of sexual sin, just so happen to be, the most common and effective method used to accomplish this end. However, just like the young man who left college to take ownership of the already established multi-million dollar corporation, if these spirits can achieve the theft of our spiritual worship by a method other than luring us into sexual sin, they will most assuredly be satisfied. They will abandon the attempt to lure us into physical sexual sin, in order to secure us in a place of distorted intimate relations with The LORD.

Let it be iterated to us again that what the Holy Spirit is really trying to convey is that **these spirits can be at work in our spiritual lives, even if they are not at work in our physical lives**! As I was writing this book, this is the revelation that really blew me away. I thought that I was just writing it to help those that are physically committing acts of sexual perversion. Then the Holy Spirit began to reveal to me that some of the spirits of sexual perversion that I *thought* I was delivered from, I was not delivered from at all! Yes, it was true that I no longer physically committed the acts, but spiritually, these spirits had still been at work in my life, distorting my intimate relationship with My Savior and my intimacy with those around me. How deceived we Christians can be at times – so blind to satan's true plans and purposes. Often times we are too wise in our own conceits *(Rom 11:25)* to receive an impartation of Yahweh's true wisdom!

Please hear what The Spirit is saying to us my brothers and sisters in Christ. Whether we are single or married Believers, there is still a great likelihood that spirits of sexual perversion are yet operative in our lives. These spirits could be manifesting themselves physically, and their works could be blatantly obvious. Or they could be, even more dangerously, manifesting themselves only spiritually, while being deceptively subtle. Either way, the assignment of these spirits of sexual perversion in our lives is still the same – to distort our intimate relationship with Yahweh God. If our intimate relationship with The LORD becomes or remains distorted, everything in our lives will be distorted as well!

Without proper intimacy with The Father, we are not strongly connected to Him. Yeshua is the vine, and we are the branches *(John 15:5)*. Thus, without that connection, we will not be able to produce abundant fruit – maybe even no fruit at all. Anything that does not produce fruit will be cut down and burned up *(Mat 3:10)*. How we interact with The LORD also affects how we interact with people. Therefore, a distorted relationship with Him is also going to distort our relationships with others, including our spouses, children, friends and everyone else. How then will we be effective witnesses for Christ? Furthermore, we as Christians are all a part of The Savior's **One** Body. Thus, distorted relations with Him, means distorted relations with one another as sisters and brothers in Christ as well. Consequently, each spirit of worship perversion plays an integral role in the disunity and dysfunction of the Body of Christ as a whole!

Are you beginning to understand the depth of this thing? It is about so much more than just you as an individual committing an act of sin. Satan is at war with the Body of Christ, in an attempt to completely destroy us all. Even though he is already defeated, his demons of sexual perversion have an important role in his greater plan to destroy as many Believers as possible. Part of what keeps us in deception concerning this issue is the confusion surrounding the question of whether or not a Christian can be *possessed* with a demon.

Although there is a correct and incorrect answer to this confusion, we do not need to specifically address this issue. *Do you know why we do not need to address it?* Because it does not matter! **Listen** – whether you are *possessed, oppressed, suppressed* or otherwise; whether the demon is living *in you, on you* or just hovering *around you* – it really does not matter. The effects are still devastating at any rate, and the way you get delivered from these demons is basically the same regardless. You must become aware of and bind every demon that is operating in your life on any level, and the question of *possession* matters very little.

Having said all of that, how will you know if these spirits are operating in your spiritual life or your marriage? I suggest that you just assume they are! I am about to make a shocking statement that might make you want to close this book and curse me, **BUT DON'T!** The statement is this: In my 15 years of facilitating this assignment to the Body of Christ, encountering thousands of Believers on all different levels of spiritual maturity, I've met only a few that were not influenced by these spirits in some aspect. Please, be not offended! Be encouraged to finally have answers to the perplexing matters of dis-integrity in The Church and to know that you are not alone in this fight. Get *M.A.D.* – **M**ake **A** **D**ecision – that it ends now in your life and in the Body of Christ!

If every Believer treats this issue as if it is a **PERSONAL STRUGGLE** and not just something that "someone else" is dealing with, we can all, as One Unified Body, be truly free to worship The Father in spirit and in truth and become that spotless bride that will usher in the return of Our Lord! If you open your heart to receive Yeshua's Truth, it will be revealed to you, as you read on. As I stated previously, I was not at first writing this book thinking that I needed to be delivered from anything of the sort. I was certain that I was victoriously free from all spirits of sexual perversion. Yet, my heart was receptive to The Truth and as the Holy Spirit wrote through my hands, I became more of a student than an author.

As you begin to read the upcoming chapters, pay close attention to the assessment of each spirit. Be especially mindful of what is written under the headings entitled, **"The Assignment"**, **"The Churchgoer Profile"** and **"The Worship Portrait"**. It is in these sections that the Holy Spirit exposes the behavior of Believers that are operating under the influence of the particular spirit being studied. These sections are written particularly for Believers that may not be committing the *physical* acts of sexual sin. It was as I wrote these sections that I most realized, I was yet in need of deliverance, and I hope it will have the same effect on you.

In conclusion, let us understand Church that for the sake of our own soul salvation, our marriages, our personal happiness and the Body of Christ as a whole, it is so important that we allow Yeshua to truly heal and deliver us, **IN TOTALITY**. If we do not allow the Holy Spirit to reveal the truth to us about our own hearts, we will be just like the person who is carrying the HIV virus but does not know it. We will be spreading infection and disease to others, while we ourselves are in danger of dying a miserable, tortuous death.

The Father will hold us accountable for our carelessness and selfishness because He forewarns us in Jeremiah 17:9 that *"The heart is deceitful above all things, and desperately wicked..."* Deceitful above **all** things? Wow, what a powerful statement! Are you sure that you have not been deceived by your deceitful heart into *thinking* that you are delivered? You better be really, really sure...

Insights from Dr. Intimacy

Are You A Virgin or Did You Marry As One?

One of the most disturbing observations of this revelation is in the case of women and men who are virgins or those who married as virgins. First of all, after reading the upcoming chapters, I am about 100% positive that you are going to realize that there are not many *authentic* virgins to begin with. And second of all, the "so-called virgin" status of many people really blinds them to the depth of perversion operating in their lives. This is also highly applicable to people that have been abstinent for an extended period of time and those that have been faithfully married for a number of years.

I have encountered many such Believers, but there is one sister in particular that stands out in my mind. She had been with only one man her entire life, and they had been married for a very long time. However, the spirit of fornication was operating in her life so strongly that it was as if she had been the most promiscuous girl on the block. I also saw a strong manifestation of the spirits of masturbation and sexual fantasy operating through her. She was totally unaware of these strongholds, and sadly too blinded by the pride of her "pure history" to even consider it.

This sister had a beautiful singing voice, and it was obvious that there was a strong call on her life to use her gift of singing to do a notable work in the Body of Christ. Unfortunately, her gift remained just that – *a gift*. It never became an *anointing* – a yoke-destroying, burden-lifting sound that could be used all over the world. Because she was not able to intimately connect with The Father, she could not allow Him to fertilize and birth out the assignment attached to her gift.

Do you have incredible gifts and talents that seem to be lying dormant, or ineffectual? Are there unfulfilled prophecies concerning the call on your life that you don't seem to be moving any closer to? Do you have a persistent character flaw or continuous difficulty in relationships with people? These could all be signs of spirits of sexual perversion distorting the intimacy with your Creator that allows for conception and birth of His will for your life.

Always remember that a problem you are not aware of is one that will never be corrected. Please don't let your lack of *obvious* sexual sin blind you to your need to develop TRUE intimacy with The Lover of Your Soul.

Chapter 6

Defining Sexual Perversion

Having a clear understanding of exactly what sexual perversion is will strengthen the foundation that we have built thus far.

It is almost time to delve into the assessments of the spirits we will be studying in the upcoming chapters, but before we move on to that, let us build on the knowledge that we have gained thus far by looking into the definitions of the words 'sexual' and 'perversion'. I do not want to leave any room for satan to deceive us. We therefore need a crystal-clear understanding of exactly what sexual perversion is.

According to Merriam-Webster's On-line Collegiate Dictionary, **sexual** can be defined as *"of, relating to, or involving sex, the sexes, or the sex organs."* The root word of perversion is pervert. According to that same dictionary **pervert** means *"1. to lead away from the proper, right, or accepted course: corrupt. 2. to use wrongly or improperly: misuse."* It also lets us know that the word **perversion** means *"1. the act of perverting or state of being perverted. 2. a deviant form of sexual behavior."* (Merriam-WebsterCollegiate.com 12/05/2004). Combining these three words, with an understanding of the Law and Righteousness of Yahweh God, into a comprehensive Christian definition gives us:

Sexual Perversion - Deviation from The Creator's ordained sexual intimacy between husband and wife; misuse of sex and/or sex organs; corruption of sexual intimacy in thought or in action, as it relates to Yahweh's plan and purpose for it.

Prior to moving on to the breakdown of the different types of sexual perversion, I would like to lay a little more ground information. The term *'sexual perversion'* will not be found verbatim, in the King

James Version of the Bible. This is simply due to the cultural and language differences of the era in which the King James Version was written. In the Old Testament, the terms 'adultery', 'harlot(ry)' and 'whore(dom)' are often used in place of what we would term 'sexual perversion'. In the New Testament, the term 'fornication', which literally translates in the Greek *'illicit sexual intercourse',* is widely used in place of what we would term 'sexual perversion'.

In some newer translations of the Bible, you may see the terms 'sexual perversion' or 'sexual immorality'. You may even see some of the ten types of sexual perversion that you will soon learn, referred to using the same names. It all depends on what translation you are reading. What is most important though, is that we are not deceived about the truth of Yah's Word, by getting caught up into minor language issues. Any person that sincerely desires to know the truth and desires to understand the *Spirit* of His Holy Word will successfully be led by His Holy Spirit past every language barrier.

Another term you will see in the assessments is **'sexual contact'**, which is used in many of the definitions that you will read. I want us to have a clear understanding of exactly what this term means. Inclusive in this term is oral sex, anal sex, manual sexual stimulation, sexual stimulation using any type of object or any type of physical contact (i.e. grinding, dirty dancing, humping with or without clothes on, etcetera) that is performed <u>with the intent</u> to sexually stimulate or cause an orgasm. This does not always, but can even include kissing, depending on how it is done. By worldly standards, *sex* has to include penetration, but by Yah's standard of Righteousness, it only has to include the motive and intent to sexually stimulate and gratify. The Father judges us by a much higher standard, according to the motives of our hearts *(1 Sam 16:7, Jer 11:20, Heb 4:12).*

<u>**Please be mindful that I am not declaring that all of the acts that are inclusive in the term 'sexual contact' are sinful**</u>. I am simply explaining what the term *'sexual contact'* means. Sexual contact is not lawful, **under any circumstances,** outside of the confines of marriage. However, most types of sexual contact are acceptable within the confines of marriage. We already discussed this, so I need not say any

more about marital sexual contact. As was stated earlier, what is lawful for you in your marriage is between you and *the god* you serve.

You will also see the terms 'law', 'lawfully' or 'legal' in some of the definitions. Often times, there are conflicts between modern law and culture and biblical law and culture. When this is the case, we should adhere to the laws and customs of the region and culture that we currently live in. The Bible tells us to obey the laws of the land *(Rom 13:1-3)*; therefore we are to be subject to the laws of whatever government we are currently under.

This is generally the case. However, because of the evil nature of the world that we live in, secular laws can sometimes, blatantly and unquestionably, cause us to sin *(i.e. the case with the three Hebrew boys in the book of Daniel 3)*. Thus ultimately, whenever we think about what is legal or lawful; we should <u>first</u> be considering what is lawful in the sight of Yahweh God, according to the Spirit of Holiness that convicts us. <u>Secondly,</u> for issues that deal specifically with the government and secular law, we should consider the laws and customs of the time and region that we live in *now*, not what *was* legal according to customs and culture in Bible times.

For instance, polygamy was an acceptable practice in biblical times, as was the marriage of an older man and young girl, but both of these practices are now illegal and punishable by law in the US. Deciphering which laws we should submit to can be challenging in this day. I was greatly disheartened to learn that a law punishing bestiality in the military was overturned by the Obama administration. We also know that gay marriage has now become "legal" in many states. Yet adhering to either of these laws would clearly violate Yahweh's laws. As a general rule of thumb, to help you properly govern your own life – if a secular law reinforces or supports a Kingdom principle or has no direct bearing on any Kingdom principle, then it should be adhered to. However, any secular law that violates, corrupts or perverts principles of Righteous, Kingdom living, should be completely disregarded! Please bear these things in mind, as you read on.

Now that I have clarified the specific terminology that will be used in the assessments, let's talk a little more about sexual perversion. Sexual perversion, by the definition given above, would include any and all sexual acts that do not take place *in privacy, between* a lawfully (*in the sight of The LORD*) married husband and wife. Understanding the definition of sexual perversion enables us to concisely outline what behaviors fall into this category. There are ten manifestations of sexual perversion that I noted that are expressly outlined and/or described in the Bible:

1. Fornication
2. Masturbation
3. Adultery
4. Incest
5. Homosexuality
6. Prostitution
7. Pornography (Sexual Fantasy)
8. Rape (Sexual Abuse)
9. Bestiality
10. Sexual Lust (Lasciviousness)

For the most part, these exact terms will not be found in the King James Version of the Bible *(which is the most widely used version)*. As I mentioned earlier, this is due only to translation challenges – not only literal translations, but the translation of meaning and symbolism as well. However, there are scriptural references that do describe these specific acts of sexual perversion, in accordance with our definition and understanding of them. Coming up in the next 11 chapters, we are going to gain a better understanding of each of the acts of sexual perversion named above, by studying a detailed assessment of each one. We will also study the assisting spirit, promiscuity.

Let me explain to you the lay out of the upcoming assessments, in order to increase your understanding. There will be nine headings listed in each chapter, as follows:

Name of the Act - Each classification of sexual perversion is also the name of a type of demonic spirit that is responsible for influencing that act of sexual sin to take place on the earth. For example, if you fornicate then "the spirit of fornication" is at work in your life. You will first see the name of the act, or spirit, listed as the chapter title; along with a scripture or two, that makes reference to it.

Some Biblical References - This section will contain a list of additional scriptures in the Bible that you can refer to for your own personal studies. Please note that some scriptures listed will only be clearly relevant, when read in certain versions of the Bible. You will have to do your due diligence to make the connections in your personal study time. A great On-line resource that allows you to compare different versions of the Bible, for free, is *www.biblegateway.com*.

The Definition - Here you will learn a brief definition of the act itself. These are Spirit-revealed definitions, as opposed to dictionary quotes. The definitions are a combination of the literal meaning and the Kingdom principles that govern and define these acts.

The Assignment - Remember, we have learned that satan's purposes always go beyond just the actual *act* of sin taking place. Ultimately, he wants us to be eternally damned and tries to cause this by clouding our understanding of our relationship with The Father. Subsequently, each type of demon of sexual perversion has a **very specific** assignment and duty in this respect that will be outlined under this heading.

The Practical Understanding – This section will be used to expound upon the basic understanding of the sin element and the literal acts that are associated with the spirit.

The Personality Profile - In this section, you will get an understanding of how the spirit affects your mental and emotional state, your personality traits and your social interaction with others.

The Churchgoer Profile - Here you learn what bearing the spirit's influence has on your likelihood to be a churchgoer, how it affects your church experience and how it affects your interaction with other Believers.

The Worship Portrait – This is the most important section, especially for those of us that were addressed in chapter five that think this book is for "someone else". This is where you will gain understanding of how the particular demon that is being discussed manifests itself in your spiritual life. This will show how your relationship with Yahweh has been distorted; in other words, it will reveal how effectively "the assignment" is being carried out by the spirit.

Insights from Dr. Intimacy – You have already seen this section in previous chapters. These are writings that contain additional nuggets of insight in the form of personal deliverance details, testimonies, articles or stories. I wanted to include these, to help you be enlightened to a different perspective that will cause you to gain an even deeper understanding. *The insights section is **NOT** optional. You will miss a lot of good meat if you skip them.*

I want you to be aware that as you begin to read the assessments, you will probably find that you have more than one of these spirits operating in your life. In essence, all of these spirits are under the authority of one greater demonic power, and therefore they all work in conjunction with one another. However, there can only be one ruler per kingdom. Although there may be more than one spirit of sexual perversion operating in your life, only one of them is what we will call **"the strongman"** (Mat 12:29). <u>This is the one that has the most control and dominates within you.</u>

Pay attention to the descriptions of how these spirits manifest themselves in your life, both naturally and spiritually, and ask the Holy Spirit to reveal to you which spirit is the strongman. This is the demon that you may experience your greatest struggles with when seeking deliverance. Also, be mindful of the fact that the dominating spirit in your life can change. For example, the strongman of sexual perversion may be different once you get married than it is when you are a single, college student. You want to identify which spirit is the strongman now and what other spirits may have been the strongman at other seasons of your life. Having this knowledge will greatly assist you in the process of deliverance that will be discussed in the last chapter.

The first two steps that will be discussed in the deliverance process are going to depend heavily on how closely you pay attention to these assessments. In step one, you must acknowledge the sins in your life and therefore must be fully aware of what those sins are. You must be able to recognize *sin as sin*. In step two, you will need to trace back over your life and track the opening that demons entered in through. For instance, maybe a wound of sexual molestation left an opening for a spirit of homosexuality to enter your life. Or, perhaps a generational curse left an opening for incest. It will work as such, so please take copious notes on the assessments, and identify what has, in the past, or currently is influencing you.

Identifying the strongman (or strongmen) is necessary because knowing which spirit is the strongman will give you insight into the severity of the particular entrance that it entered in through. In other words, it will help you discover how the strongman became so strong – what weakness did it take advantage of? In this way, you will be better equipped to tear down those fortified strongholds of satan, which usually requires healing from some issue of your past. It is a good idea to buy the coinciding workbook to this book, and use it to help you make the assessments. Use the *"Definitive Sexual Perversion Charts"* in the workbook to help you keep track of which spirits are at work in your life and which ones you think may now be, or have in the past been, the strongman. *(If the workbook is not yet available when you are reading this, please email me and request a copy of the charts.)*

The descriptions of how these demons manifest themselves in your life are very specific. You may find that some of the personality, emotional, mental, social and spiritual descriptions listed under certain spirits only describe you to a certain extent. That is simply an indication that the particular spirit that you will be reading about is not the strongman, or that you are not yet totally given over to that spirit. You should know though that the longer you allow that demon to operate in your life, the more strength it will gain and the more you will become like the description that you will read. In other cases though, concerning another spirit, the descriptions may fit you almost to a tee. It will probably be almost as if I had been reading your mind, living in your heart and spying out your business! That is how you will know who the strongman in your life is. In either case, make note of this in your journal and in the workbook.

As we take a look into how these demons manifest themselves in our lives, some of the descriptions will be a little rough. They may even be offensive to you, if you have some of these characteristics, which of course are for the most part – **negative**. However, The Father corrects those whom He loves, and He gives us wisdom in areas where we are ignorant, *if* we allow Him to *(Heb 12:6, James 1:5).* Please do not allow a spirit of offense to harden your heart against Yah's truth. People are only offended when they feel the need to defend themselves, but you need not ever defend yourself against the truth. The Bible lets us know that it is the truth that makes us free *(John 8:31-32).*

These are demons that we are talking about, not sweet little fairies. The demons are ugly, and the way that they manifest themselves in your life is ugly too! You can take comfort in knowing though that it is not so much you that is being described, as much as it is the demon operating through you that is being described. These are the same truths that I had to face when going through my own deliverance process from spirits of sexual perversion. It was hard sometimes to acknowledge how I truly acted as a person in bondage. Yet, I was always encouraged to continue on because I knew that however these demons were manifesting themselves in my life was not what my God created me to be. I knew and understood that if I could just allow the Holy Spirit to expose my enemies to me and empower me to break free from their bondage that those ugly traits about me would change.

So, please remember and be assured throughout the book that I understand what you are going through and that I am for you and not against you. Nothing that is said in this book is being said to put you down or make you feel bad or guilty. Everything that is being said is being said to expose satan and take away his power. I want to *de-power satan* in your life and **EMPOWER YOU,** with the might of the Lord God Almighty.

This is the journey that we all must take to reach the destination of glorious freedom, and that is why in the chapters leading up to the assessments, I have spoken in terms of 'we' and 'us', including myself as a partaker of these truths. However, throughout the assessments, I will be referring to YOU DIRECTLY. This is NOT because I consider myself to "have arrived" or due to me looking down my nose in judgment. My reason is that I want to speak directly to you from this point forward. This is a personal battle now, between you and the demons that are trying to destroy your destiny.

I want to stir up and agitate and weaken every demonic spiritual stronghold in your life with THE TRUTH. This is not about your neighbor, your son, your daughter, your husband, your wife, your Mom, your Dad, your sister, your brother, your extended family, your pastor, "people" in the church, "people" in the world, your haters or even the person who violated you... This is about YOU! I am going to leave nothing to chance. I am going to assume that you have some secret *little thing*, hiding away in your heart that has been sabotaging The Anointing on your life for years. I am going to speak directly to you and that *little thing*. I am going to speak directly to those demons that have been hanging around stealing, killing and destroying your effectiveness in purpose. And when I am finally finished writing this book, I am going to sit back and read it, not as an author or editor or teacher – but just like you, I will read it for myself, as someone who needs more deliverance!

Reading through the definitions, assessments and breakdowns of each of these spirits and how they manifest themselves in your life, will be hard at times because you will be forced to look at yourself in the bright light of truth, and see yourself in a way that you never have before. But my prayers are with you and so is The LORD. Please do not be afraid because you are not alone on this journey. Why should you continue to hide the truth from yourself? You are not fooling anyone else. Everyone else sees. You are the only one shrouded in deception about who you really are. So let your defenses down, and be prepared to drink the bitter waters of truth on the following pages. The end result will be sweet. I guarantee you that! As we take this journey, if we press on until the end, we will achieve deliverance and freedom!!!

*NOTE: Now is a good time to re-visit the *"How to get the most out of this book"* section in the introduction. Don't forget to print out the prayer that I suggest in the intro *(page 3)*, and recite it out loud each time before you read. And let's just recap on some key terms one last time on the next page and say a final prayer together:

Sexual Perversion

Deviation from The Creator's ordained sexual intimacy between husband and wife; misuse of sex and/or sex organs; corruption of sexual intimacy in thought or in action, as it relates to Yahweh's plan and purpose for it.

What Sexual Perversion Literally Means

Any and all sexual acts that do not take place <u>*in privacy,* *between*</u> a lawfully (<u>*in the sight of The Father*</u>) married husband and wife.

What Constitutes Sexual Contact?

Oral sex, anal sex, manual sexual stimulation, sexual stimulation using any type of object or any type of physical contact (i.e. grinding, dirty dancing, humping with or without clothes on, etcetera) that is performed <u>**with the intent**</u> to sexually stimulate or cause an orgasm. This does not always but can even include kissing, depending on how it is done.

A Prayer of Victory for Us!

Dear Father, I pray that You will strengthen us your children as we read on. I pray that our hearts, ears and eyes will be open to receive whatever it is that You want to reveal to us, as we read the remainder of this book. I pray that we will be encouraged and excited to read through to the end and that we will feel Your Enduring Love, mercy and grace surround us as we do. I also pray that by Your mighty power we will be fully equipped with desire, insight and understanding, in order to completely obey and carry out Your instructions that will be given to us, for the purpose of enabling us to be totally delivered, walking in newness of life abundantly and victoriously. In Yeshua's Mighty Name, it is so, because You Lord Yahweh Almighty have said it. Hallelujah! Thank you Yeshua!!!

Chapter 7

Fornication

"Now the works of the flesh are manifest, which are these; adultery, fornication, uncleanness, lasciviousness... as I have also told you in time past, that they which do such things shall not inherit the Kingdom of God. (Gal 5:19-21, KJV)"

Some Biblical References

Lev 18:20; 2 Chronicles 21:11, Isaiah 23:17, Eze 16:26, 16:29; Mat 5:32, 19:9; John 8:41; Acts 15:20; 15:29, 21:25; Rom 1:29; 1 Cor 5:1, 6:13, 6:18, 7:2, 10:8; 2 Cor 12:21; Gal 5:19; Eph 5:3; Col 3:5, 1 Thes 4:3; Jude 1:7; Rev 2:14; 2:20-21, 9:21, 14:8, 17:2-4, 18:3, 18:9, 19:2

The Definition

Sexual intercourse or any type of sexual contact or misconduct acted out by a person who is not married; including sexual activity with someone else's spouse. Illicit or deviant sexual behavior carried out by *any* person, married or single, with or without the involvement of a person's own spouse.

The Assignment

Sex is arguably the most pleasurable physical experience available to be enjoyed by human beings. Marriage is arguably one of the most challenging experiences. Marriage is a lifelong commitment to conform, reshape and in some cases completely sacrifice your own dreams, goals and desires for the sake of joining with someone else's. It is a sacred blood covenant that is designed to remain established for the span of your remaining years once implemented. Your reward as a married person for submitting to this challenge is beautiful, mind-blowing ecstasy through the joy of sexual intimacy. Married couples are the only people that have the Right with Yahweh God's blessing to enjoy this reward; it is His gift to the married. But fornicators usurp the responsibilities and challenges of marriage and go straight for the reward. You seek the ultimate benefit of marriage – sexual pleasure – without paying the price of marriage. **The assignment of the spirit of fornication is to impart into you the idea that you can enjoy the pleasures of God without making a commitment to be one with Him.**

The Practical Understanding

There are numerous references to fornication in the Bible. However as I mentioned in the previous chapter, biblically, fornication is a word that was used to mark a multiplicity of sexually perverse acts. This is because in essence, every act of sexual perversion is an act of fornication. We commonly think of fornication as a sexual relationship between an unmarried, dating male and female. This is the purest form of fornication, when fornication is truly the dominating spiritual influence of sexual misconduct. This is basically the context in which I will refer to fornication in this book. However, you should remain mindful of the truth that all sexually perverse acts are a type of fornication, even those that do not involve a partner and those that take place within a marriage.

Since we are thinking in terms of unmarried couples, let's go over what constitutes a legal and honorable marriage. For the most part, in biblical culture, unless you were a prostitute, an adulterous woman, a homosexual or were a victim of rape, you were considered married to whomever you had intercourse with. There was usually some type of verbal agreement between the families of the bride and groom and also a ceremony. However, these measures were not required and did not always occur. Once intercourse took place, you were considered to be married.

In our culture and times today, things are quite different. Sex is so loosely regarded that it holds very little significance at all. Therefore, to be lawfully married in the US money has to be paid, a license has to be obtained, paperwork has to be filed and a qualified person has to perform a ceremony. Of course, we must remember that when we are talking about what is lawful, we are first considering what is lawful in the sight of The LORD. No matter what the government says, The Father only honors marriages between one man and one woman. Unless you go through all of the practical steps mentioned above, with only one person of the opposite sex, you are not lawfully married in the sight of The Lord. This means that **_any_** sex(ual contact) you engage in is sinful. Just for clarification: You can only legally have one spouse at a time and must legally divorce a previous spouse before marrying again.

The Personality Profile

Fornication is such a vast issue to cover. The best approach is to break it down into three **types,** since the manifestations can vary quite a bit. You may only have the characteristics of one type, but more than likely you are a combination of all three. The purpose of separating them into types is simply to help you identify which type is dominant in you.

__Type 1 Fornicator__ - You are involved with someone that does not want to commit to marriage. Yet, you are willing to settle for an illicit sexual relationship with that person, even though you want marriage.

In this case, you are suffering from low self-esteem and lack a sense of self-worth. You probably feel like nobody loves you. You would get married if you could, but you know that you cannot make that happen. You have been, or probably will be, in many relationships like this because you are highly sensitive and insecure. A relationship with you becomes very tedious after a while, and you are prone to being on the receiving end of a break-up. If your partner does stay with you, it is unlikely that he or she will be faithful because you take the fun out of being in an uncommitted relationship. This is due to your high expectations and ever-pressing desire to marry. Because each break up makes you feel that much worse about yourself, you are that much more likely to get into the same type of relationship again.

You tend to settle for less in life. You allow others to take advantage of you without much complaint. It is not that you do not desire more, you just feel like it is out of your control to make it happen for yourself. You lack the courage and motivation to try to do better. You know in your heart that you could have more if you would pursue more, but somewhere along the way, someone spoke very damaging words over you, and you learned to settle for less. You are full of self-pity and crave major attention. You often times over-exaggerate your woes to gain notice, but even once you gain the attention of others, it is still never enough.

You are probably a person that likes being sick for the attention that it can bring you. You will for example, put up the appearance of extreme illness for something as minor as a cold or a headache. People usually *tolerate* you instead of *celebrate* you. You call everyone your "friend", but in all honesty most of those so-called friends are just "putting up with you", so to speak – you are probably totally oblivious to this though. Your constant need for attention is just a turn off to most people. However, just as you cling to your non-committing sexual partner, you so cling to others. You are a hard one to get rid of. You hate to be alone and will always try to find some way to be in the presence of others. You feel depressed and lonely by yourself.

Type 2 Fornicator - *You find that others are not "worth the trouble" of commitment and engage in frivolous dating, without any intention of even considering marriage with any of your sexual partners.*

You are an arrogant, cocky person who is selfish and cares very little about the well-being of others. Arrogance and pride are usually a cover for insecurity, and you are probably afraid of being hurt more than anything else. You may even harbor a "secret desire" to get married, but you would rather hurt first, than be hurt. You would never say that though, instead you use people for what you can get out of them and then move on.

You usually choose a **type 1** person to have sex with because being with a **type 2** person like yourself is too threatening. You want to be in control of the relationship. You feel easily threatened in life, in general, and want to be in control of everything. You are more than willing to abuse others to make yourself feel more secure, although deep in your heart you never really do feel secure.

You feel empowered to know that you have someone at your mercy and like to exercise that power by playing a lot of mind games. Sometimes you pretend to be very warm, and other times you are cold and calculating. It is all part of the game that you play – *with yourself more than anyone else.* You crave that sense of empowerment. People may sometimes see you as almost having a split personality because you are so unpredictable. Although you can be a really nice person, you do not want anyone trying to get too close to you, and you make sure of this by readily exhibiting the dark side of your personality. You are just nice enough to keep people drawn to you, but cutting enough to let them know that they should keep their distance.

You may have been the victim of a **type 2** fornicator in the past, and this is your way of avenging yourself. Undoubtedly, someone made you afraid to love. You lost something or someone dear to you, and you do not want to lose again. That is why you must stay in control. As long as you do not get too attached, you can give up the relationship easily, without a second thought. But if your heart gets involved, you will be crushed if the relationship is taken away from you – *like whatever was taken from you in your past.*

Type 3 Fornicator - *You are afraid of a marriage commitment. You desire a long-term relationship but feel it is safer to never get married, than to get married and risk divorce.*

You are currently, or have been in the past, in a relationship with someone that you would like to marry but fear that the marriage would be a failure. You fear failure in all areas of your life. You are a cautious person that is seldom willing to take risks. You also suffer from low self-esteem; you do not believe in yourself. At the same time, you exhibit a measure of selfishness because of how you hurt those that you are unwilling to commit to.

You act like a spouse in many ways, but refuse to give up the safety net of freedom that excuses you from the responsibility of a marriage commitment. Your ability to function, as if married, easily beguiles your partner into believing that you want a marriage commitment. This works in your favor because the person will probably be hopelessly in love with you by the time they realize that you are afraid of commitment. He or she will have invested so much into the relationship that it will be effortless to drag them along for years, with false promises of a future wedding.

Just as the **type 1 fornicator**, you too are a person who is full of self-pity over the many failures of your life, and you crave sympathy. You do not realize that you live in a world that you have created for yourself that you could easily get out of. In life, you are an irresponsible, unreliable person that often messes up everything you put your hand to. This is done intentionally, on a subconscious level, because you do not put forth much effort. This is due to the fact that your belief is – *if you never really try, then no one can ever say you failed.* You have many regrets over past decisions that you have made and opportunities that you have blown, but to you the end justifies the means. *The end* is that you avoid the devastation of failure. You feel that you have failed at something very important at some point in your past, and you just never want to experience that heartache again. You live not to achieve your future goals, but instead to avoid your past failures; or the failures that you observed in the lives of others.

You live in a bubble. What a life of bondage you have created for yourself. You may even have convinced yourself that it is OK to *"test out the merchandise"* for right now, regardless of the fear you feel deep down inside. You are the type of fornicator that will probably keep the same sexual partner for years, if possible, and even live together with that person, as long as you do not have to get married. You tell him or her that you will one day, but it is not in your heart to do so. If your partner is a **type 1** or **type 3** fornicator, it is unlikely that you will ever marry or break up for that matter. The relationship will probably never change – you may be trapped forever, unless someone becomes truly free and delivered!

These are the three types of fornicators, all produced by the spirit of fornication. In all of the above explanations, you are a person that willingly and freely has sex with the people you get into relationships with. You don't "struggle" with having sex, without being legally married. Having sex has become the acceptable norm for you when dating someone. Keep in mind that the main agenda of the spirit of fornication is to destroy your sense of commitment, guiding you to be in non-committed sexual relationships either because you settle for less, you're cruel or just plain afraid. However, this spirit's method of operation is different than empty one night stands or the "friends with benefits" type of scenario (what is typically called *casual sex*). This spirit aims to deceive you with a false commitment. It produces something that looks like commitment, but is not.

When fornication is truly at work, there will always be a somewhat intricate or *semi-committed* relationship connected to the sexual acts. Knowing this, you must understand that you may commit acts that fall within the parameters of the common understanding of fornication – *sex outside of marriage* – without classifying as a **type 1, 2 or 3**. For example, you may be in a *casual sex* scenario, with the awareness and conviction that you shouldn't be having sex but still do it anyway. You lack self-control and are probably apathetic and/or despondent about your spiritual walk. You continually make excuses to "get by with it". Perhaps you are a person that engages in unmarried sexual activity strictly for the pleasure of it. A relationship is not even on your agenda. You just want flesh-gratifying, emotionally detached, feel-good sex – and find nothing wrong with it. You do it because you do not acknowledge Yeshua as LORD and are blind to the truth that it is sinful. You may be engaged and believe that it is acceptable to have sex with your fiancée. You are operating in confusion and deception.

Although all of these types of sexual activity fall under the heading of fornication by definition, fornication is not the dominating spirit of sexual perversion in these cases. It is some other spiritual force, such as sexual lust, unbelief or carnality that is the mastermind behind the fornicating activities in your life. Regardless of which type of fornicator you may be, you are completely devoid of a true sense of loyalty. You can bail out of the relationship, or whatever you undertake in life, whenever you choose to, for whatever reason, without recognizable consequence.

The real deception is that as a fornicator, you can do what any married couple can do. You even possess the same creative power that a married person does but not the same wholeness, legitimacy and honor. Without the strength of the marriage bond and a legal marriage contract, your family unit will never be complete. Therefore, reproduction for you is dysfunctional. Not only reproduction in the natural, but whatever you produce in life is illegitimate and is unlikely to thrive. With marriage comes a certain type of security that you lack, and if you do have children, you will pass that lack of security on to them. Likewise, you will lack security in all areas of your life. Instability will always be around you in your health, in your career, in your living arrangements – *everywhere...*

YES – you can do what any married couple can do, but the key elements of commitment, loyalty and trust are all missing. You are enjoying a reward that you have not earned; and you can rest assured that whenever you take something that is not rightfully yours, life will take seven times more away from you that should have been yours. You are seriously selling yourself short!

The Churchgoer Profile

If you are a person that physically commits fornication, you are very likely to be a churchgoer. You *buy your own excuses* for why you are in the "situation" that you are in and often feel no shame attending church. The spirit of fornication often produces people that go to church only on holidays or special occasions. You are one of the ones jamming up the pews on New Year's Eve before you hit the club; the one that shows up on Easter for the annual fashion show; the one that makes church attendance your present to Mom on Mother's Day... Even worse, maybe you are the one who unashamedly gets drunk, booty-dances and cusses like a sailor all Saturday night and then sings in the choir Sunday morning!

If you are under this influence and you do attend church regularly, you are not reliable in your church commitments. If you are a **type 1** person, you may try to commit to everything in the church, but always find a reason to believe that none of it is going to work out for you. You get involved in all church activities, but often times turn out to be more of a burden than a blessing. You always need a ride, a free ticket, help with babysitting – anything that keeps you in the spotlight of sympathetic attention. You are the one that when other people see your number in their caller ID, they don't answer because they know that YOU NEED SOMETHING. This is not to say it is wrong to need help or that churchgoers should not help one another, but you have become victimized and helpless of your own doing – wanting to be bailed out, in order to validate your worth and fill your emptiness.

If a **type 2** fornicator, you try to play a lot of mind games with the leadership of the church. You want leadership to feel at fault for your lack of commitment. You will jump from auxiliary to auxiliary without ever really making a commitment to any of them, noting inadequacies in the auxiliary itself as your reason for leaving. You do not show up for rehearsals, but still want a part of the spotlight on the night of the big show. As a **type 3** fornicator, you will go to the same church for years without ever "joining" or making a commitment to get involved in any auxiliary or ministry. You seldom attend any special event or have any close relations with anyone in the church.

As any type of fornicator, you are a sparing giver. Supporting a ministry financially requires faith and commitment, two things that every person who is completely under this influence will lack. In essence, the spirit of fornication keeps you from making a commitment to your beliefs in Yahweh, and therefore you will see very little spiritual growth in your life.

The Worship Portrait

Under the influence of this spirit, your relationship with the LORD will be one that lacks sacrifice and commitment. As a **type 1** person, you probably want a committed, intimate relationship with

God but believe that it is unattainable. You will often long for greatness but settle for mediocrity. As a **type 2** person, you do not feel that all the sacrifices that have to be made, in order to have a meaningful relationship with God, are worth it. Your beliefs about who God is will often change, and you are likely to get involved with many different sects of religion, searching for the one that is most appealing and is the easiest to adhere to. As a **type 3** person, you fear that you will fail in a relationship with The Father and thus refuse to give it your all. You will "acknowledge Him" for years, without giving your heart.

If under the influence of this spirit, you know The LORD only casually. Although you lack genuine intimacy with Him, you expect Him to be available for the pleasures of life when you are in need. You are the type of person that only prays when sick, in trouble or in great need – in other words – prayer is a desperate last resort, instead of an enjoyable time of fellowship. Just as is often the case with a fornication based relationship in the natural, you may claim that you really love God. However, no one that is unwilling to thoroughly commit to Yahweh and sacrifice their life on His behalf truly loves Him in totality.

Think about all the sacrifice and commitment that it takes to build and maintain a marriage. A married person ceases to exist as an individual. The Bible says that the two shall become one *(1 Cor 6:16)*. A spouse literally has to die to self, in order to be a good husband or wife. We have to die to self, if we want to be a true servant of The Most High and become one with Him. Not just once, but we must die daily for the rest of our lives *(1 Cor 15:31,)* just as it is in marriage.

Every time a married person sees an area of their own desire that hinders their relationship with their spouse, they have to give it up or adjust it. It is the same way in our relationship with The LORD. But under the influence of this spirit, you will refuse to make that commitment and sacrifice. Your love for Yahweh is not at all genuine. You want His blessings, but not His ways. You want His power, but not His death. You want what is in His hand, but not what is in His heart.

If bound by this spirit, you are really deceived because you seem to be enjoying all the pleasures of marriage, without all of the sacrifice and obligation – *or the safety that it brings*. If your sex partner were to die, you would be left with nothing. The same is true in your relationship with Yah. You think you can fornicate with Him, but you will be left with nothing in the end.

Insights from Dr. Intimacy

The Myth of "Premarital Sex"

I struggled a bit when writing about fornication, trying to find the balance between the truths that I know about sexual blood covenants and the common perception in society and the church about what fornication is. There are great misconceptions in the church about fornication and marriage that has led to the staggering divorce epidemic that we are now facing. I hope in this article to shed some light that will help fill in the holes in our understanding, when it comes to the topic of fornication. I am going to start by reiterating the sentiments of the title – **THERE IS NO SUCH THING AS "PREMARITAL SEX"**.

OK, before you close the book and call me a heretic and false teacher, please consider the rest of what I am about to write. Categorically, in the Bible, there is no such thing as *"premarital sex"*. There is rape, adultery, prostitution, homosexuality, incest and *indecent proposals*. This perception that we have that fornication exclusively points to two heterosexuals having sex before they obtain a marriage license and walk down the aisle to say "I do" is completely false. As I have explained earlier in this book, 'fornication' literally means 'illicit sexual intercourse', and it umbrellas every sexually perverse act imaginable; including non-married people that have sex.

The problem is the churches insufficient understanding about what creates a marriage. That will be discussed in detail in chapter 16, so I will not delve too deeply into it now. I will sum it up by saying that in biblical times, non-married people *(referring to the Chosen People in the Old Testament and Believers in the New Testament)* fell under the labels I just mentioned – rape, adultery, prostitution, homosexuality, incest and *indecent proposals*. We all know what most of those terms mean, but you may be wondering what I mean when I say "indecent proposals". What I mean is that if a person did not fall under one of those five labels, **having sex was their marriage license** – signed, sealed and delivered. Right, wrong or indifferent, whether the families approved or not, it was a done deal!

There was no such thing as "premarital sex". The Jewish people of those days were well aware of this truth and accepted it to be so. When two people had sex without going through the proper customs, it was an indecent proposal and dishonorable union, **BUT** nonetheless valid as a marriage union. A particular movie comes to mind, as I am writing this. In the film *Avatar*, the chief's daughter was promised in marriage to someone. But she fell in love with someone else and chose to "mate" with him, in order to create and seal their union. When the community found out about what she and her new husband had done, they were all disappointed and upset. Her father and *ex*-fiancée were both furious. She had become someone else's wife without custom, tradition, approval or ceremony. It was indecent, but it could not be undone.

I know this was just a movie, but it is such a concise picture of the way things worked in Jewish culture, during biblical times. I am not suggesting that the entire ancient civilization operated under these same unwritten rules. Those that worshiped other gods lived by a different moral standard, but Yahweh's chosen people, the people that He entrusted with His covenant, lived according to these principles. Because they had an intimate knowledge of the True and Living God of All Creation, they had access to understanding and wisdom about the way life works, with a depth that other cultures did not. The Jews, *at least the upright ones*, operated according to understanding. Not mere instinct and emotion, but they operated according to TRUTH.

The Jewish people were so serious about this principle of sexual blood covenants creating a marriage union that if the dishonorable newlyweds decided to call off the marriage, the man and his family had to pay damages to the female and her family. Isn't cancelling out a recent marriage contract what we call an '*annulment*'? Isn't the man paying damages to a scorned, divorced female what we call *'alimony'*? Absolutely! So I am going to state it plainly just once more: **THERE IS NO SUCH THING AS "PREMARITAL SEX"**. But, what is the point really of me sharing this information? Is it inaccurate to label what we call "premarital sex" as fornication? No, I am not saying that. Fornication is 'illicit sexual intercourse'. In our culture, sex before an official wedding ceremony is illicit sexual intercourse. It is dishonorable and it is indecent – but it's **NOT** *premarital sex*. Armed with this knowledge, I can get to my real agenda, which is to effectively tackle two huge dilemmas that Christians face, in long-term relationships. The first of these issues is sex during the engagement period. The second of these issues is common law marriage. Let's go deep!

Sex During the Engagement Period

Whether or not it is OK to have sex while engaged is more of a dilemma than some might realize. Let's clarify that when I say *engaged*, I am referring to two single people that are both 100% committed to marrying one another, with an agreed upon date or time frame. Having a ring is not required, but I question the love and commitment of a man that will not present a ring to his future bride, and furthermore the self-esteem of a woman who would deem this acceptable. So in my professional opinion, there should be an engagement ring to solidify an "official" engagement, but that is just my say on the matter.

At any rate, once official engagement is established, the first problem is that most couples have already been engaging in sexual activity before the "engagement" is made official. Then there comes a point in their relationship when they want to "take things to the next level" and "get married", in order to make things more honorable and solidify their commitment to one another. If people could only understand that **they already took it to the ULTIMATE level** when they decided to have sex, this so-called, "premarital" engagement sex issue would not be nearly as difficult a challenge, as it can sometimes be. In most instances, you are dealing with two people that have been sexually active with each other, and probably others as well, for quite some time. You are dealing with two people that are sexually charged, alive and turned on.

They have been freely engaging in sexual activity together and are looking forward to continuing to do so for the rest of their lives – *and their suddenly supposed to stop to wait for a wedding ceremony?*

I'm chuckling as I write this. The irony of it is actually humorous to me. In essence, these are two people that are already married, in the most important sense of what marriage is, struggling to abstain from what they should be doing as a married couple. This creates a terrible inner conflict between soul and spirit, a double-mindedness that produces instability in the relationship. There is an inner, subconscious knowing that marriage already exists and yet a conscious, intellectual knowing that it is somehow illicit. As a result, the couple tries to live both married and unmarried at the same time! And for what reason do they struggle with this internal warfare? Simply because they do not understand that they are actually already married in spirit and that the marriage license and ceremony does not make it "official", it just makes it PUBLIC and HONORABLE.

Now before any engaged **fornicators** reading this start leaping for joy, thinking that I just gave engaged couples an "ALL ACCESS PASS" to have unbridled, guilt-free sex up until their wedding day – **NOT SO FAST!** I never said having sex before the wedding isn't a violation. It is wrong – just not for the reasons that people think. What makes it wrong is:

1) More than likely the couple *believes* that it is wrong. The Bible says that if you believe you are committing a sin, then you are – even if what you are doing is not violating any laws of Righteousness *(Rom 14:14, 23)*. The fact that a couple *believes* in the concept of premarital sex and yet participate in it anyway, makes them guilty of wrong-doing.

2) It is indecent and out of order. There is a proper way to do things and an improper way to do things. Having sex, thus entering into a marriage union, without full commitment to the requirements of married life, is totally out of order. It is furthermore, a mockery of the God-ordained institution of marriage.

3) It is deceptive. The couple is actually married but living publicly as if they are still unmarried. Pretending to still be single, while enjoying the

benefits of married life behind closed doors, is a lie. It is very dishonorable to your relationship and is an injustice to society as well.

4) Lastly, it greatly diminishes the quality of an individual's relationship with The LORD. A person is willfully engaging in activity that they believe to be sinful. It has caused a breech in their relationship with Him. The person knows it but doesn't care enough to correct it. That is a person that has put another god before Yahweh.

Having said all of that, I believe that I have made it clear that *"pre-wedding-ceremony-sex"* is indeed sinful, on many fronts. With that being established, I am now going to outline what an engaged couple should do, in order to get into right standing with The Father and clean up the contamination in their relationship. If a couple has been practicing *"pre-wedding-ceremony-sex"* they only have two options to fix things. One option is to cease all sexual contact *(remember what **sexual contact** is)* until the wedding ceremony is complete. This instruction is simple enough to suggest, but next to impossible to carry out for many couples. For a very sexually active couple, or one that has a wedding date that is not in the near future, this option is not optimal. The reality is that the couple is unlikely to be able to abstain for any length of time, and even if they do, it is likely to be a burden.

The second option is to break custom and go ahead and legalize and bring into order the union, by having the wedding service performed right away. Just because a marriage is signed off on already, doesn't mean that the couple cannot proceed with their original wedding plans. The wedding ceremony is a PUBLIC celebration for friends and family. It does not make the marriage anymore special, binding, legal or official. *Sure,* some people may be upset that they weren't there on the official day, but that should not be a couple's concern. As much as we'd like the approval of our friends and family when getting married, it is a very personal decision. We have every right to marry any single person we want to, whenever we choose to. And truthfully, once a couple contaminates their relationship with fornication, it is about pleasing The LORD, not pleasing the family.

If you are wondering if I think one option is preferable over the other, not necessarily. I believe that the second option is more feasible for most couples. There is nothing wrong with going through with legalizing the marriage speedily; if both partners are sure that is what they want. Besides, don't forget that in actuality the couple is already married anyway. Therefore, even if they successfully abstain from having sex, it will not cancel out the marriage covenant that they have already made. It will be a separation, not a divorce.

The first option is probably superior, in that it allows time for the individual self-development and preparation needed for married life. Besides, there was a reason that the wedding date was set for whatever particular day or time it had been set, and it may be good if the couple can stay that course. The first option also affords the opportunity for a thorough spiritual restoration of the couple, but that is **only if** they can successfully abstain. If they don't, they are doing more harm than good, and so they need to be honest about whether or not they can handle that option.

To any engaged couple that has not committed fornication, I applaud you. Don't do it! You are doing things the right way and your marriage is going to have a special blessing because of your integrity. But for those who have, above are the only two options for handling engagement fornication properly and successfully. And I strongly implore you to please, PLEASE, adhere to this advice. The fornication that you are involved in is a **MAJOR SET UP** for adultery later on in your marriage. It is causing so much unseen damage; cracks in the foundation that will later cause your married life to crumble!

Common Law Marriage

For the sake of anyone who does not know, 'common law marriage' is a term that is used to describe a couple that lives together for an extended period of time and functions like a married couple. As a general rule of thumb, without considering extenuating circumstances and non-traditional beliefs, common law marriage is very dishonorable. I do not need to go into so much detail about the dynamics of common law marriage because much of it has been covered already in this article. I will just remind you that having sex creates a marriage covenant, so essentially the couple has been married since the consummation of intercourse.

Basically, in the case of common law marriage, what we are dealing with is a couple that has been in a suspended state of *pre-wedding-ceremony-sex*. As in the previous case, the same four reasons that classifies engagement sex as fornication, applies here. In the case of common law marriage, it may be even more detrimental and out of order because there is also a fifth reason: **5) This is an open lifestyle of sin, without remorse or repentance that can cause others to stumble!** Of course, there can be exceptions, but most relationships that end up in a common law marriage start off in a total state of sin. A couple doesn't one day decide to move in together because they are committed to marriage. For the most part, they move in together because they want greater access to more frequent, spontaneous sex, help with bills, assistance with chores and a security blanket to ward off loneliness!

Seriously, just think about it – if they wanted to get married, why didn't they just do that? As a matter of fact, one website said this about common law marriage, *"A man and woman who live together and 'intend to be married' can become common law spouses. Intent to be married can be shown by the couple simply by <u>acting</u> like they were married."* The key word is *'acting'*. If a couple chooses to live together before they are even engaged, it really speaks loudly about their regard for the institution of marriage, their level of commitment to one another and their overall belief in their relationship. Otherwise, why would they *act* like they are married, instead of preparing to actually be officially married?

It is important to know that 'common law marriage' is a secular term. There is no such term or reference in the Bible. It is also good to know that most states, in the US, do not allow legally binding common law marriages. It has been outlawed in 27 states that used to recognize it, never allowed at all in 13 states and of the 9 that do allow it, there are serious stipulations that have to be met. As a whole, common law marriage is not looked upon favorably in this nation. That is a pretty strong indictment against this type of marriage. The US is a nation that applauds the marriage of homosexuals and the murder of babies, and yet invalidates the union of couples living together who are unwilling to make the full marriage commitment. **Wow**, that statement requires a – *pause for reflection...* Having said all of that, what I want to briefly cover now is the different kinds of people that end up in a common law marriage and how to address this in the lives of Christian couples. People who end up in this situation and how to approach it:

1) **_Type 1 or type 3 fornicators_**: Believers that are fornicators really need to do some deep soul-searching. They need to ask themselves how they got into the situation and if the person they are with is really who they want and need to be married to. For **type 1** fornicators, remember that they are struggling with self-esteem issues. For them it will almost always be the case that they are with the wrong person. For the **type 3** fornicators, remember that they are marriage-minded but dealing with fear of failure. They may have something redeemable. After evaluating the situation, if a person finds that they are in an unhealthy union, the relationship needs to be ended quickly. If the couple believes that they have something worth keeping together, they need to go through premarital counseling and if all goes well there, validate their union quickly.

2) <u>Unbelievers and backsliders</u>: This is similar to the above scenario and the advice is almost the same. However, being in a total state of separation, at the onset of such a relationship, does change the dynamics slightly, since spiritual accountability is measured in accordance with a person's level of understanding. If a couple got into this situation as an unbelievers or in a backslidden state, and then become true Born Again Believers that want to live right, their main focus should be on growing in their relationship with The LORD and trusting Him for wisdom and guidance on validating the marriage or ending the relationship. However, if only one person becomes enlightened and the unbeliever wants to stay married, then the Believer needs to consider that. It is not always easy to undo what's

been done and no one should carelessly savage someone else's life, for the sake of correcting their own.

3) *People who had issues obtaining the legal paperwork*: My question to them would be: why did you give up on obtaining the paperwork? Is living right just not worth the trouble? Is your husband or wife just not worth the trouble? Or, are you hiding something illegal? With 50 states in this nation, there should be somewhere that a couple who really wants to get legally married, to be able to make it happen. If there is no state in this nation that will allow that couple to get married, it could only be due to a legal conflict – like a divorce that was never completed or missing identification paperwork. This is just completely unacceptable for a Christian. Take care of it ASAP, or accept the fact that you cannot get married, end it and move on!

4) *People who object to government marriage licensing for religious reasons or anti-government rebellion:* In a situation like this, a couple has probably carried out the duties of marriage as faithfully as any traditionally married couple, just without the license. This kind of couple would also be completely free of guilt because they truly believe that they are honorably married. I can certainly understand how some people may not want the dirty hands of the government in any way associated with their marriage union. However, it is just a formality, and even Yeshua said that we should render unto Caesar what is his *(Mat 22:21)*. Whether it is for religious reasons or anti-government rebellion, refusing to get a marriage license is in direct violation of the biblical mandate to obey the laws of the land *(Rom 13:1-7)*. As Christians, we are citizens of the Kingdom of Heaven. Therefore, let us be blameless before sinners, not provoking them to speak evil of our good. I encourage a couple like this to immediately take care of obtaining their license; just be a good example.

5) *Engaged couples that felt pressured to live together for "practical" reasons*: "OK Christian... is this what you tell yourself to help you sleep at night?" This is completely unacceptable. If two people really care to please God, they will be officially licensed as a married couple within 30 days of reading this or living at two different addresses! If one person

in the union is ready to do the right thing and the other person isn't, the convicted person should err on the side of Righteousness – **somebody should move out**. If separating does not move the fiancée to action that is probably a clue that the engagement needs to be called off. There is nothing else to say about that!

Conclusion of the Matter

I know I spent a lot of time on this, but I believe that the information in this article is going to disarm the demon of marital disunity and divorce in the lives of every couple who applies what is written herein. So please, take very serious all that you just read. For every engaged couple and common law couple that has read this, **I implore you to act quickly**. If the relationship is over, deliver a swift death blow to it and start your healing and restoration process. *(Please visit this link for help with the break-up process: http://wp.me/p1VniQ-bd.)* If it is redeemable, legalize and validate the union right away.

For the couples that choose to redeem the relationship, my only mandate is that you go on a 30 to 90 day consecration from sexual relations, and whatever else you want to abstain from, for the sake of purifying your union. **THIS IS REALLY IMPORTANT**. The state of fornication that you have been in has invited many demons into your relationship. There is a lot of contamination and a lot of doors that are open. You don't want to carry this any further into your marriage! That is why it is so important that you take at least 30 days out to read this book from cover to cover, together with your soon-to-be spouse. Also, be sure to go through premarital counseling. Even if you have been before, go again. After these steps, you may find that you need more time before you make your union official, or that it is not a good idea to move forward with the union at all. Don't be afraid of that. It is better to call it off now than – 10 years, a house, 2 bank accounts and 3 kids later. For every couple that needs to go through separation, whether temporarily or permanently, go to chapter 16 and read the *Insights from Dr. Intimacy* article. You will learn how to get spiritually divorced and be truly cleansed of soul ties. It will make everything a lot easier and help put you on the path to a beautiful marriage in the future.

Chapter 8

Masturbation

"Run away from sexual sin! No other sin so clearly affects the body as this one does. For sexual immorality is a sin against your own body." (1 Cor. 6:18)

Some Biblical References

Num 25:1; Job 17:9; Psalm 7:3, 18:20, 18:24, 18:34, 24: 3-5; 28:2, 47:1, 63:4, 77:2, 88:9, 119:48, 134:2, 141:2, 143:6; Prov 10:4, 12:25, 31:10-31; Ecc 4:5; Mat 5:32, 15:19, 19:9; Mark 7:21; Acts 15:20, 15:29, 21:25; Rom 1:29, 3:13; 1 Cor 5:1, 6:12-13, 6:18, 7:2, 10:8; 2 Cor 12:21; Gal 5:19; Eph 5:3; Col 3:5; 1 Tim 1:6;1 Thes 4:3; James 4:8; 1 John 1:1; Jude 1:7; Rev 2:14, Rev 2:20-21, 9:21

The Definition

The act of sexually stimulating yourself, usually until orgasm is achieved, without another person's touch.

The Assignment

The spirit of masturbation is a particularly deceptive and clever one. People who do not want to accept the truth about masturbation being a sin use excuses like, *"I'm not hurting anyone; It's my body and my business; I'm not thinking about doing anything wrong; It's better than having sex with someone. It's natural to masturbate, even children do it!"* However, those who use these excuses are missing the true intention of the spirit that has them bound. Intimacy is a process between two people, who *labor together in love*, focused on how to satisfy one another's needs and reward one another with climatic ecstasy. Masturbation usurps this process; negating the reliance on another to fulfill your needs and aiming straight for the desired end. **The spirit of masturbation is assigned to bring you to a place where you feel as if you do not need The LORD, do not need to obey Him or do things His way. It decreases your spiritual stamina and causes you to seek the path of least resistance for attaining your desires. This spirit is all about a false sense of empowerment and self-control to get what you think you desire, as a cover for feelings of inadequacy and isolation.**

The Practical Understanding

A lot of people debate over whether or not masturbation is actually a sin. Many people want to confine the Word of Yahweh to our limited English language and vocabulary. Because in their hearts they desire to indulge sin, they feign ignorance due to the fact that every evil act is not noted in black and white in the Bible. However, the Bible tells us in Romans 1:18-19, *"¹⁸But God shows his anger from heaven against all sinful, wicked people **who push the truth away from themselves**. ¹⁹For the truth about God is known to them instinctively. God has put this knowledge in their hearts."*

Admittedly, there is no scripture in the Bible that says, "Thou shall not masturbate". So hey, if you want to chance standing before God on judgment day with your hand in your pants, you can try this *omission of specific language* out as your defense! However, for those who hunger and thirst after Righteousness, you are getting ready to get your fill: the **Bible Truth** concerning masturbation. Since there is no scripture that uses the word "masturbation" *(simply because there is no word-for-word translation between the languages)* let's examine some scriptures where it can clearly be read between the lines.

"Run away from sexual sin! No other sin so clearly affects the body as this one does. For sexual immorality is a sin against your own body." This scripture in 1 Corinthians 6:18 has often been debated as to its relevance toward masturbation. This is because verses 15 and 16 of this same chapter, as you will read further down, make specific reference to female prostitution. However, in order to fully understand

a scripture, you have to examine it within the context of the entire passage that it is connected to.

That is why I want to take a look back to 1 Corinthians, chapter 6, beginning at verse 9. By doing so, we can find some pretty strong references to masturbation. Since this is a long passage, let's look at the scriptures a few at a time. *"⁹Don't you realize that those who do wrong will not inherit the Kingdom of God? Don't fool yourselves. Those who indulge in **sexual sin**, or who worship idols, or **commit adultery**, or are **male prostitutes**, or **practice homosexuality**, ¹⁰or are thieves, or greedy people, or drunkards, or are abusive, or cheat people—none of these will inherit the Kingdom of God."*

The author of this text makes specific mention of several different acts of sexual perversion: sexual sin, adultery, male prostitution and homosexuality. Homosexuality we understand clearly to be sexual relations or attraction between two people of the same gender. Male prostitutes are clearly men who exchange sex for money or favors, most often with other men and often as a part of ceremonious idol worship. Adultery is understood to be sex between a married person and someone other than their spouse.

Then we are left with the term "sexual sin". What is the author referring to with this term? This text was written during a time when it was culturally acceptable for men to have as many wives as they wanted to. This means that a man could not "technically fornicate" in the way we think of fornication, which is "sex outside of marriage". If a woman was single and agreed to have sex with a man, they were married – *unless she was a prostitute or committing adultery*. With female prostitution already being addressed directly in verse 18 and adultery already being addressed in verse 9, what else are we to believe the term "sexual sin" means here, as it is certainly not fornication as we think of it?

Now let's look at verses 11-14. *"¹¹Some of you were once like that. But you were cleansed; you were made holy; you were made right with God by calling on the name of the Lord Jesus Christ and by the Spirit of our God. ¹²You say, 'I am allowed to do anything'—but not everything is good for you. And even though 'I am allowed to do anything,' I must not become a slave to anything.* ¹³*You say, 'Food was made for the stomach, and the stomach for food.' (This is true, though someday God will do away with both of them.) But you can't say that our bodies were made for sexual immorality. They were made for the Lord, and the Lord cares about our bodies.* ¹⁴*And God will raise us from the dead by his power, just as he raised our Lord from the dead."*

In this passage in verses 11-14, the author expounds upon his reference to being "greedy", made earlier in verse 9. By doing so, he is trying to help us understand that just because we have been made "clean", does not mean that we are exempt from the bondage of sin. You can eat and eating in and of itself is not bad. However, you can also overeat and overeating can be deadly. Let's face it; overeating is suicide on a payment plan. Carelessly subjecting your body to unwholesome, damaging activities is sinful. In other words, just because the body functions enable you to do an activity, doesn't mean that you should do it. The author gives this simple, practical example about eating because it is easy to relate to.

Then the author wants to build upon this understanding and apply this same concept to sexual immorality, in the next passage, making the point clear once again: **just because you can do something, doesn't mean that you should do something!** ¹⁵*Don't you realize that your bodies are actually parts of Christ? Should a man take his body, which is part of Christ, and join it to a prostitute? Never!* ¹⁶*And don't you realize that if a man joins himself to a prostitute, he becomes one body with her? For the Scriptures say, "The two are united into one."* ¹⁷*But the person who is joined to the Lord is one spirit with him."*

So now, looking at verses 15 and 16 in consideration of the entire message being portrayed, the specific reference to prostitution is no more the "focus" of this passage than any of these other specific references. What is more important than the reference to prostitution are these clauses from 13, 14 and 17: *"But you can't say that our bodies were made for sexual immorality [like you can say the stomach was made for food, which makes engaging in sexual immorality even that much worse]. They were made for the Lord, and the Lord cares about our bodies.* ¹⁴ *And God will raise us from the dead by his power, just as* he raised our Lord from the dead... ^{17} But the person who is joined to the Lord is **one spirit with him**." These clauses are important because the truth of the matter is that ALL sexual sin causes you to become <u>one</u> with somebody. Whether done rightly through marriage or wrongly through homosexuality, prostitution or adultery – sex makes you one with the person you join with.

This truth is just as applicable in the case of masturbation, as with any other sexual act. Your body belongs to the Lord and is designed to die to self and sin, after you have been cleansed and set apart. This is apparent because in the middle of a passage that has nothing to do with natural death or resurrection, the author makes a clear indication of your body being raised from the dead. This is the death of flesh, death to self, death to your own will and your way that the author is talking about. When you let your body die to sinful ways, The LORD will raise your dead body up as a standard of Righteousness for all to see! Yet, instead of dying to self and becoming "one spirit" with The Lord, you are exalting your own sinful life and becoming one with the will of your flesh. And so finally, we can read verses 6:18-20 with full understanding.

"^{18}**Run from sexual sin! No other sin so clearly affects the body as this one does. For sexual immorality is a sin against your own body.** ^{19}**Don't you realize that your body is the temple of the Holy Spirit, who lives in you and was given to you by God? <u>You do not belong to yourself</u>,** ^{20}**for God bought you with a high price. So you must honor God with your body.**" Paul clearly and deliberately covered each type of "sexual immorality" *(the general term that is used for all sexual activity not done with your spouse)* in this passage: adultery, male prostitution, female prostitution, homosexuality and masturbation (sexual sin). The specific illustration of prostitution in verses 15 and 16 is only used to help paint a clear picture of sexual perversion that everyone can undeniably agree is sinful. He follows this illustration by pointing out that we are to be "one spirit" with the Lord.

I don't believe that if Paul could have translated this passage into English himself that he would have included a break between the two clauses in 17 and 18, "one spirit with him" and "Run from sexual sin!" This is one continuous thought, leading us into understanding that masturbation, which is what I believe he is referring to when he uses the term 'sexual sin', is just as perverse as prostitution and all of the other acts of sexual immorality mentioned in this chapter. It is not at all by coincidence that this clause is followed, in verse 19, with these words: **"You do not belong to <u>yourself</u>..."**

The text could have said, *"You do not belong to a prostitute..."* Or, *"You do not belong to an adulterer..."* Or, *"You do not belong to a homosexual..."* But instead, it clearly states, **"YOU DO NOT BELONG TO YOURSELF!"** This is a vivid picture of the act of 'self-sex' and taking liberties with your own body that are not harmonious with your estate as The Temple of the Holy Spirit. Child molesters always begin their disgusting acts by touching a body that does not belong to them, attempting to cause corrupt sexual pleasure. Your body DOES NOT belong to you; when you masturbate, you are molesting your own body! Even worse, you are molesting The LORD's body because your body belongs to Him!

You see, Paul wanted to ensure that no matter what kind of sexual addiction you are dealing with, you will know that this text applies to you. Yes, even you who freely indulge yourself sexually. Now you have to consider this: Does masturbation honor The LORD with your body? Can you see yourself at the throne with the 24 elders, who will be casting their crowns before Him in worship, bowing and saying, *"Holy, Holy, Holy..."* while you are indulging in your own flesh, enjoying sexual lust by your own hand? That is what you have to ask yourself.

The Personality Profile

The scriptural foundation has now been laid to give you the necessary level of understanding to acknowledge masturbation as a sexually sinful act. Moving forward, let's talk about what it actually is physically and how it shapes your life. Masturbation is for the most part, thought of as sexually stimulating yourself with your hands. This activity would be inclusive in defining masturbation, but not complete. It can also involve stimulating yourself with some type of object, or it can be as simple as purposefully allowing your clothing or bedding to rub up against your genitals in a sexually stimulating way.

It does not even have to involve contact with your genitals at all. If you know how to flex and relax your genital muscles in a sexually stimulating way or how to fantasize yourself into an orgasm, that too is masturbation. Remember, it is not so much what you do or how you do it, as much as it is *why* you do it – what is the intent of your heart? So for the broadest understanding of which acts fall under the umbrella of masturbation; it is **any intentional sexually stimulating activity done without the involvement of another person touching you**.

As a masturbator, you were probably teased a lot as a child and may have been neglected by your parents in some sense. You learned to be a loner at some point in your life. Masturbation is similar to fornication in that it yields sexual pleasure without commitment, but is different in that it is a totally selfish act. Therefore, if masturbation is your strongman, you are undoubtedly a very selfish person in many ways. You are very impatient. You are also a stubborn, arrogant and controlling person.

In a sense, masturbation takes more creativity than intercourse, in that you have to accomplish alone what usually takes two people. This means that you probably can be characterized as a self-starter and person of ingenuity. However, your ability to get things done without assistance only adds to your arrogance. Being able to give that type of sexual pleasure to yourself invokes a false sense of empowerment and isolates you from the need of other people. You are therefore inclined to give yourself the credit for every pleasurable thing you acquire or experience in life. This produces a nature of being unappreciative. Your mindset is that even though someone may have helped you, you never *needed* their help anyway. As far as you are concerned, you don't *need* anyone's help. Although you feel as if you do not need anyone, the truth is you are one of the loneliest people on earth. The isolation from people is only a cover for feelings of inadequacy.

This is because masturbation leaves a void. It is like someone who gets a GED instead of a high school diploma. Even though both pieces of paper provide you with the credentials to say you have completed your education, a GED leaves you void of the experience that completing high school affords you. You miss the memories of connecting with friends in school, attending a prom, being honored at a graduation ceremony and the joy of sharing a life-changing experience with peers and loved ones – not to mention a lifetime of high school reunions you will never attend and stories that you will never be able to tell your children! When considered from this perspective, even though a high school diploma and a GED give you the same end result; there is a vast gulf of difference in the level of enrichment that these two experiences provide.

Likewise with masturbation, although you achieve orgasm in the end, there is a huge empty chasm where the experience of intimacy should have been. You are void of the memory of an enriching experience that made a difference in your life and somebody else's life – human connectedness. You already feel void before you start the act of masturbation and that sense of void is only magnified when the act is complete. Because of this void and your past and present woes, you are full of self-pity. Even though you are full of woe, you will not let anyone comfort you, yet you are a failure at comforting yourself.

The spirit of masturbation lures you further and further into a state of inadequacy. You feel as though you work hard for everything in life, yet do not see the results that you desire. The harder you work, the greater the void becomes because all of your effort is still not producing the desired result. You fail to realize that success is not about 'working hard' but instead is about 'working right'. Through masturbation you are expending your efforts in the wrong way; looking for the "path of least resistance" to achieve your goal. You avoid the risk of vulnerability that is present when having to labor in love in intercourse with a partner, but **with the absence of great risk, there is also the absence of opportunity for great reward.**

The sense of inadequacy that you feel begins to take over all aspects of your life. The isolation from others seems like a good way to protect yourself. By performing only for yourself and by yourself, you can keep your inadequacy from being exposed to others and offer yourself some relief. However, that is a deception. The truth is, you set a standard for yourself that is so high, it is impossible to ever achieve. You judge yourself more harshly than anyone else ever would.

You make yourself devoid of the encouragement and affirmation of others by isolating yourself and spend the majority of your waking moments beating yourself down mentally and emotionally. By isolation, I do not necessarily mean that you keep people away from you physically *(although you may)*; I mean more so emotionally and mentally. No one gets close to you. No one gets to know the real you. It is a harrowing, lonely, weighty existence. In an attempt to make yourself feel better; you masturbate seeking to escape pressures and cares through the release of orgasm, but the pleasure is fleeting. It is like unplugging a bath drain to drain the water, but leaving the faucets fully open so that more water continues to blast into the tub – you never really seem to feel any lighter.

Even in relationships, you are selfish. It is hard for you to focus on making your significant other feel good in sexual affairs or everyday life. Your foremost thought is always how to pleasure yourself. If both you and the person you are in a relationship with practice masturbation, you will have intercourse less frequently as a couple. Masturbation trains your body to expect a certain type of feeling in order to climax, and when it does not get that feeling, it is not satisfied. If you are truly bound by this spirit, even after climatic sex, you still need to masturbate to feel satisfied. This is because masturbation desensitizes the body to the touch of others and makes it responsive to your own touch instead. The more you practice masturbation, the harder it is going to be for anyone else to please you sexually.

When you get right down to it, masturbation is all about control. You try to control your life through the act of masturbation and you end up being a control fanatic in general. You want to control every aspect of your life and everyone involved in your life. As a masturbator, you are convinced that the way you do it is always best. As a result, you are extremely critical. You lack tolerance for the shortcomings of others and are seldom satisfied with what anyone does for you; it is never good enough. If you feel someone has not put in enough effort, you are upset about that. If someone goes the extra mile, you feel it was not necessary, even if what they do is done in an effort to please you. If you tell people what to do for you, you are depressed because they did not do it for you without being told. But if they do it without being told, you are displeased because it is not done the way you would have done it yourself. When you cannot have control of what is going on around you, you just look for a way to masturbate again. What a cycle of misery!

Masturbation is highly addictive! You can never quite achieve what it is that you are trying to achieve in masturbation. You want that feeling of inadequacy, isolation and loneliness to go away, but it is such a trap. What you are really craving is connectedness and intimacy. The Bible says that it is not good for man to be alone *(Gen 2:18)*. Masturbating will never satisfy the need for human connectedness. The truth is the more you do it, the more inadequate you feel because your desire is never satisfied, no matter how much you masturbate. But you are blind to this truth, as you have thoroughly convinced yourself that you do not really need anyone.

You will try to become more innovative with your acts of masturbation. You will use all different types of devices and aides trying to fill that void. You will try to make it last longer and include sexual fantasies. However, the harder you work while still not getting the desired end result, the worse you feel – the worse you feel, the more you want to masturbate. The more you masturbate, the more isolated, selfish, arrogant and unappreciative you become. You cannot wait to get alone to masturbate again, just for the sake of that five second orgasm that makes everything go away, for just a moment!

The Church-Goer Profile

As far as whether or not people who practice masturbation go to church regularly, just think about this: **How often have you heard someone talk from the pulpit about masturbation?** Most people, when they do talk about it, will not even use the word 'masturbation'. It is such a 'hush-hush' topic. Masturbation is such an easy sin to pull off in secret, and that makes it likely that you are a churchgoer. As-a-matter-of-fact, people that practice masturbation are probably innumerable in the church.

Masturbation goes totally against The Father's perfect plan for sexual intimacy: It does not teach us that we are to worship Him alone; it does not in any way symbolize our blood covenant with Him; it does not teach us anything about being intimate with Him; it totally robs us of the creative power that we have when joined together with Him in spirit. This means that under the influence of the spirit of masturbation, you are spiritually unfruitful. If you are a Believer, you may try to fast, study and pray a lot, yet never quite accomplish much in the things of the Kingdom – quickly becoming impatient with *"the process"* and lacking spiritual stamina. Your ministry work is stagnant, and you seem to always have some excuse for it.

You probably want to control everything in the church. You may not forthrightly say anything because of your feelings of inadequacy and desire to isolate yourself, but in your heart you always *have a better way* to run the church. You are too arrogant to submit to leadership. If you ever happen to get into a position of leadership, you are king. You are unappreciative for the help and honor that people try to give you and very, very critical of everyone and everything. You are not really a pleasant person to be around. Fellowship with you can be "intense" at times. You are very uptight and make people feel drained.

The spirit of masturbation creates selfish people who are oblivious to the needs of others and want things their way, and people who will break protocol to get it. You are prone to complaining about everything, and this spirit is responsible for quite a bit of the rebellion that is stirred up against leadership. This means that you regard very lightly the words of your pastor or leaders in church. In general, your church experience is a very disconnected and unfruitful one. You may often feel as if you don't even know why you bother to go and are inclined to be a renegade church-hopper. Instead of allowing the Holy Spirit to lead you to your place of assignment, you will hop from church to church looking to find the one where 'they do it your way'.

This often times leads to rebellious people who start ministries not ordained by Yahweh, just for the sake of being able to control things. You probably have thought about starting a church yourself, *hmmm...* The problem is that pastoring is all about connecting with and caring for God's sheep. If you do start a church, it is bound to be a mess – a cold, un-loving place that is void of Yahweh's presence. It will probably be a very unique ministry, and surely you will know how to deliver a good, revelatory word. You may even be able to emulate a fake worship experience, but you and your entire submitted flock will be just a bunch of spiritual masturbators, getting off on your own praise, not realizing that God is not feeling anything!

The Worship Profile

The mindset of the spirit of masturbation is this: If you can give yourself sexual pleasure, you can give yourself anything. However, sex is something that was designed by The Creator to be performed between two people. Sex, as ordained by The LORD, is all about intimacy, selflessness and lack of control. Masturbation is about just the opposite. Under the influence of the spirit of masturbation, you will deny The Father the one thing He desires most, which is **true worship**. Worship like sex, is all about intimacy, selflessness and losing control in the presence of Your Lover. However, under the influence of this spirit, you will never do that.

Instead of worshiping Yah, you worship yourself. Spiritually, masturbation is nothing more than an act of self-worship. Even though you beat yourself down emotionally, you still exalt yourself above The LORD. You have an ungrateful spirit and often times feel like He has failed you in some way. You even go so far as to say that He owes you something. This is because He does not do it the way you would do it yourself – and *your way is of course the best way*. Because you are blinded by your own inadequacy and fear of vulnerability, you will easily rebel against Yahweh God, just like, as a churchgoer, you will rebel against your leader.

A classic example of the spirit of masturbation at work in someone's life in the Bible is, King Saul. In verse 3 of 1 Samuel 15, The LORD says this to Saul, "*³Now go and completely destroy the entire Amalekite nation—men, women, children, babies, cattle, sheep, goats, camels, and donkeys.*" However, what Saul actually does is revealed in verses 7-9, "*⁷Then Saul slaughtered the Amalekites from Havilah all the way to Shur, east of Egypt. ⁸He captured Agag, the Amalekite king, but completely destroyed everyone else. ⁹Saul and his men spared Agag's life and kept the best of the sheep and goats, the cattle, the fat calves, and the lambs—everything, in fact, that appealed to them. They destroyed only what was worthless or of poor quality.*"

Let's take a look at what transpires after that in verses 10-23, "*¹⁰Then the LORD said to Samuel, ¹¹"I am sorry that I ever made Saul king, for he has not been loyal to me and has refused to obey my command." Samuel was so deeply moved when he heard this that he cried out to the LORD all night. ¹²Early the next morning Samuel went to find Saul. Someone told him, "Saul went to the town of Carmel <u>to set up a monument to himself</u>; then he went on to Gilgal. ¹³When Samuel finally found him, Saul greeted him cheerfully.* **"May the LORD bless you,"** *he said.* **"I have carried out the LORD's command!"** *¹⁴"Then what is all the bleating of sheep and goats and the lowing of cattle I hear?" Samuel demanded. ¹⁵***"It's true that the army spared the best of the sheep, goats, and cattle,"** *Saul admitted.* **"But they are going to sacrifice them to the LORD your God. We have destroyed everything else."** *¹⁶Then Samuel said to Saul, "Stop! Listen to what the LORD told me last night!" "What did he tell you?" Saul asked. ¹⁷And Samuel told him, "<u>Although you may think little of yourself</u>, are you not the leader of the tribes of Israel? The LORD has anointed you king of Israel. ¹⁸And the LORD sent you on a mission and told you, 'Go and completely destroy the sinners, the Amalekites, until they are all dead.' ¹⁹Why haven't you obeyed the LORD? Why did you rush for the plunder and do what was evil in the LORD's sight?" ²⁰***"But I did obey the LORD,"** *Saul insisted.* **"I carried out the mission he gave me. I brought back King Agag, but I destroyed everyone else. ²¹Then my troops brought in the best of the sheep, goats, cattle, and plunder to sacrifice to the LORD your God in**

Gilgal. *"* ²²*But Samuel replied, "What is more pleasing to the LORD: your burnt offerings and sacrifices or your obedience to his voice? Listen! Obedience is better than sacrifice, and submission is better than offering the fat of rams.* ²³*Rebellion is as sinful as witchcraft, and stubbornness as bad as worshiping idols. So because you have rejected the command of the LORD, he has rejected you as king."*

Wow, what a telling passage of scripture! Note how Saul *"set up a monument to himself."* This is a manifestation of the self-worship of masturbation. Note also how The Lord says to Saul, *"you may think little of yourself."* This is a manifestation of the plague of inadequacy that the spirit of masturbation takes advantage of. Notice Saul's argumentative debate with the Prophet. He knew that he had rebelled against the Lord's instructions, but he felt justified because he thought <u>he had a better way</u>. Instead of doing **exactly** what The LORD told him to do, Saul had a different idea that he thought was better and persisted that he was right. If we look finally at the last verses, we see that The LORD was utterly disgusted with Saul and that he viewed his actions as being as evil as witchcraft and idol worship. Wow!

Instead of relying on Yahweh to give him the desires of his heart, Saul got everything he needed on his own *(or so he thought anyway)*. He was so use to his own touch spiritually that he was completely unaware of how unpleased The LORD was with Him. But this is so typical because as was stated earlier, masturbation is about satisfying your own needs so much so that it causes you to be oblivious to the needs of others. You think less about how to please Yahweh and more about what He can do to please you or about how you can please yourself. Ultimately this spirit isolates you from the need for The Father, and thus causes you to be cut off from all that is inclusive when in intimate relationship with Him. Just like the case with Saul, you will eventually be rejected by The LORD because of your rejection of Him.

Masturbation is a dangerous spirit indeed and not at all the least among the spirits of sexual perversion. But maybe you are a Christian that masturbates without conviction. Maybe after all that you have just read, you are still not convinced that you should pursue deliverance from this spirit. You may truly think that it is OK to pleasure yourself in this way. If that is you, let me just give you this to chew on. The next time you lift your hands in the air to praise your Holy God, picture how messy your hands are, stained with your own body fluids, after completing your indulgent sexual act of self-worship. Then remember this verse: *"³Who shall go up into the mountain of The Lord? Or who shall stand in His Holy Place? ⁴He who has* **clean hands** *and a pure heart, who has not lifted himself up to falsehood or to what is false, nor sworn deceitfully. ⁵He shall receive blessing from The Lord and Righteousness from the God of his salvation. (Ps 24:3-5, AMP)"* Notice how clean hands are directly associated with purity of heart. How clean are your hands after you masturbate? Are these truly the same hands and heart that you will lift before The Lord in worship? Think about that – *Selah*.

Insights from Dr. Intimacy

Do Chemical Reactions in the Body Play a Part in Sexual Sin?

I'm so glad you asked! I seem to find in Christianity two extremes of thought concerning scientific research – completely under-rated or completely over-rated. Even though this book is exploring primarily the spiritual aspects of sexual activity, let's not forget that sex is still, in its most basic form, a physical act. There are many physical factors that impact our sexual energy. Hormones, the central nervous system and blood circulation are among the most prevalent factors. There are times that you may be suffering from a spiritual attack when you feel uncontrollably aroused. There may be times when wounds from your past are driving you to desire acts of sexual sin. However, I do not want to give you the impression that every time you feel sexually stimulated, you need to rebuke the devil or plead the blood against your body *(laugh)*. There is nothing wrong with you, if you desire sex. I would rather say, it is cause for concern if you don't desire it!

Therefore, when a sexual impulse arises in your body, before you run off to find the holy water, consider if it is something that is merely physiological. External stimuli can easily activate sexual impulses in the body. What were you watching or reading or listening to when the impulse hit you? What were you wearing? Wearing tight clothing can easily cause sexual impulses. Wearing no clothing at all, especially when lying down, can cause them as well. Perhaps there is a certain food or supplement that you are in-taking that is stirring up your hormones. Detoxing, workouts and even some medicines can alter the functions of your body and cause you to experience sexual impulses.

Knowing when to rebuke the devil and when you just need to exercise some control and discipline over your body is very important. Rebuking a devil that is not present will not offer you any relief. On the other hand, not rebuking a devil that is present will cause you to suffer defeat. You have to begin to pay attention to what is going on in your life, and not use *"the devil made me do it"* as a cop-out for lack of good, old fashioned discipline. If you are sitting on his lap, don't find it strange when you feel him erect! If you are meditating on the last time you had sex, then don't rebuke the devil when you start to feel horny! Instead, you need to take those thoughts captive. You need to be accountable for your own actions and take those thoughts captive. Stay in safe places; think on pure things!

God designed our bodies for marriage and sexual intimacy. Your body is a sex machine just waiting to operate at full capacity. In this sex-crazed society, it won't take much to get your engines revved up. Respect the sensitivity of your body's sexuality and avoid sexual stimulants. This might mean giving up some things you enjoy – certain movies, music and books or spending time with your fiancé in isolated settings. This is especially true for women around their menstruation, anyone who plays sports or trains aggressively and especially those that preach. All of these activities release hormones that lead to an increased sex drive. I know this is challenging. However, if you really want to live a pure life, these are sacrifices that you are going to have to make. Once you know that you are doing all that you can do on a practical level, it will be much easier to identify the legitimate areas of spiritual warfare in your life. Then you can stop blaming everything on *the poor ol' devil!*

Chapter 9

Adultery

"But whoso committeth adultery with a woman lacketh understanding: he that doeth it destroyeth his own soul." (Provs 6:32, KJV)

Some Biblical References

Exodus 20:14, 34:16; Lev 18:18, 20:10; Deut 5:18, 22:22; Psalm 51:1, 106:39; Proverbs 6 & 7; Isaiah 57:7; Jeremiah 3:2, 3:6 -9, 3:13, 5:7, 7:9, 13:27, 23:10, 23:14, 29:23; Ezekiel 16:17, 16:22, 16:38, 18:6, 18:11; 18:15, 22:11, 23:1, 23:17, 23:37; Hosea 3:1, 4:2, 4:13-14; Matthew 5:27-28, 5:32, 12:39, 15:19, 19:9, 19:18; Mark 7:22, 10:11-12, 10:19; Luke 16:18, 18:11, 18:20; John 8:1, 8:3-4 Romans 2:22, 7:3, 13:9, 1 Cor 6:9, Heb 13:4; James 2:11, 2 Pet 2:14; Rev 2:22, 17:2, 18:3, 18:9

The Definition

Voluntary sexual intercourse or other sexual contact between a married person and a person other than their spouse.

The Assignment

An adulterer breaks the established marriage covenant with their spouse and creates an illegitimate covenant with someone else. The adulterer contaminates both the person that they have the affair with and their spouse; selfishly using them both to fulfill his or her needs, while not committed to fulfilling the needs of either of them. Under the spirit of adultery, you are very valuable to satan because of your ability to draw others away from serving The LORD. **The spirit of adultery is assigned to cause you to be unfaithful to The LORD and to selfishly use Him. This is done in an effort to eventually cause total separation from Your Creator and complete divorce.**

The Practical Understanding

Adultery is the only act of sexual perversion that is listed as forbidden in the Ten Commandments and is mentioned by Yeshua several times in the Gospels. One of the reasons that adultery is mentioned so frequently and strongly in the Bible is because, as was stated earlier, in biblical times adultery was a word that was used to describe a number of different acts of sexual perversion, in the Old Testament. Just as the word 'fornication' is widely used in the New Testament, 'adultery' being referred to so commonly in the Old Testament is again a manifestation of the difficulty of word-for-word translation, from one language to another.

After centuries of study, we now have more specific and accurate labels for different manifestations of sexual perversion. These labels help us to more clearly identify how demonic spirits are operating in our lives and how to target the weak areas of our Christian walk. Having said all of that, let us get a basic understanding of what adultery is and what it is not. The obvious definition is clear to us – a married person having sex with someone other than their spouse. But, there are other ways that adultery can manifest itself in one's marriage.

If you are married, pornography would definitely fall under the umbrella of adultery for you. Through pornography you are creating a sexual connection with another person. People watch pornography because it is sexually stimulating. As a married person, you should only be receiving sexual stimulation from your own husband or wife. That is why Yeshua states in Matthew 5:27-28, *"[27]You have heard the commandment that says, 'You must not commit adultery.' [28] But I say, anyone who even looks at a woman with lust has already committed adultery with her in his heart."* Pornography is commonly accompanied by masturbation and on-going sexual fantasy. Long after the video is no longer being viewed, you are repeatedly committing adultery in your heart and mind.

There is also the most subtle form of adultery that has, as of lately, claimed more formerly faithful wives than you might imagine.

Many husbands have experienced this as well. This form that I am talking about is commonly referred to as *emotional adultery*. This happens when you develop <u>and nurture</u> strong feelings of attraction, love or friendship with someone other than your spouse. A frequent doorway for this type of adultery to enter into one's marriage is through the forging of an internet relationship, which often times at the onset seems like such an innocent and safe way to make an emotional connection with someone. It also frequently occurs in close working relationships, between close family friends and with spiritual leaders or mentors as well. Really, any on-going communication between two people can lead to this type of adultery, if not carefully monitored.

For the broadest understanding of what adultery is – always remembering that you are to consider first the motive of the heart, before you consider anything else – it is anyone or anything that you become intimate with. Yes, I said any THING too! Marriage is a sacred covenant that you enter into with a promise to your spouse to love, honor and cherish them **ABOVE ALL ELSE**. Furthermore, don't forget that marriage is designed to be the symbol of our relationship with The Creator. Just as NO one or NO thing should ever come before Yahweh in your life – aside from your intimate, personal relationship with Him – NO one or NO thing should ever come before your spouse!

You should not have a closer friend; you should have no secrets; you should have no greater love; no greater intimacy; no greater oneness; no greater loyalty, commitment or connection of any kind; than that which you have with your spouse. This includes people – especially your family and even your children. This includes places – such as your job and even more especially the church. And this includes things – such as sports, hobbies and even ministry pursuits! Don't get an intimate relationship with The LORD confused with public ministry. Your intimate relationship with Him should always come before your relationship with your spouse – your public ministry ***never should***!

Any bond or intimacy that you create, with anyone or anything, that takes away from the esteemed **FIRST** place of honor that should be reserved and dedicated to your spouse alone, is a betrayal and a violation of your sacred marriage covenant. Let me put this disclaimer out there: I am not endorsing the use of this revelation to offset a free-fall of divorces on the grounds of "non-sexual adultery". However, I believe that the absence of this understanding is destroying more marriages than any other weapon in this present day. The spirit of adultery is present in more marriages than we can possibly conceive. Surely, when the spirit is present and prevalent in subtle, non-sexual manifestations of adultery – it is likely that sexual adultery will follow. That is why it is so important that you grasp this broader understanding of what adultery really is.

One last point on adultery is about understanding *what it is not*. When I wrote the first version of this book, I stated that an unmarried person who has sex with a married person could be labeled as an adulterer. However, upon further study I have learned that this is a secular view of adultery but is not the biblical view. Biblically, you can only commit adultery, if you yourself are married. If you are unmarried and have sex with a married person, you are a fornicator, not an adulterer.

To add validity to this point, I ask you to consider that what truly defines adultery is the violation of an established covenant. The terms of an established covenant are the **exclusive responsibility** of the parties that entered into that covenant. The marriage covenant is between the husband and the wife that agreed to it. No person outside of that covenant can break it or violate it because... *well that's just it –* they are **outside of it**. The other woman or other man that a husband or wife engages in emotional or sexual intimacy with has nothing to do with that spouse's covenant. Therefore that person would not be considered an adulterer (unless they are married as well) but would instead fall under the category of fornication. I just wanted to clarify this, in order to help you accurately identify which spirit is operating through you.

The Personality Profile

So now that we have this broad and probably somewhat shocking view of adultery, let's examine how this spirit shapes your life and your character. First of all, let's understand that when adultery is your strongman, you are not likely to have one night stands. There is something very crucial that you need as an adulterer that you should be able to get from your spouse but are not getting. It could be something physical, spiritual or emotional. Whatever the case may be, there is a void that is not being filled. Your spouse may even be magnifying the void that is in your life, and therefore your affairs are typically flings.

I am not writing this to invite you to escape taking responsibility for your own actions, but it is important for you to understand all the tactics that the spirit of adultery is using to keep you bound. Adulterous affairs are rarely birthed out of sexual impulse and lust alone. You are not looking for sex; you are looking for a deeper relationship than what you have at home. There is something that you feel you need and this spirit has deceived you into thinking that cheating on your spouse is the way to get that need met. However, there are many married individuals that experience voids and needs in their lives that do not commit adultery. So why are you so prone?

You are a person that leans and depends on others to give you a sense of wholeness and worth, entirely too much. You are afraid of being alone long-term. You are afraid of being tested and experiencing pain. You do not know what your breaking point is, and you do not want to find out. You just want someone to be there for you to make it all better. You more than likely experienced a lot of let downs and instability in your childhood, and thus there is a part of you suspended in the past that never matured. Subsequently, you can display a lot of childish behavior at times.

The let downs of your past also cause you to put high expectations on the person you are having the affair with. You feel that you have already been let down enough in your life. You are, for some reason, disappointed by your spouse, and so you expect your mistress or [5]*mantress* to make up for what your spouse lacks. You expect people to make up for the voids in your life in general. "Everybody owes you something". This is displayed through the high demands that you put on people to perform.

You may even be a **double-strength adulterer** – meaning that not only are you cheating on your spouse, but you are doing it with a person who is also married. Who broke your heart in the past and made you feel justified in violating your sacred covenant and/or connecting intimately with another person's spouse? Someone has hurt you deeply. It could have been in your childhood or in a relationship, but someone who you believed owed you love and respect did not give it to you. For this reason, there is a part of you that feels that you are just giving back what was dealt to you; you feel justified in a sense.

You do not believe in yourself or the possibility that anyone could ever really love you. Probably due to your upbringing, you are a person who lacks strong morals and integrity. On the one hand, you admire the commitment of marriage, but on the other hand, you violate it at will. This lack of respect that you have for marriage has its underlying cause in your lack of respect for yourself. You have a strong, burning desire for whatever it is that you feel is missing in your life. You want it anyway and anyhow you can get it, and that makes you a dangerous person. You are a backstabber of the worse kind. Depending on your level of desperation, you may even sleep with your spouse's friends and relatives and/or the spouses of your friends and relatives. This is what you become, as you continue on in the way of adultery.

As you continue on in adulterous affairs, you become more and more destitute in your moral standards, and this begins to affect every area of your life. You have to lie to cover up your adulterous activities; that makes you a liar. You have to scheme and deceive to keep your adulterous activities going, and that makes you a conniver. Someone who lies and connives will easily steal, so you may even be a thief. Unfortunately, the truth is that you cannot be trusted; not only by your spouse but by people in general. This spirit can even drive you to

---

[5] This is my word used to define a male that is having an affair with a married woman.

commit murder, if you feel a sexual partner who tries to interfere with your marriage is threatening your security!

You were probably a fornicator before you got married, and it is highly likely that you and your spouse engaged in illicit sexual activity with one another, before taking your marriage vows. You took the vows but never got delivered from the spirit of fornication, and now two spirits of sexual perversion have you bound. You like the security of being in a committed relationship, but you are unwilling to remain loyal to that commitment. You want loyalty but are not willing to give it in return. More than likely, you are reluctant to divorce your spouse or end it with your other; you'd be crushed to find out that either of them is pursuing another person. You are a user who lives by a double standard.

The spirit of adultery in your life plays on that same sense of inadequacy that was mentioned when discussing the spirit of masturbation. You are never really satisfied because the truth of the matter is; you want it to work out with your own spouse. You want that loyalty and commitment that you signed up for when you walked down the aisle, but you are too much of a selfish coward to put in the effort to make it work. The really sad part about it is that people who are inclined toward adultery, usually make such great husbands and wives once purified. If you would just deal with your issues and allow Yeshua to heal you, you would have so much to offer a spouse. Disloyalty is just the opposite of who you really are.

As a matter of fact, you may be one of the most cowardly of all adulterers – one of the ones who have become committed to your "other", but refuses to get a divorce! You see, you actually have a loyal nature underneath it all, and if you stay with your "other" long enough, you are going to direct your commitment and loyalty away from your spouse and toward that person. You have become deeply involved with this other person. Your "other" seems to be a dream come true. It has been months, or maybe even years, since you have touched your spouse sexually.

You have completely divorced your spouse in your heart and in your mind, but still want to selfishly hold onto the security of remaining married on paper. This is such a disgraceful injustice. You are selfishly using your spouse and your "other" to give yourself the ultimate security, while giving neither of them the same. There is such a great void inside of you that you are scared to death to lose anything. You are much like the **type 3** fornicator, and sadly, if either your spouse or your "other" does not take the initiative to put an end to the relationship with you, you are likely to stay in this state for years.

PLEASE, GET HELP. YOU ARE BETTER THAN THIS, SO MUCH BETTER!!!

The Churchgoer Profile

Whether or not a person who is under the influence of the spirit of adultery will be a churchgoer can really go either way. If you do attend church regularly, you already know of The LORD and have made some sacrifices to be committed to Him but have a wandering heart. You feel like God has already, or will at some point, let you down and you are determined to keep some type of "security plan" on the side. You are a covenant breaker and cannot be trusted by Him. He wants to give you His all but already knows that you will not be loyal.

However, you try to play The LORD, just like a cheater plays their spouse. You are a person who comes to church and *"plays the role"* of someone who is sanctified. You are usually one of the loudest praisers and most faithful attendants, yet you have no real intimacy with The Father and are very critical of others that do because you are envious. Thus you will experience stagnancy in your spiritual life. You must fake the anointing because you are not willing to commit to Yahweh enough to get a real anointing. You pray, fast, read the Bible and preach the Gospel all without Holiness.

You use the same deceptive tactics in church to fool others, as you would at home to fool your spouse. You are one of the most notorious liars. You will lie right from the pulpit and swear on the Holy Ghost without conviction. Sometimes you get so good at lying that you even begin to believe your own lies after a while. You are a religious

Pharisee who is satisfied to maintain only the *appearance* of Holiness, and you are totally deceived about your fast approaching appointment in divorce court – **Yahweh's divorce court**!

Or maybe you don't attend church regularly. You desire to have a real relationship with The Father but just do not believe that He will love you. You were probably raised in church or know of Yeshua but are backslidden. On the occasions that you do go to church, it is just a formality. You get nothing out of it and think about any and everything but the preached Word while in church. You usually come late and leave early and spend a lot of time outside of the sanctuary while there. You may have a seeming breakthrough from time to time but immediately after service go seeking out sin. Remember that you are also a fornicator, so you have no real commitment to The Most High and will drop Him in a hot second when you do not feel a sense of oneness with Him. He is only part time, just like a mistress. You just do not understand that Yeshua is totally committed to you and truly loyal.

You are a dangerous person for other Believers to hang around. Just as an adulterer in marriage will draw others into their covenant-desecrating activities, so will you do anything to draw devout Believers away from serving The Father. You are very skillful at convincing other Believers to sin with you. You are a deceptive, conniving and backstabbing member of the church – backstabbing The LORD and robbing Him of His tithes and offerings!

The Worship Portrait

It is noted at the beginning of this chapter that adultery is mentioned frequently in the Bible because it was once a word used to describe a number of different sexually perverse acts. However, there is something else that is very distinct about adultery as well, which is the fact that committing adultery involves the breaking of a covenant. We talked about our covenant with Yahweh a little bit in chapter 2. Yeshua's precious Blood was brutally spilled, in order to establish our covenant with Yahweh. As Believers and followers of Christ, our entire relationship with The LORD is based on covenant.

The spirit of adultery is working against a person's commitment to Yah. Under the influence of this spirit of adultery, you will begin to yield to the worship of other gods. Whatever this spirit can get you to direct your attention toward and serve, it will do so. This is done so deceptively though because most often times what you end up worshiping is your own fears, inhibitions, hang ups and issues. We as Christians often times let our past wounds and negative experiences control our lives.

The reason the Bible makes it clear that adultery is particularly offensive to The LORD is because He is such a faithful and ever unchanging God *(1 Cor 1:9)*. We also discussed in chapter 2 how a blood covenant can only be broken by death or the establishing of a new covenant that cancels out the former. That is why the scripture says that by committing adultery, we destroy our own souls *(Prov 6:32)*. By breaking that covenant with Him through the spirit of adultery, we are literally pronouncing ourselves dead unto Yahweh!

The most common form of spiritual adultery toward Yahweh is similar to the natural "non-sexual" adultery that I wrote about earlier: It is carnality. Carnality, according to Dictionary.com is defined as, *"1. Pertaining to or characterized by the flesh or the body, its passions and appetites; sensual: carnal pleasures. 2. Not spiritual; merely human; temporal; worldly"*. Any activity that is not done with conscious deliberateness toward growing closer to The Father is a carnal activity.

Now that does not mean that every carnal activity is sinful. Washing the dishes is certainly not done with the purpose of developing intimacy with Yeshua, but is rather a necessary non-spiritual activity. 'Carnality' and 'sin' are therefore not synonymous. But the scripture says *"to be **<u>carnally minded</u>** is death (Rom 8:6)."* To engage in necessary, non-spiritual activities, out of obligation to the things of this life, is not wrong. However, when such carnality **<u>fills your mind</u>** and consumes it to the point that it takes away from the esteemed first place of honor that should be reserved and dedicated to Father God alone, then it becomes a betrayal and a violation of your sacred Blood covenant with Him. It becomes spiritual adultery.

The plan of this spirit is detrimental indeed. Understand that a wife that is divorced by her husband, due to her unfaithfulness, loses all of the rights and benefits of the marriage. She loses her husband's name, intimacy with him, her inheritance, her covering, her protection, the right to live in his house – every blessing and favor the marriage yielded is lost. When we give way to the influence of the spirit of adultery in our relationship with The LORD, we risk being divorced by Him and losing everything. Whatever controls you is your master and whatever is your master is what you will serve and worship. Are you a spiritual adulterer?

Insights from Dr. Intimacy

Christian Women and Adultery

I have observed a disturbing epidemic lately, in the instances of devout Christian women committing adultery and divorcing their husbands. This is a very dear topic to me, and thus I am compelled to share the revelations that I received about this attack on Christian marriages. There are a number of these situations that have been brought before me. What has been most disturbing to me about this is that the women who have fallen prey to these attacks seem like the most unlikely candidates. The type of women that you read about in 1 Peter 3:1-2,

"^{1}*In like manner, you married women, be submissive to your own husbands [subordinate yourselves as being secondary to and dependent on them, and adapt yourselves to them], so that even if any do not obey the Word [of God], they may be won over not by discussion but by the [godly] lives of their wives, ^{2}when they observe the pure and modest way in which you conduct yourselves, together with your reverence [for your husband; you are to feel for him all that reverence includes: to respect, defer to, revere him – to honor, esteem, appreciate, prize, and in the human sense to adore him; that is to admire, praise, be devoted to, deeply love and enjoy your husband]. (AMP)*"

I prayed to Yah, for insight in scripture, about the spiritual wickedness behind this trend. And He led me to look at 1 Peter 3:7 and 1 Samuel 30:1-6. *"⁷Husbands, likewise, dwell with them with understanding, giving honor to the wife, as to the weaker vessel, and as being heirs together of the grace of life, that your prayers may not be hindered. (1 Pet 3:7 NKJV)"* You see, a woman that is fulfilling the mandate of 1 Peter 3:1-2 becomes dependent on her husband and that is what makes her the weaker vessel. This scripture is not referring to physical weakness. There is nothing in the context of this chapter that would suggest that. It certainly is not referring to the wife being spiritually weaker. That is made clear with the clause, *"as being heirs together of the grace of life"*: stated in the New Living Translation as, *"but she is **your equal partner** in God's gift of new life."*

But if not physically weaker or spiritually weaker, then what is Peter teaching us here? He is teaching us that a woman becomes the weaker vessel emotionally, or *"emotionally tender"*, in order to fulfill her role as helpmeet. Therefore Peter, who was a married Apostle, exhorts Christian brothers to, *"...live considerately with [your wives], with an intelligent recognition [of the marriage relation]... (1 Pet 3:7a AMP)"* In other words, live in consideration of what she has to sacrifice emotionally to become that submissive, dependent, adaptable, quiet-spirited, obedient woman that blesses you, as a helpmeet.

Now keeping that entirely in mind, let's look at 1 Samuel 30:1-6 (NIV), *"¹David and his men reached Ziklag on the third day. Now the Amalekites had raided the Negev and Ziklag. They had attacked Ziklag and burned it, ²and had taken captive the women and everyone else in it, both young and old. They killed none of them, but **carried them off as they went on their way**. ³When David and his men reached Ziklag, they found it destroyed by fire and their wives and sons and daughters taken captive. ⁴So David and his men wept aloud until they had no strength left to weep. ⁵David's two wives had been captured—Ahinoam of Jezreel and Abigail, the widow of Nabal of Carmel. ⁶David was greatly distressed because the men were talking of stoning him; each one was* *bitter in spirit because of his sons and daughters. But David found strength in the LORD his God."*

Reading this text is where my understanding came together: the women were left unprotected and taken captive by an enemy! The Holy Spirit said that this is what is happening in many Christian homes. The woman in 1 Peter that strives to be that perfectly, submissive wife leaves herself vulnerable, by **willingly** becoming the weaker vessel. There are certain attacks that she is simply not equipped to protect herself from because she has willingly become dependent on her husband.

During times of war in those days, when a woman was taken captive, she was forced to marry one of her captors or forced into prostitution. In other words, in her captivity she became an adulteress. It was not a decision that she made or a path that she chose for herself. But the enemy got a hold of these women that were left uncovered and unprotected by their husbands and thus the enemy, *"carried them off as they went on their way."*

The wives of today that are being affected by this same enemy spirit that you see operative in 1 Samuel 30 – this spirit that is assigned to steal the wives and children of the soldiers of the Kingdom – are being carried away too! The way of living for these loving wives is to serve The LORD and their husbands. But once an enemy has taken someone captive, they take the person **their way,** as the scripture says! In captivity to satan's attacks, these women become what they do not want to be and do what they do not want to do.

Christian men – Apostles, Prophets, Evangelists, Pastors and Teachers especially – beware! This spirit wants to steal your family. And guess what? Only a woman that is emotionally neglected can fall prey to such an attack. Look at verse 6 again, *"...for the men spoke of stoning him because the souls of them all were bitterly grieved, each man for his sons and daughters."* You see, no mention was made of these men grieving over their wives. They did not honor their wives. They only cared for what the women could add to them, but cared not for the women themselves. Yet understand that if you fail to dwell together in understanding with your wife; honoring her as the woman that voluntarily made herself weak for the sake of loving and respecting you, thereby allowing the enemy to steal her – you will lose not only her but all that she gave birth to in your life as well. *Selah*

Most of the time, a woman taken captive in war is never seen or heard of again. She becomes someone else's wife. The scripture even refers to the husband as 'master' in 1 Pet 3:6 (AMP). And so although taken captive against her will, because she has the heart of a true wife, she will serve and honor her new husband, just as she did you. And yes, The LORD will bless her because she was a victim of circumstance. Fortunately in this text, David honored his wives and was determined to pursue the enemy and reclaim them. **Because of his love for his wives**, his prayers were not hindered. Yahweh answered his prayer, and all of the women and children were recovered.

Men, if you have found yourself in a similar scenario, pursue your wife immediately, before the enemy carries her out of your reach. If your marriage has not been affected by this, do not allow it to be. Love, honor, cherish and desire your wife above all. If your wife is long gone and has become the wife of another or her heart is beyond your reach, forgive her and yourself. Examine how the enemy got in and stole your family. Cover her in prayer, regardless of the outcome, and move forward with the revelation knowledge of what it will take to be successfully married in the future – *if you so choose to remarry*. Even if you do not marry again, you can help others protect their families.

NOTE: I am in no way suggesting that every woman who commits adultery falls into this category. There are many reasons that people commit adultery, some worse than others. This article speaks to a specific cause of adultery that is applicable in some cases, for the benefit of those affected by it. If it applies to you, I am sure you can discern that. If it doesn't, you must search for answers in prayer about why adultery occurred in your marriage.

Chapter 10

Incest

"None of you shall approach to any that is near of kin to him, to uncover their nakedness: I am The Lord." (Lev 18:6, KJV)

Some Biblical References

Gen 19:30-37, 38: 15-24, Lev 18:6-17, 20:11-12, 14, 17, 19-21; Eze 22:11; 1 Cor 5:1, 5:5, 2 Cor 2:5, 7:11

The Definition

Sexual intercourse or other sexual contact between persons so closely related that law or custom forbids their marriage.

The Assignment

A person involved in incest takes an already existing relationship that has an established purpose and twists it into something else. This ultimately destroys the quality and purity of the pre-existing relationship and leaves something perverse in its place. The spirit of incest is a contaminating, deluding spirit. It corrupts entire sectors of the Body of Christ and aims to cut them off from the other members. A member separated from the whole will quickly die off, and so ultimately this spirit wants to cause total separation from the Body of Christ and birth out cults. **This is a very dangerous spirit whose ultimate assignment is to pervert the love of The Father in your heart. Yahweh God is LOVE; to pervert your understanding of love and relationship is to completely undermine any possibility of you having an authentically intimate relationship with The LORD.**

The Practical Understanding

Understanding the literal meaning of incest is not difficult to grasp. Sexual relations of any kind with a close relative – regardless of penetration – would constitute incest. By reading Leviticus chapter 18, we get a very clear picture of who can be defined as a close relative: *biological mother or father, step mother or father, full or half-sister or brother by either mother or father – whether or not you were raised together, biological grandchild, step sister or step brother, aunt or uncle, aunt or uncle's spouse, daughter or son-in-law, sister or brother-in-law who is married to one of your siblings, sister or brother-in-law who is the sibling of your spouse, step daughter or son, step grandchild.*

What I find most interesting about incest is **the reason** for it being such a detestable act in the sight of The LORD: *"For whoever commits any of these abominations, the persons who commit them shall be cut off from among their people (Lev 18:29, AMP)."* There was a time earlier in scripture, when it was not only permissible to marry a close relative, but was actually *preferred*. In Genesis 24:4, Abraham sends his servant to find one of his relatives for his son Isaac to marry, *"ᴬBut you shall go to my country and to my relatives and take a wife for my son Isaac."* Abraham's wife Sarah was actually his half-sister. As we study incest a bit further, it will be revealed to us why it became a detestable thing in the sight of Yahweh.

Before we go on though, let's clearly establish that incest occurs for different reasons. There is incest that occurs purely for the sake of fulfilling a sexual desire – this type would fall under the category of lust. There is incest that occurs through the sexual violation of an underage person, by an older relative – this type would fall under the category of rape or pedophilia. Lastly, there is incest that occurs when two relatives develop an abnormally intimate relationship, which emulates that of an average couple – this is the type that is actually targeted in this chapter. Incest operating at its maximum capacity aims to pervert not just sex, but even the entire sacredness of being in love in a relationship.

The Personality Profile

As a person who commits incest, you have a difficult time appropriately relating to other people. You are a withdrawn individual that feels rejected. Due to this, you are reluctant to seek out new relationships and that is part of the reason why you prefer to "keep it in the family". You lack understanding of what love really is and have warped concepts concerning life in general. This is undoubtedly due to a misrepresentation of love in your childhood. Someone who claimed that they loved you did not express or exhibit love as it ought to be, but because you trusted them you accepted their display as true love.

You cannot quite put your finger on it, but you know that something is "not right" with you. You may often hear people tell you that you are *crazy*; that *something is wrong with you*; that *your mind is not right* or some similar comment. You are probably so used to hearing it by now that you do not even bother to refute it. You have become numb to the effects of such words, and they do not move you at all. You just accept such to be true, even though you still do not know why it is true.

It is unlikely that you would be in a relationship with more than one family member, unless you are being sexually abused. Remember that incest attempts to emulate, as closely as possible, a legitimate love affair and therefore monogamy is highly likely in your relationship with your family member. You are only likely to be in a relationship with more than one family member, if the first relative relationship did not work out for some reason. In this case, you are inclined to try a relationship with another family member, as opposed to seeking out a relationship with a stranger. That would be way too risky for your taste; too much uncertainly to face. You have been hurt so often that for the most part, you are not even willing to give anyone else a chance.

If you suffered molestation in your childhood, especially if it occurred over a long period of time, you are much more inclined to fall into this type of relationship. People who are molested at a young age tend to define themselves by that molestation. Molestation shapes your thinking and molds your perception of relationships in a very perverse way. You know that the incest you are involved in is not right; at the same time you think to yourself, *"Can it really be wrong?"* The reason for this mental duplicity and confusion about your incestuous relationship is that you were built on incest. I knew a young lady that was regularly molested by her biological father. She was eventually convinced that she was in love with him and did not want to end her sexual relations with him, even when she became an adult. After her father finally married and ended the relationship with his daughter, she went on to "fall in love" with several more family members.

Another trigger for incest is being raised in an overly strict, religious environment. Sexuality is a natural and healthy part of life that cannot be denied expression. As a child begins to go through puberty, if he or she is made to feel dirty or abnormal for their sexuality, they will become very misguided about how to handle it. The sexual desires that they feel will not go away, no matter how much the child is threatened or punished. The child will eventually begin to view his or herself as a social deviant because of their desire to express the sexuality that they cannot suppress. This often leads to younger siblings being molested or leads to siblings and/or cousins who are close in age engaging in consensual sexual activity.

Whether you were molested or driven to incest through the crazed ranting of hell fire and brimstone by the religious adults in your life; you feel that the relative that you are in a relationship with is the "only person in the world" who understands you. They accept you the way that you are. They do not make you live up to a false standard of expectations. You feel loved and received by him or her. They made you feel special when no one else did. You feel incomplete and being connected to this family member intimately gives you a sense of wholeness. It is like they *fill in the missing parts*. The spirit of incest is really aiming to make you feel like you are "in love". Incest is not an act that is derived out of lust, as much as it is derived out of a warped sense of love.

Being in incestuous relationships has taught you to live a life of secrecy. Everything is always a secret with you. You probably do not even like to tell your age. You are a paranoid person that is always fearful of "being discovered". You tend to think that people are always plotting against you (and your sexual partner). Friendships do not usually last long with you, unless it is with a really naïve and unsuspecting person, who is not a threat or someone who knows about and accepts your relationship of incest. You cannot allow anyone else to get too close to you, or they might "find you out".

If you have other family members outside of your love interest, you may be constantly at odds with them and try to stir up a lot of strife. You do not want your sexual partner to be drawn to, or form intimate relations with, anyone else in the family beside yourself. You portray everyone in a negative light to him or her because you are an outrageously jealous person. You are jealous of everyone and everything, and you try to destroy anything that makes you feel insecure or inadequate. This destructive, jealous behavior extends itself across every element of your life and all people that you encounter. You are particularly destructive if and when your sexual partner attempts to be in a relationship with another person.

The Churchgoer Profile

Most people who physically commit the act of incest will not have a relationship with Yeshua. These are broken, bitter and delusional people who want to give **ALL** of their love to the family member that they are involved with. If you are a person who is under the influence of this spirit and do have any type of relationship with The LORD at all, it is a twisted one for sure. Whether you are under the influence in only a spiritual sense, or actually participate in it literally and physically, you are highly likely to be involved in occultism and new age religion.

Mild or indirect occultism – such as organized, biblically-based false teachings, informal idol worship, as well as separatist religious organizations and denominations – is actually the most prominent manifestation of the spiritual influence of incest in the religious world. It is an easy trap for you to fall in to, since you lack understanding of who Yah really is. Your perception of Him is just as warped as your perception of love. For Yahweh is LOVE *(1 John 4:8)*; to misunderstand love, is to misunderstand God completely.

If you are actually a "Christian" churchgoer, you are constantly under a veil of deception. You undoubtedly experience persistent feelings of condemnation and guilt. There is something off about your relationship with The LORD. You know it, but are not quite sure what it is that you know. Something just does not feel right. You are not free. You feel bound and ashamed and want to hide away in a delusional state of denial.

Under the influence of the spirit of incest, you are very jealous about Yah. You try to *possess* God and do not like to see others have a relationship with Him because you want Him all to yourself. You believe that Christianity is some type of exclusive club for you and The LORD alone; as if you are the only person in the world that He loves. You are that way about your pastor as well. You are probably also the type that frowns on fellowship with other church members and other church ministries. In your mind, your church is the best and only church; your pastor is the best and only pastor. You like to keep your circle small and intimate. You are really into cliques and clubs – and *your clique is the best and only clique worth being a part of.*

You are not a productive member of the Body of Christ because you reject unity, unless it is with your own little group, which is generally operating under the same twisted spirit that you are! Medically, we know that when close relatives conceive, they usually miscarry or give birth to deformed children. As it is in the natural, so it is in the spiritual – whatever you produce is either unlikely to survive or is deformed. Not only are you unproductive, but you also try to keep others from producing or try to destroy what others do produce. You are so green with envy to see anyone else grow spiritually or be elevated in ministry and the things of the Kingdom of Yah.

You keep that air of secrecy about you, while spreading much discord and disunity in the church. Yet you are deceptively defiant and proclaim boldly that you have done nothing wrong. Oddly enough, although you don't want anyone to join your circle, you invite them anyway. You may invite someone to visit your church and then treat them contemptuously once they come. You want them to *see* what you have but not *partake* of it. As a leader that operates under this spirit, you will often try to oppress and even get rid of any follower that thinks outside of your boxed-in mentality and does not promote the agenda of making your name great. This is nothing like the heart of The Father. You are so far from The LORD that you have not even begun to **know who He is...**

The Worship Portrait

I want to look now a little more deeply into the detrimental driving motive behind this spirit. Leviticus chapter 18 – which is a written record of the direct Word of The LORD to Moses – is dedicated almost entirely to defining the acts of incest. Verses 6 through 17 serve this purpose. But then in verse 24, The LORD begins to speak His heart concerning not just "the acts" of incest but also "the why" of its wickedness. It reads:

"^{24}'Do not defile yourselves in any of these ways, for the people I am driving out before you have defiled themselves in all these ways. ^{25}Because the entire land has become defiled, I am punishing the people who live there. I will cause the land to vomit them out. ^{26}You must obey all my decrees and regulations. You must not commit any of these detestable sins. This applies both to native-born Israelites and to the foreigners living among you. ^{27}All these detestable activities are practiced by the people of the land where I am taking you, **and this is how the land has become defiled**. ^{28}So do not defile the land and give it a reason to vomit you out, as it will vomit out the people who live there now. ^{29}Whoever commits any of these detestable sins will be cut off from the community of Israel. ^{30}So obey my instructions, and do not defile yourselves by committing any of these detestable practices that were committed by the people who lived in the land before you. I am the Lord your God'."

Several times in this passage of text, The LORD emphasizes that these acts were committed by the other nations – the Egyptians from whom the Israelites came out of and the Canaanites to whom they were going. The Heathens made a regular practice of incest, in order to increase their own numbers and make their own names great, ***reproducing after their own kind***. Often times the heathens would take the deformed or unwanted children produced through incest and burn them as a blood sacrifice offering, to a pagan god named Molech. Molech was primarily a god of the Ammonites. The Ammonites were descendants of Benammi, a child that was conceived through the incest of Lot and his younger daughter.

Before the Israelites were called out of Egypt, they practiced these same detestable acts. However, when Yahweh is ready to elevate you and bring you into a new place, what was once tolerated will no longer be deemed acceptable. You see, this was a time that Yah was ready to make a distinction between His chosen people and the rest of the world. In other words, He was saying, *"This is the way that the heathens live, those who are NOT called by My Name nor mandated to live by My decrees."* This interpretation can be confirmed in Leviticus chapter 20, another chapter that deals heavily with the acts and consequences of incest. In the last clause of verse 26 it reads, *"...I am the LORD your God, who has **set you apart from the nations**."*

The spirit of incest wants you to reproduce what comes from within your own corrupt spiritual bloodline. This is what defiles the land; when the same corrupt DNA is being reproduced over and over again. Intercourse with close relatives is going to afford a great opportunity for this, not to mention that intimate relationships also allow for the transfer of mindsets, ideals, beliefs and behaviors. The Israelite bloodline was contaminated from the start, with Abraham marrying his own sister. While the Jewish people may have lived somewhat better than the Canaanites, they fell far short of the lifestyle that Yahweh God wanted them to portray as His Holy, set apart people.

What The Father wants is to decontaminate your bloodline, by causing you to reproduce what comes from within His Loins. Through the Israelites, He wanted to make *His own name great* and manifest *His glory* to the nations of the world. Notice also that in verse 18:26 The LORD emphatically **BREAKS** the pattern of incest with this statement,

"...This applies both to native-born Israelites and <u>to the foreigners living among you</u>." He made an invitation to **anyone** of **any nationality** that was willing to follow His decrees, to become a part of His chosen people!

Under the influence of the spirit of incest, you are going to miss the greatest and most important element of your walk with Christ. I am speaking of *the great commission,* as it is referred to, found in Mark 16:15-16, *"¹⁵And He said to them, 'Go into all the world and preach and publish openly the good news (the Gospel) to every creature [of the whole human race]. ¹⁶He who believes [who adheres to and trusts in and relies on the Gospel and Him Whom it sets forth] and is baptized will be saved [from the penalty of eternal death]; but he who does not believe [who does not adhere to and trust in and rely on the Gospel and Him Whom it sets forth] will be condemned.'"*

In Luke chapter four, Yeshua says that He was **anointed** to preach the Gospel *(to anyone and everyone that would listen).* The endowment of The LORD's power only comes when we are willing to share it with others. By His very nature, The Father wants to save ***everyone***; He wants to love ***everyone***; He wants to share His power with ***everyone***. He will have no part of anyone that attempts to shut others out from His blessing or cut others off from relationship with Him. By doing so, you diminish the work of the cross and the Glory of The Son of Man.

God longs to be connected to all of us, not just you! The Father wants a chosen "people", not a chosen "person". While you go before The LORD in bitter discord, complaining about those that don't "love" Him as much as you do – you are offering up the children of Yahweh to be burned in the fire, just like those who gave their children to Molech! You may think your selfishness for Him is birthed out of Love, but be careful of this spirit because it is only deceptively *"disguised"* as love. If you operate under this spirit, there is no real love in you, and you probably do not have any fellowship with Yeshua at all.

The Spirit of Incest in Organizations

You need to consider very carefully what you are about to read. Incest is very prevalent in our society, in both the literal, physical sense and the deeper, spiritual sense. Once a spirit has gained access into your sphere of influence, it has the opportunity to manifest itself in any way that it chooses. This is why you need to be very careful about what you expose yourself and your family to. Perhaps after reading this, you will not find it at all perplexing that there is incest occurring in your family.

Think about everything that you just read about the spirit of incest. One of the driving motives behind the spirit of incest is to keep "outsiders" cut off. *Exclusivity* is synonymous with incest. With that in mind, think about a lot of these "exclusive" clubs and organizations that are only open to people of the same mindset of those who head up the organization. Some examples of this are the Masons, Eastern Stars, the KKK, Illuminati and even fraternities.

You might be surprised to see the names and types of those organizations associated with one another, but let us consider the similarities. All of the above organizations have a strong generational influence. Usually, the members of such organizations are, for example, the 5th or 6th generation of their family to be a part of it. These organizations keep their activities very private. The members marry within the organization. They make it difficult, if not impossible, for "new people" to join. They look down on other organizations and often other classes of people. They often charge hefty dues that exclude many from even considering a membership. Those that are members pride themselves on the membership and are not quick to invite others to become a part of the group, at the risk of it becoming common.

These manifestations just scream INCEST! Often times within these groups, not only is incest operating spiritually, but there is a high occurrence of natural incest as well. I know this is a hard thing that you are reading, but I have to challenge you so-called Christian "disciples" on your involvement in such organizations. Christianity is the most **non-exclusive** organization in the world; it is open for any and every one to join, for FREE. Now when I say "Christianity", I am referring to the true Body of Christ, not the man-made organization. As a matter of fact, the spirit of incest is the driving force behind man-made denominations and organizations.

It is proven in scripture. 1 Corinthians 1:10-13 and 31 read, "*[10]But I urge and entreat you, brethren, by the name of our Lord Jesus Christ, that all of you <u>be in perfect harmony and full agreement in what you say, and that there be no dissensions or factions or divisions among you, but that you be perfectly united in your common understanding and in your opinions and judgments</u>. [11]For it has been made clear to me, my brethren, by those of Chloe's household, that there are contentions and wrangling and factions among you. [12]...each one of you [either] says, I belong to Paul, or I belong to Apollos, or I belong to Cephas (Peter), or I belong to Christ. [13]Is Christ (the Messiah) divided into parts? Was Paul crucified on behalf of you? Or were you baptized into the name of Paul?... [31]So then, as it is written, Let him who boasts and proudly rejoices and glories, boast and proudly rejoice and glory in the Lord.*"

In this text is written a **clear and direct denouncement of denominations,** as Paul makes it clear that we should boast in NO NAME except that of The LORD. 'Denomination' is defined as: *a class or kind of persons or things **distinguished by a specific name** (www.dictionary.com).* It comes from a root Latin word whose meaning is "to choose or designate". So who gave the Corinthians, or anyone for that matter, the right to choose or designate which group of people is most acceptable to The LORD? Are these not the same people that were reprimanded by Paul for condoning *INCEST* in their church? "*[1]It is actually reported that there is sexual immorality among you, and of a kind that even pagans do not tolerate: A man is sleeping with his father's wife. [2]And you are proud!... (1 Cor 5:1-2a NIV)*" Furthermore, three times in his letters to this group, Paul had to address idolatry!

It says in John 3:16, "*For God loved **THE WORLD** so much that he gave his one and only Son, so that **EVERYONE** who believes in him will not* *perish but have eternal life."* The only requirement for becoming a member of the Body of Christ is desire and belief. **NO ONE IS EXCLUDED.** No one has to pre-qualify or be referred or be a family member of so-and-so. Everyone is welcomed to come just as they are and everyone has the same rights to the full benefits of membership. What Yahweh does in the church, He does openly for all to see and in the book of Acts it says, He added members daily *(Acts 2:41-47)!*

Brothers and sisters, if we are to be *disciples* of Christ, then we must model our lives after His. If you are a part of any organization – clique, club, fraternity, sorority, church, denomination, group or otherwise – that encourages exclusivity, boasting of the group's name, strict membership guidelines, membership dues and secrecy, then you are under the influence of the spirit of incest! As a Christian, you are already a member of The Body of Christ. You have joined the most honored, distinguished and elite group in all of creation! Why then would you lust after the prestige of some other, lesser, base association? These organizations are not of The LORD. They separate and divide and bring glory to the name of the group, instead of to **THE NAME THAT IS ABOVE ALL NAMES**. When Yeshua returns, He will be returning for ONE spotless and pure Body; not corrupt, scattered bits and pieces that are hiding behind fancy membership names.

Take heed to this warning! For in scripture, in the book of Mark 5:9 there is a case where a demon possessed man is encountered by Yeshua. And when Yeshua confronts the demonic force inside of the man, it is recorded as such, *"⁹Then Jesus asked him, "What is your name?" "My name is Legion," he replied, "for we are many."* Is it only a coincidence that by a simple rearranging of the letters in the word 'denomination' you can create the sentence: I Demon Nation? Or is The Spirit of God speaking, teaching us that with these man-made organizations, we are dealing with the same kind of demonic force that possessed this man: A unified, collective body of demons that operate as one? *My (singular) name is Legion, for we (plural) are many – I* **Demon Nation** *(in other words, I am an entire nation of demons)!*

Chapter 11

Homosexuality

"Do not practice homosexuality... it is a detestable sin." (Lev 18:22)

Some Biblical References

Gen 19:5, Lev 18:22, 20:13; Deut 22:5, Judges 19:22-23; Rom 1:24, 26-27; 1 Cor 6:9-11; 1 Tim 1:10

The Definition

Strong attraction toward persons of the same sex; sexual intercourse or other sexual contact with persons of the same sex.

The Assignment

A homosexual trades in the honor of his or her role in nature for that of another. Homosexuality is about more than just having sex with a person of the same gender. It is the unspoken renouncing of one's significance in the cycle of existence and harmony of creation. **The spirit of homosexuality is assigned to rob you of your understanding of your true identity in The Creator. Robbing you of your identity leaves you barren and unable to give birth to Yahweh's will or to reproduce His Kingdom. It also leaves vacancies in the plan of creation or places unequipped individuals in positions that they are not designed to effectively fulfill.**

The Practical Understanding

Disclaimer

Being "politically correct" when addressing any homosexual agenda has become more relevant these days. I hear terms like 'gay', 'bi-sexual', 'transsexual', 'transgender', 'cross-dresser', 'drag queen', *'lesbian' and many others. To be frank, I do not know how to distinguish between many of the newer terms. As I began writing this chapter, I considered studying the terms to get an understanding of the precise meanings. However, I realized that understanding these words is not my assignment. Spending time studying such things would distract me from my true purpose, which is to reveal the spirit that is operating behind all of these terms. I am here to expose darkness, not to be politically correct. If I offend anyone with political incorrectness, I ask your apologies in advance. My heart is full of compassion for every person that reads this book, and it is never my intent to hurt the human heart as I expose the workings of satan. It is my intent to use truth to strip satan of his power; at times his victims get caught in the cross-fires of this war. Yet I assure you that I mean no offense.*

I feel compelled to say that I am sorry that so many "so-called" Christians are mean and abusive toward gays. I have heard preachers use words like "fag" and "butch" right from the pulpit. It breaks my heart and incites righteous indignation within me. This is not the love of Yeshua, who showed compassion to the masses of people, no matter what their issue was. In spite of these evil and deceived people, please know that The Father loves you. He does not approve of a homosexual lifestyle, but He does love you just the way that you are. The taunts of these hateful people are not a reflection of how Yeshua feels about you, His love and desire for you or how I personally feel about you. So please, let me take liberty to study <u>the spiritual truths</u> about homosexuality, and I will leave it to all you civil rights activists out there to straighten out what is, and what is not, politically correct.

****

Having put that disclaimer out there, let's now get into the heart of the matter. As in the case of masturbation, the Bible's position on homosexuality is hotly debated. In the case of masturbation, I can understand the confusion, but on the topic of homosexuality where is there really any room for debate?

"^{22}*Do not practice homosexuality, having sex with another man as with a woman. It is a detestable sin. (Lev 18:22)*"

"*¹³If a man practices homosexuality, having sex with another man as with a woman, both men have committed a detestable act. They must both be put to death, for they are guilty of a capital offense. (Lev 20:13)"*

"*²⁶That is why God abandoned them to their shameful desires. Even the women turned against the natural way to have sex and instead indulged in sex with each other. ²⁷And the men, instead of having normal sexual relations with women, burned with lust for each other. Men did shameful things with other men, and as a result of this sin, they suffered within themselves the penalty they deserved. (Rom 1:26-27)"*

"*⁹Don't you realize that those who do wrong will not inherit the Kingdom of God? Don't fool yourselves. Those who indulge in sexual sin, or who worship idols, or commit adultery, or are male prostitutes, or practice homosexuality, ¹⁰or are thieves, or greedy people, or drunkards, or are abusive, or cheat people—none of these will inherit the Kingdom of God. (1 Cor 6:9-10)"*

"*⁹For the law was not intended for people who do what is right. It is for people who are lawless and rebellious, who are ungodly and sinful, who consider nothing sacred and defile what is holy, who kill their father or mother or commit other murders. ¹⁰The law is for people who are sexually immoral, or who practice homosexuality, or are slave traders, liars, promise breakers, or who do anything else that contradicts the wholesome teaching ¹¹that comes from the glorious Good News entrusted to me by our blessed God. (1 Tim 1:9-11)"*

The Bible **speaks expressly** about the wickedness of homosexuality. I have heard the arguments that attempt to make null the above scriptures, as a case against homosexuality. Those in favor of "Christian homosexuals" say that these scriptures are referring to ritual acts of sex being done as an act of worship to a false god and male prostitution. *Ok, let's say I was to accept that argument.* Then what about the condemned men of Sodom, who became synonymous with homosexuality? The argument here is that they were filled with sexual lust and violent, atheistic immorality – unlike the loving, monogamous relationships of today's homosexual activists. *Ok, let's say I was to* *accept that argument.* One more question then: If it cannot be emphatically proven in scripture that Yahweh <u>dishonors</u> loving, homosexual relationships – where is the proof in scripture that He <u>does honor</u> them?

I have never failed to find a clear confirmation in at least two places in scripture, for every thought or idea of doctrine that is impressed upon my spirit. As a matter of fact, it is my own personal guideline for any doctrine or spiritual concept that I believe is being revealed to me. If I cannot find a scriptural reference or practical example in at least two places in the Bible, I continue to research it before I will really embrace it. The Bible CLEARLY ENDORSES marriage between one man and one woman. The proof is all throughout scripture. But where is the proof that The God of the Bible endorses loving, homosexual relationships?

Please show me one example in scripture of a loving, sexual relationship between two men that were called Righteous. Please don't try to use Jonathan and David. There is nothing in text that would suggest that they were sexually involved. David clearly enjoyed having sex with women! Please don't insult The Christ by saying Yeshua and John were gay, simply because John leaned on him at the table. I sometimes lean on my Mother, and yet never once have I had or even thought about having sex with her! People can love each other, without having sex or sexual desire. The greatest love on the planet is arguably that of a mother for her child, and yet no good mother ever translates that love into sexual desire for her child or tries to become the wife of that child!

Please show me even one example of two women that lived together as a married couple, which Yahweh called blessed. And please explain to me how the union of two men or of two women, measures up to this scripture: *"[15]And did not God make [you and your wife] one [flesh]? Did not One make you and preserve your spirit alive? And why [did God make you two] one? Because He sought a godly offspring [from your union]. (Malachi 2:16)"* It is undeniable that The LORD created us **male** and **female** and mandated us to become one flesh, in order to procreate. His plan for marriage is plainly laid out before us.

Even if we never had a Bible to read, nature itself proves that The Creator's design is for male and female to come together and reproduce. This is how He designed it, and this is what He blesses.

Having said that, I will not try in any way to make void the love that homosexuals share with each other. I do believe that there is a measure of love that homosexuals feel for each other. It may be as strong, if not in some cases even stronger, than the love of two heterosexuals. But by this same argument, I can justify the pedophile that falls mutually in love with his 11 year old neighbor and takes her away to be his wife. I can justify the man that wants to marry his best friend, which just so happens to be his dog. I can justify the man that is equally in love with both his wife and his mistress and wants to keep them both. If we use love as an argument to eradicate the Righteous standards of scripture, then I guess we can all do _what_ we love and _who_ we love, without conviction or consequence!

I will not labor anymore to establish the sinfulness of homosexual relationships. I believe for anyone that desires to walk uprightly before The LORD, the truth that has been presented is sufficient. For all others, like the men of Sodom, there is nothing that can be said to dissuade you. You have made your choice. So, now let's discuss a little bit more about what homosexuality is practically.

The dictionary describes homosexuality as a strong attraction for the same sex. That definition is too broad. A definition that broad lends itself to labeling everyone that has ever had a sexual thought about the same gender as homosexual. An attraction, which is simply a feeling, would not in and of itself put you in the category of homosexuality – anymore than being attracted to someone underage categorizes you as a pedophile or getting sexually aroused when you see two dogs have sex justifies labeling you under bestiality. Be that as it may, you are certainly "at-risk" of becoming homosexual if you experience strong, same-sex attraction. And perhaps you are actually homosexual, just having not given in to the physical act of sex as of yet. If you are doing it in your heart and mind, you have already lost the battle. Reading the information in this chapter will help you determine how strongly this spirit is operating in your life. It is at least certain though that if you are unsure or "still in the closet", you are not yet totally given over to this spirit. Once it completely has you under its influence, you will proudly and boldly take a public stand.

The question is often posed, *"Can someone be born gay?"* This is a good question and the answer is a simple and emphatically clear – *Yes and No*. Yes, in the sense that you can be born with an inexplicable inclination toward "reverse-gender" behaviors and same-sex attraction. Let me explain how I know this. I have given birth to seven children. At the time that I am writing this, my youngest is 5 years old and my oldest is 18. Having had the experience of being involved in training this small army of humanity, I can with certainty say that human beings are born with a vast array of personality traits. These traits range greatly from those most honorable, to those least desired.

One of my children for instance, is the very epitome of joy, and she has always loved to share this joy with any and every one. Since infancy, she has had the ability to transfer feelings of joy to others because she has such a strong energy of happiness emanating from her being. At the same time, she is insanely jealous – more so than any of my other children. Her longing to make people feel good also causes her to demand to be the center of attention at all times. Now I have another child that is naturally strong and independent. He has from infancy, preferred to be alone. He taught himself to walk at eight months of age, while I was busy trying to teach him to crawl. Yet, he was an unusually angry baby – throwing terrible tantrums, getting easily frustrated; and banging his head in fits of rage. He was always like this, although he had no diagnosed medical issues of any kind. He had the ability to try the patience of a saint with his anger issues!

Here is more: a daughter that was a critical snob from birth, but is somewhat justified because she is exceedingly more mature and intuitive than her peers; a son who is extremely sensitive and easily hurt emotionally, yet very fun-loving; a son that is insatiably inquisitive but worries all the time; a daughter that is the most intelligent but naturally melancholy and withdrawn; and another child that was labeled as gay from as early as eight months old. People always said he looked and acted like a girl, no matter how hard I tried to "beef up" his masculinity. Oh boy! So if the question is, *"Can someone be born with negative personality traits and emotional challenges?"* – **why, heaven's yes!**

As was stated earlier in this chapter, an attraction, same-sex or otherwise, is no more than a feeling. That is why people fall in and out of love in marriage. They *felt* attracted to their spouse at one point, and then at another time no longer *felt* attracted. Attraction is a fluid emotional state that can be easily affected by external influences and deliberately controlled. With any abnormal or unpleasant personality trait, characteristic or emotional state that a human being may be born with, every attempt should be made to correct it. Homosexual tendencies are no different.

My son that had the anger issues is now 11. He had many troubled years at school because of his anger. Should I have just allowed him to succumb to his anger because *he was born that way*? Should I have just told his teachers after he threw books across the room, *"Well that is just who he is"*? No! He would have been in juvenile detention by the time he was eight. I had to teach him how to manage his strength and use it to his advantage. I used prayer, love, biblical teachings and sought professional help as well. My friendly daughter that will walk up to a total stranger and hug them like they are her long, lost relative; should I let her think it is okay to be friendly to everyone? Should I not teach her to curtail her friendliness for the sake of keeping her safe from predators? And concerning her jealously – do I not have a responsibility to teach her that though she is a gift from God, she is not His only gift to the world?

You see, my point is that just because someone is born with an inclination toward homosexuality, does not mean that the person should not be redirected toward what has been the established order and law of nature since creation. All human beings are born in an imperfect state. Yet if I have a child that is born blind, would I not do everything that I could to give her sight if it is possible? If I have a child who is born deaf, should I not pursue obtaining hearing aids so he can hear? Blindness or deafness does not diminish the value of my child at all. Yet they are abnormalities that will indeed make life much more challenging and difficult for that child. Therefore, if it can be corrected without harming the child in some detrimental way, I will opt for that correction.

The one thing that I am certainly not going to do is pretend that there is no issue, or try to force my child to believe that he or she is "typical", when all of creation is evidence against that. This will only serve to shroud that child in confusion and darkness. It will render him or her helpless in their ability to make accurate decisions, with mindfulness of the maladies that will make life more challenging for them, in certain instances. By helping them confront their differences and challenges head-on, I empower them to either eradicate those challenges or to overcome them by using other strengths!

So that is the 'yes' part of the answer; now to address the 'no' part. Using the example of my formally angry child, *(who is almost as gentle as a lamb now, by the way)* let us continue. I said that he was born with an inclination toward feeling angry and frustrated. If he grew up to kill, could I then say he was born a killer? No. He was born with a bad temper, which was not his choice. How he responds and reacts to that anger *is* his choice. If he responds to feelings of anger by killing someone that is a choice that he makes. Feeling angry is not sinful; killing someone on the other hand, is indeed wrong. Homosexuality is the same. Having feelings of attraction toward someone of the same sex is not sinful, responding to those feelings through sexual contact with the same sex, is indeed wrong.

So yes, you can be born with an inclination toward homosexuality. But in order for your feelings of same-sex attraction to cross the border of sin – you have to deliberately and consciously act upon them. This also means that you cannot become homosexual through molestation. If someone puts heroin in your food and exposes you to the drug that does not by default make you a drug addict. You will only become a drug addict if you **choose** to yield to the temptation that the experience produces in you, to use heroin again. You then become a drug addict by choice.

Also, I must tell you about a door of homosexuality that might make you want to throw stones at me. It is masturbation. *What,*

Masturbation? Yes! Now understand clearly that I am not stating that you are gay if you engage in masturbation. However, I am stating that it can open the door to homosexual attraction. This is not a difficult principle to wrap your thoughts around when you think about it practically. When you masturbate, you are achieving sexual pleasure through interacting with your own sex organs. Typically you are either looking at your sex organs while you masturbate or visualizing them.

Essentially you are being sexually aroused by touching, looking at and interacting with your own male or female anatomy. This creates an attraction to that particular anatomy. If you are a female, you are getting aroused by your own female sex organs. The transition to visualizing another female's sex organs is then easy and arousal is inevitable. Subconsciously, you will relate seeing another female, to the memory of the enjoyable experience you had touching the female body. The fact that the body you touched was your own cannot be differentiated by your hormones. Your body's chemistry learns to respond to certain triggers. Masturbation will teach your body to be triggered by and respond to the same sex. This is also true to the same degree for a male.

The bottom line is that homosexuality is a choice, **your choice**. You can be assured that The Creator did not make you gay. Remember that homosexuality begins with a feeling of attraction. Everyone has the freedom to choose how they feel. Anger, joy, peace, hatred, bigotry, love, excitement, sadness, attraction – these are all emotions over which you have complete control. You are going to have to determine when these feelings of attraction began and discover what triggered them. Then make a decision about how you really want to feel. Yahweh can change your desires, if you really want Him to.

The Personality Profile

It is almost hard for me to write this section because most homosexuals have such great inner strength. It is then difficult for me to take your positive characteristics and attribute them to this spirit of homosexuality. Just know that the fact that you are under the influence of this spirit does not at all diminish the value of your positive qualities. It is up to you to reclaim the good in you, and use it for good.

Under the influence of this spirit you are stubborn and defiant, but these two qualities have made you a survivor. On the other hand, they also make you very hard to minister to. In your past, with much negativity, others tried to define who you were and who you would become. One day you said *"I'm not going to take it anymore!"* You began to search out for yourself who you really are. Homosexuality is what you settled upon, and now you are determined to not let anyone dissuade you.

Most others would have crumbled under the pressure of the hardships that you have endured, but through homosexuality you found a way to survive. You are not going to let anyone take that from you. For this reason, you are a very strong person but also extremely argumentative. You will boldly stand against friends, family members and all of society for what you believe in; which is *"your right to be you"*. You have finally found your niche in life, and you are staying in it! Like has been said, you are stubborn and defiant, but for you it is all about survival and maintaining your sanity.

Circumstances made you feel as if this is the only way. You have and will continue to sacrifice greatly, in order to secure your lifestyle. For instance, you know that you can never produce a baby with your gay partner; in most places you will never be considered legally married, and you will have to face day in and day out the taunts, discrimination and abuse of a society that cast its eyes down on homosexuals. Nonetheless, it is all worth it to you in return for the acceptance that you have been longing for. Even before you were gay, you have always been considered an outcast, a freak or a reject. Now you have found a way to be accepted as such amongst your own kind. It is not acceptance by everyone, but it is enough for you.

Homosexuals are a group of people that have experienced a lot of rejection. A great number of homosexuals were victims of rape, molestation or some other form of abuse in their lifetime. You are probably no exception. You feel as if having a relationship with someone of the same sex will enable you to finally be understood. You are seeking someone who can relate to you and your pain. The spirit of homosexuality thrives on low self-esteem, rejection, low self-worth and identity crisis. You harbor all of these characteristics. You are currently, or were at some point in the past, convinced that you are good-for-nothing and worthless. Thus it is *(or was)* easy for you to desire to be someone or something else. It is these negative emotions that are empowering this spirit of homosexuality in your life.

Maybe you are one of the ones that believes you were born gay. If so, perhaps homosexuality is a generational demon that was passed down to you. It could also just be indicative of the fact that feelings of rejection and worthlessness were imparted to you at such a young age that you cannot ever remember a time that you felt good about yourself or had confidence. It might also be the case that sexual abuse occurred in your life at a young age that you may or may not remember. Maybe you are one of the ones that says it's a lifestyle choice; your preference. If this is your stance, you did at one time believe in yourself. You had an understanding of who you were once upon a time and wanted to try and work at being a successful *you*. However, somewhere down the road your hopes were thwarted.

Defiance and boldness is what the public sees – a happy, successful person that can accomplish anything a heterosexual person can. But, on the inside there is turmoil. That little child within you is still crying out for real acceptance as a "normal" person. That person inside of you that was verbally, emotionally, physically and/or sexually abused is still hurt, angry and confused. You are still unsure of who you are, no matter how much you say that you have got it all together.

You will play the role as long as you have to, but if there were really a way out, you would take it. Somewhere inside of you, you wonder what it would be like to be "straight". You probably still remember childhood ambitions to have a normal spouse and live a traditional American family life. You suppress these feelings, but they do exist within you. Often times nobody knows, but feelings of depression and suicide hit you so strongly. You just want to give up the facade and take off the mask, but you still do not know exactly **who** lives underneath it all. Homosexuals have the highest suicide rate among any other group of Americans. The average life expectancy for a homosexual is said to be less than 50 years of age. You do not "live", you merely "exist". The spirit that has you bound is hoping that in the end, you will give up and die never understanding how awesome you truly are.

Perhaps you are reading this and you have not made that bold proclamation of homosexuality. Maybe no one ever empowered you with the truth that homosexuality is merely a feeling and that your emotions are always within your control. From reading the above profile, you may be more certain than ever that you are highly "at-risk" for giving in to living a homosexual lifestyle. The profile may fit you to a tee; only you have not yet taken that final step of getting into a relationship. Well now you know that you do not have to give in to homosexuality. You have a choice. If it is a lifestyle that you desire, and you have no Christian conviction about living that life, then you have no reason to fight. But if you know deep down in your heart that this is not the life that you want to live; that this is not the life that Yeshua wants you to live – reclaim the good in you, and use it to pursue your true purpose!

The Churchgoer Profile

Many practicing homosexuals are atheist due to their anger toward God for the abuse they have suffered in their lifetime. Yet there are plenty that claim belief in God as well. If you are a churchgoer that is bound by the spirit of homosexuality, you are unproductive. The spirit of homosexuality comes strongly against your ability to produce in the spirit. If two people of the same sex lay together, the creative power of intimacy is made null and void. Orgasm may still cause the body to go through the process that enables conception, but there is no sperm and egg to come together. It is the same in the spirit; not being able to reproduce the Kingdom of Yahweh is what the spirit of homosexuality is all about.

The spirit of homosexuality is not only seeking to destroy your ability to conceive and give birth to Yah's Kingdom but also to distort your understanding of who you are in Christ. Under the influence of this spirit, you do not perceive or accept your true identity. You are blind to the greatness and glory with which The Father created you. Because you are unable to see any greatness or worth in who you truly are, you try to be something that you are not. What this ultimately means is that you are not fulfilling your purpose in the Kingdom. The Body of Christ is suffering, due to the vacancy that you should be filling.

This is what ultimately causes you to be unproductive. You cannot reproduce something that you truly are not. A horse can be made to look like a donkey, but it still has the DNA of a horse and therefore can never give birth to a donkey! **You cannot reproduce what you are only pretending to be. Instead of fulfilling your role in the church, you are poorly emulating someone else's.** Unfortunately you do not believe in your true self or your ability to produce anything of worth. This identity crisis caused by the spirit of homosexuality produces double-mindedness and hypocrisy.

Because you do not really know who you are in Christ, you are forever trying on a new personality and way of living. There is often times an over-exaggerated effort to prove that you are "happy" and "confident". This means that you are often times showy and loud in church. You want to prove that you have it all together and great effort is put into proving this. You will probably be involved in a lot of activities in the church, as part of your effort to prove yourself. You only hope that your air of togetherness and confidence will gain you acceptance and often times it does. The spirit that operates within you has blinded you to the truth that the God Who Created You is the only one that will ever truly know and understand who you are.

Nonetheless, you are probably one of the most loved people in the church, at times. Your charisma and false-confidence attracts those seeking to be entertained. That is why homosexuals are often given positions of leadership in church. Leaders in churches that lack discernment and/or the willingness to stand for Holy integrity will elevate you simply because you are well-liked by others. You may even be a preacher that has a large ministry. However, you do not produce spiritually and do not bear the fruits of the Holy Spirit. You are a carnally-minded and shallow-spirited churchgoer that will tolerate just about anything in your ministry.

Just as is the case with practicing, natural homosexuals, those under the spiritual influence of homosexuality harbor those feelings of rejection and uncertainty deep within. The truth of the matter is; you are depressed and on the brink of losing it all at any moment. Your experience in the church is a masquerade of something that you only wish you were. You are a know-it-all, you look deep, you sing loud, you fall out in worship... But, it is all faked. Your experiences are superficial and empty of heart and soul.

The Worship Portrait

The spirit of homosexuality effects men and women differently in terms of their intimate relationship with The LORD. To understand this, you need only to think about it practically for a moment. Consider the **stereotypical** roles of males and females when it comes to sex in a relationship. Men are typically more sexually aggressive but lack intimacy. They prefer quantity over quality. Females, on the other hand, are often times less aggressive in their sexuality. They enjoy sex only under certain circumstances; aiming for a much more fulfilling and intimate connection when having sex.

With homosexuality there is a role reversal of gender-related activities and styles. For instance, gay women may play traditionally male aggressive sports and wear men's clothing. A gay man may act effeminately, talk with female antics, enjoy doing hair and make-up and dress in drag. I again disclaim any intentional political incorrectness if I am propagating a negative gay stereotype by making these comparisons. I am only doing so to paint a spiritually symbolic picture for understanding's sake. This is because the reverse gender characteristics in the natural, effects your overall perception of yourself and how you relate to others, Yahweh included.

This means that if you are a female under the influence of this spirit, your worship with Yah will have much less meaning and intimacy. Women typically find it easier to achieve intimate worship with The LORD. With the Body of Christ being referred to as a "bride" and often relegated to a female personification, it is easier for a woman to see herself in an intimate relationship with Him. But under the influence of this spirit, you will have a more male-like view of intimacy. As a male on the other hand, you may enjoy an ease in pursuing intimacy with The Father. The typical fear of appearing effeminate in the expression of worship will not affect you, if you are a male under the influence of the spirit of homosexuality.

The truth of the matter is though that gender is irrelevant when it comes to your intimate relationship with The Creator. The Bible teaches us that there is neither male nor female for those that are in Christ *(Gal 3:28)*. I believe that the main purpose for The Church being given a female personification is to help us understand how much Yahweh desires our fellowship in His presence. In 1 Corinthians 11:8-9 it reads, *"⁸For man did not come from woman, but woman from man; ⁹neither was man created for woman, but woman for man."*

This is reminding us that at creation, Elohim said that it was not good for the man to be alone *(Gen 2:18)*, and He made the perfect companion for the man. When the man saw his companion he was pleased. How Adam saw Eve is how The Creator sees you. He made you just for Himself. He made you as His perfect companion and after He created you, He was pleased with what He had made and declared that you are good!

You do not need to try and reassign your gender in order to fit into a false perception of what you think will make you happy. Because remember that ultimately, this spirit wants to cause barrenness in your life. Both sperm and egg are required to come together, in order to conceive and reproduce. A man can pretend to be a woman and even have gender reassignment surgery. But, he will always genetically be a man and will never be able to conceive a baby with another man. And, like wise for the woman who pretends to be a man. You see, if you pretend to be something other than what Yah made you, you cannot give birth to all of the great things He has planned for your life. If your seed is never reproduced, your name will be cut off from existence – it will be omitted from the Lambs Book of Life.

One of the greatest tragedies resulting from the influence of this spirit is how people are abandoning their true assignments to fulfill a purpose that is not theirs. I believe that this is one of the greatest factors in the high divorce rate we have in America today. Looking beyond the physical act and just considering the non-sexual influences of this spirit; look at what has happened in homes. So many women have become masculine in their mannerisms and how they run the home, and likewise the men have become effeminate. The spirit of homosexuality strips a man of his priestly authority and robs him of his ability to cover his home. It then re-deposits that authority in the woman. She is thus stripped of her soft beauty and supernatural ability to nurture and heal with just a look or touch.

A man cannot adequately fulfill a woman's assignment and a woman cannot adequately fulfill a man's. But this is nothing new; we see a clear picture of this in scripture in the relationship between King Ahab and his wife Jezebel *(1 Kings 21:25)*. Their relationship could be used as a model of what the spirit of homosexuality looks like when operating in a heterosexual relationship. What we cannot miss is how it ultimately affected their intimacy with The LORD though. Ahab was misdirected, wimpy and confused – chasing after prophets that would tell him what he wanted to hear because he had no connection with Yah. Jezebel on the other hand was an idol worshiper to the core of her heart. This spirit wants to destroy your understanding of who you are and how to relate to Yah, thereby killing your assignment and purpose!

Intersexuality

I would be remiss to not address the issue of intersexuality in this chapter! 'Intersex' is a term that is used to describe a person that has congenital defects affecting the sex and reproductive organs. Often this results in varying degrees of ambiguous genitalia. In these cases, the person cannot be definitively categorized as male or female, according to our established definitions of the sexes. In some of these cases, chromosomally the person is clearly an XX (female) or an XY (male). Other times, it cannot be clearly determined if the person is genetically male or female. Intersexuality is not to be confused with homosexuality *(feelings of same-sex attraction)* or being transgender *(feelings of being psychologically opposite of the sex of the body you were born in)*. Intersexuality is a legitimate medical condition or birth defect that is just as real and challenging as down syndrome, cerebral palsy or any other congenital defect.

I was blown away when I first learned about this. It was brought to my attention through the prayer requests of people who had encountered my ministry resources. I remember the distress of this one sweet Christian lady whose "grand-daughter" (as they chose to raise the child as a girl) was a medical hermaphrodite. The child had both male and female sex organs and both XX and XY chromosomes. That was not nearly as challenging to me though as the "Christian couple" that I met with this issue. Upon first seeing them, they appeared to be a lesbian couple. After learning of my book, they began to open up to me about their situation. The "male" person in the couple believed that he was intersex and that his mother had erroneously assigned him female gender at birth.

I remember trying to keep as straight a face as I could. The last thing I wanted was for judgment to come across in my tone or expression. They were so sincere, and it was obvious that they truly loved each other. I had no prior experience with this kind of thing, so I was in no position to advise them to one end or the other. Yet it just was not setting well with me, what they were saying. Something just did not feel right. He had no proof that he was intersex, and she was formerly a practicing lesbian. To make matters worse, they chose to live together as a married couple. They stated that they were without choice because they could not marry, due to him being documented as a female on his birth certificate.

Now, what am I to say about a situation like this? This was many years ago, and since that time I have encountered others that are confirmed intersexuals. Sometimes these anomalies are apparent at birth. In other cases, the intersex condition does not become apparent until puberty or even later in life, *if at all*. In this couple's case, he said he always felt male. He never accepted his female gender assignment. He said that he never felt gay – like a woman that was attracted to other women. He stated that instead, he had always felt like a straight man that was attracted to women but trapped in a female's body.

And this is what it is often like for intersex people that go through life trying to conform to a gender assignment given them at birth that is not consistent with what their physiology settles into, as they grow and one gender becomes the more dominate. A great deal of mercy is necessary in these cases. We take special care, to compensate with kindness, those that have physical disabilities, and this should be treated no differently.

Yeshua said in Matthew 19:11-12, *"[11]But He said to them, Not all men can accept this saying, but it is for those to whom [the capacity to receive] it has been given. [12]For there are eunuchs who have been born incapable of marriage; and there are eunuchs who have been made so by men; and there are eunuchs who have made themselves incapable of marriage for the sake of the kingdom of heaven. Let him who is able to accept this accept it."* In this text, Yeshua was referring to people that had sexual abnormalities that prevented them from entering into a marriage covenant. In the Bible, proper consummation was required in order for any marriage to be valid. Therefore, if a person was unable to engage in intercourse by its natural design (full penetration of the penis into the vagina), that person was rendered a eunuch and unfit to marry. Some were eunuchs from birth; some through physical trauma or violence; some by choice.

Yeshua made reference to this with great compassion, stating first and foremost that very few people would be able to accept a status as a eunuch. Within the full context of the passage, Yeshua was teaching on Yahweh's perfect design for marriage and sexuality. I believe that the point Yeshua was making is that any sexual union, outside of The Father's perfect design, is stripped of the honor and glory with which The Creator crowned Holy matrimony. So then if a marriage or sexual union cannot bring glory to The Father, it becomes void of its spiritual purpose – an empty, flesh-gratifying act of compromise. Remember that marriage, in its entire splendor, is a replica of our intimate relationship with The Creator. At the end of the day, sex is the only thing that sets marriage apart from all other relationships. Therefore, the title of **marriage** becomes obsolete if a person can **never** have **full intercourse** with their *"supposed"* spouse. Yeshua was basically saying here, *"If you cannot have sex according to The Father's design for it, then you should not have it at all"*.

So after all of this time, I finally realize what it was that bothered me so much about the couple's union. Were they in sin? That is not even the greater issue to me. They were married in their hearts and stated that, if legally allowed to, they would have gone through the steps to make it official, and I truly believe that they would have. That being the case, as a married couple, they had the right to live together and engage in sexual activity. So I won't be quick to condemn the relationship as sinful. What I saw that bothered me was a spirit of compromise. I saw two people with powerful calls on their lives that were unwilling to accept the lot that The LORD had given them.

First of all, this young man is undeniably a eunuch. He is unable to perform the sexual duties of a man, according to Yah's design for it. Secondly, the scripture says that all things should be done decently and in order. It may be all well and good for people that don't claim Christianity to shack up so long that they finally get the "common law marriage" status. But not so for The LORD's people! Remember that this was discussed at the end of chapter seven, when exploring fornication.

The LORD declared to Moses in Exodus 4:11, *"¹¹The LORD said to him, "Who gave human beings their mouths? Who makes them deaf or mute? Who gives them sight or makes them blind? Is it not I, the LORD?"* In other words, sometimes Yah allows us to be born with physical limitations, for the purposes of His glory. If our physical limitations prevent us from doing something then it is not hard to figure that there is something else that we should be doing. A blind person cannot drive a car. A mute person cannot sing a song. A eunuch cannot have sex according to The LORD's design.

If a person has no legs and therefore has difficulty getting a job, does it make it okay for him to steal? Of course not! No disability or physical limitation should be used as a free pass to live a life of compromise and sinfulness. Now I do believe that love covers a multitude of sin *(1 Pet 4:8)*. The Father's love for this couple, their love for Him and their love for each other will keep them in Yeshua's fold. But the situation that they are living in is stripping them of His glory.

They both have powerful calls on their lives, but the man's intersex condition is preventing them from doing things decently and in order. If Yahweh wills for the two of them to be married, does He not have the power to get them the paperwork they need, in order to do it honorably? And if that paperwork is delayed, does it mean that they should live in fornication in the meantime? Jacob waited for Rachel for seven years; seven years! This couple chose the low road. They chose the way of compromise, and it hurt to see the call on their lives suffer.

If you are a single, intersex Christian reading this, my insight for you is to do all of the necessary practical things. First and foremost, get officially diagnosed by a medical doctor, if you have not already. Learn the extent of your condition and what can be done, if anything, to correct it. If it is medically possible to determine a sex, submit to the sex that The Creator genetically assigned to you, even if you have to accept a gender change. *(For example, if you were raised male, but tests reveal that you are clearly XX, and you have felt female during your lifetime).* If you can't handle this, then you have to surrender to a life of celibacy because to be in a relationship with the same sex would be homosexuality for you. Yet to be in a relationship with the opposite sex would be homosexuality to your partner because they perceive you as the same sex as they are! Confusing I know, but you understand exactly what I mean. *(If you are already married in this situation, then stay as you are. I believe The LORD will honor you and your marriage, if you entered into it unaware of your condition.)*

Now if it is medically impossible to definitively determine your gender, pray to The Father for guidance. Then choose a gender, have peace about it, and stick to it. If you can stay single, that is what Yeshua advises you to do. However, if you cannot accept a life of singlehood, you have to do all things in decency and order. Make sure your legal identification reflects the gender that you choose to live as, even if you have to go so far as to have your birth certificate amended. When you do enter into a relationship, be honest with your mate. You have to give your mate the option to choose whether or not they can accept your condition. Lastly, do not live a life of fornication. Get legally married and live honorably before The LORD.

For parents that are facing this situation with their children, my insight about doing the practical things is the same. Get as much medical information as you can. If it can be determined genetically what sex the child is, regardless of how the child looks, raise the child with the gender assignment that is consistent with their genetic make-up physically *(accept in the case of complete AIS – this is more complex).* The LORD has the ability to cause the child's physical body to line up with their hormonal chemistry. If it cannot be determined, pray about it, make a choice and live in peace. But do not; DO NOT lie to your child!!! They need to be raised with a full awareness of their disability. They need to learn how to cope early and not have a traumatic upset in their teen or adult life.

Do not; DO NOT have reconstructive, cosmetic surgery performed on your child – *unless surgery is necessary for health reasons.* Your child is likely a eunuch and will be used in a special way by The LORD. Having "pretty", normal-looking genitals is of little concern. Besides, that is a decision that the child should make when they are old enough to fully understand sexuality, gender and concepts of relationships and marriage. Waiting also gives them a chance to go through puberty, after which time everyone can be sure of which gender will dominate. It furthermore gives time for the advancement of medical technology. The longer you wait, the more advanced and effective the techniques and equipment available will be for such surgery. This is of course, if your child even wants surgery, which can permanently mutilate and render useless, otherwise good-feeling genitalia that is at the very least, able to experience pleasure. A life of singleness is a hard choice; no one should make that choice for a person born with these challenges. Put the case before The LORD. Raise a confident, loving, sanctified human being. And you never know, Yah may even straighten everything out as the child grows. But if not, you need to train them up in Righteousness and then let them make a decision about their own future.

I know this is an extremely difficult trial for anyone facing it. I pronounce no judgment on anyone in this situation. This is only basic wisdom that I have shared, but truly no one knows what you go through. What I do know is that there is a way to live righteously and abundantly in the midst of all challenges. If we truly love Yeshua and want to be His disciples, we will deny ourselves, take up our crosses and follow after Him *(Mat 16:24)*. We will find strength to live a life that is pleasing to Him, when pleasing Him is what we're really after. And remember always that to whom much is given, much is required. For those that have a high-calling on their lives, great sacrifices will have to be made. But such sacrifices are always worth it – look at Apostle Paul, the greatest of all time, and he was a eunuch by choice!

Chapter 12

Prostitution

"A prostitute is a dangerous trap; a promiscuous woman is as dangerous as falling into a narrow well." (Prov 23:27)

Some Biblical References

Gen 38:24; Lev 19:29, 20:5-6, 21:7, 21:14, Deut 22:21; 23:17-18, 1 Kings 15:12; Prov 23:27; Isa 23:17; Jer 3:2, 3:8, 13:27, Eze 16:16-41, 23:3-49, 43:7, 43:9, Hosea (ALL); Micah 1:7; Nahum 3:4; Rev 17:2

The Definition

The act of offering oneself as a sexual partner in return for monetary compensation or some other favor or gift.

The Assignment

A prostitute uses his or her natural gifts, talents and beauty to bring pleasure to those that would only abuse them. Instead of using their strengths to pursue their purposes, they waste the essence of who they are on uselessness – trading the priceless for the worthless! **The spirit of prostitution is assigned to affect your ability to see your worth in Christ or simply as a human being. It causes you to sell yourself short and miss the higher calling of Yahweh God on your life. You also miss out on the beauty of being in an authentic relationship with a God who truly loves you; not for your value, but instead for your worth.**

The Practical Understanding

When we think of prostitution, we usually envision a Vegas back street, with scantily dressed women walking up and down, wearing wigs, popping gum and running to any car that stops nearby saying, *"Hey baby! Can I show you a good time?"* That is definitely a true depiction of prostitution, but it is not a complete one. As a matter of fact, it is actually the least common of prostitution's manifestations. The spirit of prostitution also has you bound if you get into a relationship with a person just for material or financial gain or the status of the person. Even if you marry the person, the spirit of prostitution is still in your life because of your motive for marrying him or her. This manifestation of prostitution is very prevalent in the worlds of professional sports, politics and entertainment.

Being a stripper is also a form of prostitution. As a stripper, in exchange for money, you are performing sexually explicit moves for others to view. Those that are watching, watch intently for the purpose of being sexually stimulated and pay money to do so. Remember, sexual perversion is about a lot more than penetration. Just the intent to sexually stimulate makes you guilty before The LORD. Furthermore, if you consider yourself a model or actor/actress because you pose nude or perform pornography for money, please do not be deceived. The spirit of prostitution also brings on these acts. The spirit of prostitution also binds any male who behaves in any of the aforementioned ways.

A prostitute, by all of the above descriptions, fails to see his or her true worth. Why would you sell off something as priceless as your sexual intimacy? Sex is the most intimate act that you can involve yourself in and is the act that creates the greatest vulnerability. Why would you marry someone just for the money or status? Do you lack the confidence to earn your own money? Do you fail to believe that you can achieve greatness apart from someone else?

Unfortunately, many people are forced into prostitution through human trafficking. Human trafficking is reported to be a 32 billion dollar a year industry globally, with an estimated 12.3 million victims world-wide. The average age for entrance into the industry is 12 years old, and 80% of the victims are female. This is a very serious situation that we, as the Body of Christ, should not turn a blind eye to. It affects the church, just as much as it affects people outside of the church.

I had the privilege of having a series of in-depth sessions with a former victim of human trafficking. She was inducted into the industry at 15 years of age; taken away from her home and remained a victim for 20 years. What I was shocked to find out is that 17 out of those 20 years, she was an active member of several churches! They knew of her occupation and gladly received the large tithes and offerings donated by her and her pimp. No one tried to help her get out of the industry. What was even more disturbing was to learn that as her profession became known in the church world, she was employed to supply "working-girls" for church leaders after they finished preaching!

This is a true story, not Hollywood hype. What is really sad is that many young girls are being manipulated into the industry. We as a community need to keep a watchful eye on our children. Some warning signs that a child may be a victim of human trafficking are:

- Your own intuition; listen to your inner voice
- Reports from the child's friends and peers
- The child mentions prostitution in conversation
- Unexplained money, gifts or clothes
- An expensive drug habit
- Absence from home, friends and school
- Uncharacteristic changes in dress, schedule or associates
- Relationships with older men and women
- Unwillingness to answer everyday questions
- A suspicious job
- Frequent brushes with the law
- Prostitution in their neighborhood

If you or someone you know is a victim of human trafficking, please contact me. I can put you in touch with a dear friend of mine who is a human trafficking activist and former victim. She can help you start the journey of recovery.

The Personality Profile

Note: Buyers of prostitution do not fit this profile. If you are a person who pays for sex, you are going to fall somewhere in between the profile of a rapist and that for sexual fantasy. Please take note of this.

To onlookers, prostitution seems like an easy lifestyle to get out of, but you feel hopelessly trapped in a life full of use and abuse. Sometimes that entrapment may be literal, if you are a human sex slave. But most often times, it is a psychological entrapment. The entrapment comes not because of an inability to just walk away from the lifestyle and do something else, but comes instead from the inability for you to recognize worth in yourself. More than likely, you believe that there just is no way out, and you probably do not seek a way out.

As a prostitute, you have no real sense of self-respect or self-worth and do not at all value your life. That explains why you are willing time and time again to put your life in danger – by being alone with deranged people that you do not know; by living a dangerous lifestyle; by risking the contraction of AIDS or some other disease; etcetera. The average age of death for a prostitute is 34, and a prostitute is 51 times more likely to be a victim of a violent homicide when compared to other Americans.

Believe it or not, prostitution is also addictive. It is a high in its own right and provides a false sense of being in control. The temporary escape that it provides from your shattered self-image, and allowing you to feel valuable since someone is willing to pay money to spend time with you, is an addictive entrapment. You are in control *(so it seems)* when you are able to bargain what your sexuality is worth and demand your payment.

Prostitution can enter into a person's life through wounds of abuse whether verbal, physical, sexual or just emotional. The sense of entrapment that you feel now, bound by a life of prostitution, is the same sense of entrapment that you felt at the time of your life when you were being abused. It is unfortunate that you were deceived into a life of prostitution by this spirit because the lifestyle that you are living increases the likelihood that you will now be abused again and again and again. The average prostitute is raped eight to ten times per year. Abuse causes you to feel like you are defective, and anything defective lacks value. The initial abuses that you suffered, before prostitution entered your life, began the process of diminishing your worth in your own eyes. The more abuse you suffer, the less and less worth you will see in yourself.

Under the influence of this spirit, you are usually a hypocrite, because you always have to present yourself a certain way in order to look appealing to the potential buyer. Yet, you seldom match internally what you portray externally. You have learned to live a life of fantasy and falsehood, a life of pretense, not knowing who you truly are. You become whatever will earn you a buck or a gift for that moment. To others you may seem really tough and hard, but that is just more pretense. You have to appear this way because you live a competitive and dangerous lifestyle. Although you appear tough outwardly, inwardly you are more fragile than an empty eggshell. It is not unlikely that you are a victim of drug or alcohol addiction because often times *a high* is needed to help you keep up the guise and escape your reality.

What is your reality? Your reality is a life that is full of torment. You do not desire to live the lifestyle that you are living. You would give up the financial gain that it provides for you in an instant, if you could discover any worth in yourself other than your sexuality. Sometimes you convince yourself that you are really providing an important public service that helps people. Other times you say that prostitution is your way to make a living in a tough world. But as was already stated, your life is all about pretense. The longer you indulge in this lifestyle, the less you are able to differentiate between what is real and what is pretense. Whereas many of the other acts of sexual perversion make a person feel that they are in control, prostitution makes you feel helplessly out of control (*outside of the temporary upper-hand that you sometimes have when engaged in the negotiation of a sale*).

You may be a disloyal person to friends or family because you find it hard to form "authentic", meaningful bonds. You are unappreciative and selfish because you only perform for what you will gain and then you move on. This prevents you from ever really connecting emotionally. Even with those that you are not performing acts of prostitution with, you have a hard time bonding and connecting. All of your relationships are superficial, not surpassing the physical appearance you hide behind. You are so used to spending only a few fantasy filled moments with individuals that you are always expecting every relationship to end abruptly.

Even if you have children, you cannot escape the feeling that "it will all be over soon". No matter what occurs in your life, whether you enjoy it or despise it, you are still bound by the sense that it will all be over with soon. This sense that "all is temporary" takes away the enjoyment of the good times in life but helps you endure the rough times in life. Ultimately though, it leaves you without any stability whatsoever and devoid of any sense of reality.

Our bodies are the only (tangible) things on this earth that truly belong to us as human beings. From birth until death, no matter what else we may gain or lose in life, our bodies should always be our very own. That makes your body a priceless treasure. Yet, you sell your own body and therefore you have given up the only thing of true worth that you ever really owned. It leaves you with nothing, and you are constantly down on yourself and beating yourself up because of this. It makes you almost insane to think about it and that is why you try not to.

You are probably a very talented person. You may have some unique ability to sing or draw or lead – some special quality that stands out. You probably like helping people solve their problems as well. People that like to help others are more inclined to get involved in prostitution because this is an act that requires you to give of yourself over and over again. These are good characteristics and qualities about you. Unfortunately, you are taking what Yah has given you and wasting it on those who will never appreciate it. Instead of using your gifts and talents in a meaningful way that will help you fulfill your purpose in life, you waste all that you are for money that is not even worth the paper that it is printed on.

I iterate again, your life is one that is full of pretense, lacks stability and is totally out of control. All you want is your worth back, but how can that happen? Take heart because you too can be victoriously free! Your body was never really yours anyway. It was bought with the Blood of Yeshua and belongs to Him *(1 Cor 6:20, 7:23)*. He has redeemed you and will also restore all to you, if you will just turn to Him wholeheartedly!

The Churchgoer Profile

Practicing prostitutes are not likely to participate in any regular religious beliefs. You just do not see the point in *wasting God's time* on someone of no worth like yourself. Besides, in your mind, if there even is such a deity, he would only be temporary pretense to you. If you are a churchgoer that is operating under the influence of the demon of prostitution, in your spiritual life, you have very little stability in your walk with The LORD. One month you want to be a praise dancer, the next a minister, the next a missionary and the next a Sunday school teacher.

Just like natural prostitutes, as a spiritual prostitute you fail to see your true worth in Christ. For this reason, you spill your gifts and talents any and everywhere, allowing people to pimp you spiritually. In other words, you will allow people to benefit at your expense, without getting your true reward in return. You probably have been abused in life and in ministry. You will settle for less out of people, life and even God when you are worth so much more. You usually find it hard to say no to anything that has even miniscule value. You will involve yourself in many religious activities that are not conducive to your growth in the anointing.

Although you are most often times the type of person that will do anything for anyone, you are always looking for something in return. You feel that an injustice has been done you, if you do not get your payoff. As nice as you are most of the time, people will see the ugly come out of you in the event you do not get the **small** payoff you were expecting. I say small because you are always selling yourself short. The greatest rewards can often times not be measured, but surely you measure every payoff.

You would like to have a relationship with The LORD, but you are unable to receive or return His unconditional love. You believe in your heart that it is not real and will not last. Yeshua is just a momentary pleasure for you, just like everything else in life. You perceive Him to be a fake and a phony, a user just like everyone else. You will not even give Him a chance because you are afraid. This feeling is what will keep many naturally practicing prostitutes from even going to church, but if you are a literal prostitute that goes to church, you still retain these feelings toward The Father.

You are secretive, deceptive and hypocritical and unfortunately cannot be trusted. Just like a prostitute in the natural lives a life of pretense, so do churchgoers that are operating under the spiritual influence. The longer you operate under the spirit of prostitution, the more detached you will become from the Holy Spirit's truth. It becomes easier and easier to *pretend* that you are an evangelist, a pastor or a prophet. It is easy for you to *pretend* that you live a consecrated, Holy life that is pleasing to The LORD. However, the truth of the matter is that you probably live a wretched life that is full of the most treacherous sins, and you know it too. This is not a conflict with your character though. Due to your extremely superficial relationship with God, there is no loyalty to Him or His ways anyhow. Nonetheless, you have to keep up the front. You must always look appealing and continue to advertise what you are selling.

You are at risk of becoming part of non-Christian religions and cults that claim belief in God, but have little to no Holiness standard. This is because this would be a more comfortable setting for you. You are putting your spiritual life in danger, but since you see little to no worth in yourself; it really does not matter to you. You feel as if you might as well get out of religion, whatever you can. It is so sad that you are blind to the great worth that you truly possess inside.

The Worship Portrait

The following passage of scripture, taken from the New Living Translation of the Bible, so perfectly describes how the spirit of prostitution impacts your intimacy with Yahweh. All that I can say to help prepare you for what you are about to read is that failing to realize your true worth in Christ causes you to believe that The Father does not and could not ever truly love you; that He could never have any need of you. This is what is causing you to fail in your relationship with Him.

Ezekiel 16:4-30, NLT

"⁴On the day you were born, no one cared about you. Your umbilical cord was not cut, and you were never washed, rubbed with salt, and wrapped in cloth. ⁵No one had the slightest interest in you; no one pitied you or cared for you. On the day you were born, you were unwanted, dumped in a field and left to die. ⁶But I came by and saw you there, helplessly kicking about in your own blood. As you lay there, I said, 'Live!' ⁷And I helped you to thrive like a plant in the field. You grew up and became a beautiful jewel. Your breasts became full, and your body hair grew, but you were still naked. ⁸And when I passed by again, I saw that you were old enough for love. So I wrapped my cloak around you to cover your nakedness and declared my marriage vows. I made a covenant with you, says the Sovereign Lord, and you became mine. ⁹"Then I bathed you and washed off your blood, and I rubbed fragrant oils into your skin. ¹⁰I gave you expensive clothing of fine linen and silk, beautifully embroidered, and sandals made of fine goatskin leather. ¹¹I gave you lovely jewelry, bracelets, beautiful necklaces, ¹²a ring for your nose, earrings for your ears, and a lovely crown for your head. ¹³And so you were adorned with gold and silver. Your clothes were made of fine linen and were beautifully embroidered. You ate the finest foods—choice flour, honey, and olive oil—and became more beautiful than ever. You looked like a queen, and so you were! ¹⁴Your fame soon spread throughout the world because of your beauty. I dressed you in my splendor and perfected your beauty, says the Sovereign Lord. ¹⁵"But

you thought your fame and beauty were your own. So you gave yourself as a prostitute to every man who came along. Your beauty was theirs for the asking. [16]You used the lovely things I gave you to make shrines for idols, where you played the prostitute. Unbelievable! How could such a thing ever happen? [17]You took the very jewels and gold and silver ornaments I had given you and made statues of men and worshiped them. This is adultery against me! [18]You used the beautifully embroidered clothes I gave you to dress your idols. Then you used my special oil and my incense to worship them. [19]Imagine it! You set before them as a sacrifice the choice flour, olive oil, and honey I had given you, says the Sovereign Lord. [20]"Then you took your sons and daughters—the children you had borne to me—and sacrificed them to your gods. Was your prostitution not enough? [21]Must you also slaughter my children by sacrificing them to idols? [22]In all your years of adultery and detestable sin, you have not once remembered the days long ago when you lay naked in a field, kicking about in your own blood. [23]"What sorrow awaits you, says the Sovereign Lord. In addition to all your other wickedness, [24]you built a pagan shrine and put altars to idols in every town square. [25]On every street corner you defiled your beauty, offering your body to every passerby in an endless stream of prostitution. [26]Then you added lustful Egypt to your lovers, provoking my anger with your increasing promiscuity. [27]That is why I struck you with my fist and reduced your boundaries. I handed you over to your enemies, the Philistines, and even they were shocked by your lewd conduct. [28]You have prostituted yourself with the Assyrians, too. It seems you can never find enough new lovers! And after your prostitution there, you still were not satisfied. [29]You added to your lovers by embracing Babylonia, the land of merchants, but you still weren't satisfied. [30]**"What a sick heart you have, says the Sovereign Lord, to do such things as these, acting like a shameless prostitute."**

Selah...

Insights from Dr. Intimacy

The Prostitute and Her Redeemer:
A True Love Story

There was once a young prostitute that brought great wealth to her master. She was his most profitable working-girl. He had taken her from her parents when she was only 10 years old. By the time she was 18, she was both young and experienced and very beautiful; indeed a rare combination of qualities in the world of human-trafficking. One day her pimp sent her on a job. He gave her a sealed envelope and told her to put it away until she was with her caller and that the caller would tell her when to open it. She took the envelope and put it with her belongings and then went on her way to the location where she was to meet her caller.

When she got to the location, she felt a little strange. It was not like the other places she had been. It had a warm feeling, almost like being home. She could smell delicious, hot food cooking. She was a bit taken aback by it and had to pull herself together for her "performance". She rang the doorbell, and when the gentlemen opened the door, he seemed very familiar to her. She felt like she knew him but could not remember from where. He gave her the same warm feeling that she had gotten when she walked up to the house.

Again having to force herself to stay focused on her job, she began her routine to get the gentleman aroused. But he quickly stopped her, informing her that he desired for her to join him for dinner. She was delighted because the food smelled so good. Before he allowed her to the table though, he asked her to go to a room that he had prepared for her and change into one of the outfits in the room. He instructed her to bathe before changing.

When she walked into the room, it was beautifully decorated with all of her favorite things. She even saw replicas of some of her favorite childhood toys. Her eyes got a little watery as she went into a luxuriously white bathroom, where a bath was already full of hot water, scented oils and bubbles. She wondered if the man had some kind of fantasy that he wanted to fulfill; a fantasy of child porn or something. She thought he might bust in the door as she bathed, so she kept the door unlocked, expecting his entrance.

After spending a good amount of time soaking, she realized that the man was not going to come into the bathroom. She finished her bath. Feeling wonderfully clean and refreshed; she went into the room and opened the closet. There was a closet full of the most beautiful clothes; not at all the kind of things that she was used to wearing. She loved everything so much that it was hard to choose what to wear. She tried to find the sexiest thing in the wardrobe, but there was nothing sexy to find. Everything was elegant and feminine and perfectly sized.

When she went back to the room where she had last seen her caller, he was there waiting to escort her to the table. He complimented her on how beautiful she looked and gently asked her if she liked her room and clothes and all of the things he had bought for her. She told him that she was very pleased. Finally sitting down to the delicious meal, she found herself at a prepared table full of her favorite foods. He made her plate, and they ate. He talked with her as they ate, and she could not help but to relax around him. She began to feel very comfortable and enjoyed talking with him. When he brought dessert to the table, it was the same cake that her mom used to make for her every year on her birthday. She could not contain herself anymore and began to sob.

"Who are you? Why did you bring me here?" She cried.

"I brought you here to celebrate your birthday." He replied.

"But today is not my birthday." She said.

"It can be, if you want it to." He said gently.

"What do you mean? You want me to pretend it's my birthday and jump out of a cake naked?" She asked in a confused tone.

"No! I want to make it your real birthday; a day that will be as if you become born again. You see, I have loved you since your birth. I know everything that happened to you. I have been watching over you

*every day, waiting for just the right time to make you all mine. Open the envelope that your **former** master gave you."* He instructed her.

The girl looked down at the table, and surprisingly, the envelope was in front of her. She slowly tore it open to find a check inside, with an unbelievably large sum written on it. The check was written out to her and signed by her pimp. *"You mean, you bought me?"* She asked.

He then responded, *"I did not **buy** you, I **redeemed** you. I have wanted you for the longest time, but your worth was so great that your master did not want to give you up. As it turns out, you did not rightfully belong to him after all, but I had to go to a Higher Power that had the authority to allow me to redeem you. The One that I appealed to told me that I could have you, but that the price was great. I was the wealthiest King in the universe and lived in a magnificent Kingdom, having rule over everything and everyone. But in order to redeem you, I would have to give up everything I owned and all of my power. You are so precious to me that I decided no price was too great. For the cost of losing you, would far outweigh the price paid to have you. So I did what I had to. I gave up everything, that I might redeem you from your cruel master and life of bondage. The check that is in your hand is all of the money that he earned from your bondage, plus seven times that amount in interest. It belongs to you and is yours to keep."*

By this time, the girl was crying uncontrollably, *"Is this for real? Do you mean I never have to go back to my master? What do you want from me?"*

He answered her sincerely and with love beaming from his eyes. *"It is real, only if you believe in me. I love you. All I want is for you to make this the first day of the rest of your life and become my wife. If you agree to receive my love forever and to love me back, then yes – you never have to go back to your former master. For I AM Your True LORD; My Name is Jesus (Yeshua)."*

****

I was involved with prostitution for almost ten years of my life, from the ages of 15 to 24. My experiences never reached the extreme of living in a brothel or working a street corner; they were probably minor in comparison to many people who live this lifestyle. Yet, I did have "an agent" at one point, I got paid to have sex and I have had sexual encounters with more people than the average person ever will.

That is my story. Yours may be different, but you don't have to actually practice prostitution to feel like a prostitute. There are many situations in life that can make you feel used and abused and ashamed. So often, we allow other people's bad choices concerning us, to influence us to make our own wrong choices. Life can begin to feel so out of control. And perhaps, the worse form of prostitution of all is when we sell ourselves short, by not believing in our own worth to The Creator that made us.

Whatever the case may be; the above story is for you. Going to church does not mean you have a real relationship with The Father. You may be just like the young lady in the story, living a life of bondage, under the hand of a cruel master. The Savior can and will redeem you from your life of religious pretense. However, if you never receive Him as **Your Lover**, then you will never be His. Your old master, the devil, does not want to let go of you because of your great worth. Yet, you can stop getting spiritually pimped, by choosing to truly become Yeshua's bride today. He gave up everything to redeem you: Now what are you willing to give up, in order to receive His redemption?

"[4] "Fear not; you will no longer live in shame. Don't be afraid; there is no more disgrace for you. You will no longer remember the shame of your youth and the sorrows of widowhood. [5]For your Creator will be your husband; the Lord of Heaven's Armies is his name! He is your Redeemer, the Holy One of Israel, the God of all the earth. [6]For the Lord has called you back from your grief — as though you were a young wife abandoned by her husband," says your God. [7]"For a brief moment I abandoned you, but with great compassion I will take you back. [8]In a burst of anger I turned my face away for a little while. But with everlasting love I will have compassion on you," says the Lord, your Redeemer. (Isa 54:4-8)"

Chapter 13

Pornography (Sexual Fantasy)

"But I say, anyone who even looks at a woman with lust in his eye has already committed adultery with her in his heart." (Mat. 5:28)

"If your sinful nature controls your mind, there is death. But if the Holy Spirit controls your mind, there is life and peace." (Romans 8:6)

Some Biblical References

Gen 6:5, 8:21; Leviticus 19:2; Josh 1:8; Job 31:1, Ps 1:1-3, Prov 6:25, 27:20; Isa 57:8, 65:2, Eze 3:2, 3:7, 16:30; Mat 5:28-29, 15:19; Luke 1:51; Rom 1:21, 8:5-7, 12:2; 1 Cor 2:16; 2 Cor 10:5; Eph 5:12; Phil 2:5; 2 Timothy 4:5; 2 Pet 2:14; 1 John 2:16

The Definition

Pornography – Pictures, writings, audio recordings or videos involving nudity, sexual intercourse and/or other sexual activity, designed to arouse and sexually excite.

Sexual fantasy – Indulging in mental images that are of a sexual nature.

The Assignment

A person that views pornography loses his or her ability to perceive people with purity. Everything becomes corrupt and defiled in that person's mind. What is innocent to others; is evil to them. **That is essentially the assignment of this spirit; to corrupt your spiritual vision and rob you of your spiritual discernment. Through corrupting your mind, this spirit can contaminate your heart. This will eventually cut you off from even the very possibility of having an intimate relationship with The LORD because it is only the pure in heart that** can see Him. If you are not close enough to see Him, surely you are not close enough to be one with Him!

The Practical Understanding

When it comes to sexual perversion, the devil wanted to make sure that he did not leave anybody out! There are some people that are just too shy or inhibited to actually engage in sex with a partner. There are also those that are physically incapable of having sexual intercourse. But even if you fit one of these descriptions, you must still be on guard against sexual perversion. The spirit of pornography and sexual fantasy is especially designed to make sure that even if you do not physically have sex, you will still suffer some degree of sexual perversion in the flesh. That is only one aspect of this spirit though. It affects anyone who is involved in sexual sin because it has a very important assignment, which is to **corrupt the mind**.

These two acts, pornography and sexual fantasy, fall under the same heading because they are one in the same. I really could have entitled this chapter "Sexual Fantasy" alone. Essentially, all pornography consists of, is the acting out of someone's sexual fantasy, with the intent to aid you in creating your own. This spirit's intent is to fill your mind with sexual images. By corrupting your mind with sexually stimulating thoughts from an external source, it can accomplish the goal of inducing you to use your own creativity to produce sexual sin in your heart. Once this happens, you will no longer need to engage in pornography to view sexually explicit images. The images will be fed to your mind directly from within the evil that resides in your own heart.

Let us clarify what types of acts would constitute pornography. Pornography includes any type of picture, movie, book, magazine, radio show, live activity (such as a strip tease or phone sex) and/or internet site; even a letter or conversation that is designed to feed sexual images to the mind. In our society, we may think of pornography as something that we pick up at an "adult movie" store or view on an "over 18 only" website. However, Yah's standards are much higher. No amount of sexually explicit or suggestive media is expedient to take in.

This means even a nice romance novel, that letter or sexual poem you wrote to or received from someone you were dating and many seemingly *"innocent"* TV shows and movies fall under the category of pornography. Any type of media or activity, which contains <u>any degree</u> of erotica that would produce a sexual image in your mind, is pornography!

Pornography is another sin that some would argue is acceptable, especially when used as a tool to stir passions before having sex with your spouse. However, Yeshua tells us in Matthew 5:28 that if we even **look** at a person with lust in our hearts that we have already sinned. The Apostle Paul also tells us in Ephesians 5:12 that, *"It is shameful even to <u>talk</u> about the things that ungodly people do in secret."* If it is shameful for you to even <u>talk</u> about these things, how much more shameful to *think* about and *look* at them?

Sinful pornography is still **sinful pornography**, even if you are watching it with your spouse. Remember that marital love-making is designed to be a replica of your worship with The LORD. It should be an intimate, heart-to-heart experience; as opposed to a merely flesh-gratifying, physical experience. True intimacy is more erotic than any pornography could ever be. So let me just break the news to you: If you need to indulge in pornography, in order to experience arousal before having sex with your spouse; if you feel that watching pornography is maybe not "necessary" but is a desired enhancement to your marital sex – YOUR MARRIAGE IS IN SERIOUS TROUBLE!

Believe it or not, even over-indulgent conversations between husband and wife that stir sexual images, <u>at times other than when they are actually engaged in the act of sexual intimacy,</u> are induced by the spirit of pornography! What would be the motive behind you meditating on images of having sex with your spouse, while you are at work? Why would you get yourself all hot and bothered with such images, while you are away on a business trip? This will cause pheromones to be released from your body; a scent that is undetectable to the nose but recognized by the brain of others "in heat". The next thing you know, you go from fantasizing about your spouse to flirting with the secretary. Or, you end up renting a porn movie in your hotel room and masturbating.

Even if you did not fall into some type of physical sexual sin from these fantasies, they will still corrupt your intimacy with your spouse. By the time you finally come together to engage in intimacy, it will not be *intimate* at all. You will be replaying the fantasy in your mind. Then, instead of being totally absorbed in that moment of being together with the one you love, you will be reliving the moment in your office when you were burning with lust. You will be focused on what *you* fantasized about, the position *you* wanted it in and how *you* wanted to do it – when you should be focused on *pleasing your spouse*. When you should be connecting to his or her spirit, becoming one and creating a **new** experience; you will instead be reliving a dead, self-fulfilling fantasy.

Sexual fantasy is **any** sexual thought, whether produced externally through pornography or live-streamed from within your heart, which you intentionally meditate on and allow to arouse you. The greater of the two, when it comes to externally or internally produced sexual fantasy, is definitely the latter. This is because sexual fantasy seeks to corrupt not only the mind but also the heart. Pornography is only used as a method to influence you to give in to sexual fantasy.

Sexual fantasy is not a passing thought. We all struggle with strange and fleeting thoughts and images at times. It can only be labeled as sexual fantasy when you really begin to entertain and meditate on the thought. When you spend minutes, hours, maybe even days imagining on sexual acts; when you turn a thought into an entire and detailed mental scenario – that is how you can tell that you are bound by sexual fantasy. You are definitely in a greater level of bondage if the images are being fed to your mind from within your heart *(Mat 15:19)*.

The scriptures make it clear that pornography and sexual fantasy is not acceptable behavior for Righteous, Christian living. You have to understand that the five senses are the gateways to your mind. Pornography uses these gateways. And although there may be no direct danger in looking at or listening to erotica, there is great danger in thinking about it. Pornography is the leading proponent of prostitution, rape, child porn and molestation in the U.S. It is also indirectly responsible for the destruction of many marriages and families.

After so many fantasies and so many videos, if you are physically fit enough to do so, you will eventually act out what you have seen in your mind. And it is not a far jump from paying to watch sex on a video – to paying to watch it in a strip club – to paying to have a lap dance – to paying to listen to it on the phone – to paying for sex with a prostitute. All of these acts are driven by some sexual fantasy and **what you think about is what you will eventually become!**

The Personality Profile

Now that we have this broad understanding of what pornography truly is, let's talk about how this spirit shapes your life. If the spirit of sexual fantasy is your strongman, you are a daydreamer for sure. The spirit of sexual fantasy is connected to other spirits of fantasy. If you daydream about sexual fantasies, you probably daydream about other things as well. You are probably just a daydreamer in general. For this reason, you are a person that is detached from reality. It is hard for you to decipher between what is false and what is real.

Because of your constant fantasizing, you get very little accomplished in life. You spend more time fantasizing than you do planning and putting plans into action. You are a procrastinator, always putting things off to the last minute. You are a poor planner, if you even make plans. You probably miss a lot of appointments, find yourself constantly running late, losing and misplacing things and are just generally disorganized. You are probably a poor housekeeper. Everything around you is junky and disorderly. You are clumsy and careless, dropping and breaking things often. You are what people would call a "scatter-brain".

You likely talk to yourself when you are alone. I don't mean that you talk to yourself, as in the sense of an encouraging pep talk. I mean talk to yourself, as if you are having a pretend conversation with someone. You might rather be alone than with people because you get so much enjoyment out of engaging in fantasies. You get more enjoyment out of fantasy than any other activity in life. Sexual fantasy is another spirit that will drive you into isolation. However, if you do find yourself around people a lot (maybe due to career, ministry, or promiscuity), you still have this ability to be "alone" even when in a room full of others.

You are very skillful at tuning people out, and you do so without even realizing it. Many otherwise meaningful conversations and moments are sucked into the vortex of fantasies in your mind. You have a tendency to "drift off" into vain thoughts, often times not even remembering what you were thinking about when you "come to". You are literally like a zombie sometimes. Being in a relationship with you can be very frustrating, due to this.

You are probably a very creative person and detail oriented. Fantasies draw you into the detail of thought, and thus you are probably more detailed than most people when you work on something. The catch here is – *your unlikelihood to actually finish something.* You have this awesome creative mind but cannot concentrate on one thing long enough to bring it into fruition. Focus is very difficult, if not impossible for you. You fall asleep easily; you can drift off to sleep in a moment. A mind that cannot stay focused has a hard time staying awake. You probably do not dream often either, when you do sleep. You do not need to dream when you are asleep because you live in a perpetual dream-like state. Furthermore, a dream is an *uncontrolled* series of mental images. For fantasy to be optimal, you must be able to control how the images play out!

In your natural life things are probably totally out of your control. Your career, education, health, relationships, finances and living arrangements – every aspect of your life may be completely out of control. You are just really unaware of how you are living and how you are managing, *or failing to manage,* your life. But none of this matters to you because you live in a world that exists within your own mind. And there, in that world that you have created, everything is just what you want it to be. In your land of fantasy, you have got it all under control. An out of control life may have been the open door that allowed this spirit access to you in the first place. You wanted to exist somewhere that you could be in control. This is a spirit that is common amongst those that have suffered abuse. Fantasy is a way to escape abusive situations and regain control in an otherwise state of hopeless despair.

Under this spirit, you do not see things as they are but instead see them as you want them to be. Your perception of reality is completely distorted, and often times other people cannot relate to you at all. To have a common understanding with others requires an awareness of "actuality". This awareness is missing in you, and therefore you find it difficult to work with others or to get others to work with you. You may be a great leader, have great plans and ideas, but fail to relate to people realistically enough to be effective.

Although sexual fantasy is a really opportune act of perversion for those that, for some reason, are incapable or unwilling to engage in sexual sin with a partner, it does not stop there. Most people that are bound by sexual fantasy also engage in other acts of sexual perversion. If you were to survey those that commit any of the other acts of sexual perversion, you would be hard pressed to find even one that does not engage in sexual fantasy. The images in your mind create a craving in your body that longs to be fulfilled. Masturbation is probably the sin you commit most frequently, in conjunction with the sexual fantasy because it allows you to maintain that sense of control. However, it will not stop there. Although the spirit of sexual fantasy can cause you to isolate yourself, it can also drive you to seek out fulfillment of your fantasies.

Whatever it is that you are fantasizing about, whether it is child molestation, rape, sex with animals, homosexuality or otherwise – if you are drawn deep enough into the fantasy, you will become detached enough from reality to think that you can do it and still be in control. Sexual fantasy can get so bad that it can lead you into a state of psychosis or delusion, where the real world ceases to exist for you. You will get to the point that you are committing all types of crazy and dangerous, possibly illegal acts, without realizing the consequences or effects of those acts. You will be completely unaware of what is going on around you, in the real world, because the act itself that you are doing is of no significance to you. It is the fantasy that you are playing out that is driving you and bringing you pleasure.

This is such a dangerous, dangerous spirit. If you are addicted to pornography or sexual fantasy, and you still have enough presence of mind to understand what I am saying, I beg you to put this book down right now and repent. How many more times will you watch child porn before you actually molest someone? How many more strip clubs will you visit before you hire a prostitute to fulfill your lust? How many more videos of violent sex will you watch before you rape someone? How many more times before you find yourself doing something that you never thought you were capable of? Ask Yeshua to save you from this spirit! You could be just days or even moments away from completely losing your grip on reality; destined to rot away in insanity, like so many lost souls wandering the streets homeless and behaving strangely.

The Churchgoer Profile

It seems like churchgoers and pornography almost go hand and hand. Maybe not literally, but you have to understand that the majority of the "so-called" Christian world is steeped in man-made religious practices that have absolutely nothing to do with Righteousness or relationship with a Savior. Religion is not about an actual standard of right-living but is instead about a code of appearances. This means that any activity that can be done in secret, without violating that code of appearances, is very appealing to the religious at heart. Pornography falls safely within those margins, and therefore it is highly likely that sexual fantasy and pornography addicts will be found in the church.

As a Church-goer that is bound by the spirit of sexual fantasy, you are easily distracted from the things of Yah. Fantasy is a mesmerizing, bewitching spirit that pulls on you constantly. Once it enters into your sphere of influence, it is very difficult to remain focused on anything. The visions and the plans that The Father lays out before you, are often replaced by imagination and procrastination. The mandate to "deny yourself, take up your cross, and follow Christ *(Mat 16:24)*" is a very unappealing one that cannot at all compete with the pleasures of dwelling in your world of fantasy.

Like many bound by some of the other spirits of sexual perversion, you are more likely to become involved in some type of occultism or witchcraft because of your detachment from reality. You bear little or even no fruit at all. Your life is full of carnality and evil. Even many sinners will note your behavior and say, *"Aren't you supposed to be a Christian?"* You totally lack the character of Christ and have no light. You are dull in your spiritual hearing, dim in your spiritual eyes and your heart is hardened.

Because of your inability to perceive the Word of God, you are often subject to confusion and double-mindedness. You are stagnant in your growth and remain spiritually immature, even after being in church for many years. You get very little accomplished, if anything at all. This is because you spend more time fantasizing about how your life in Christ is going to be than actually working toward **applying** the principles of The Word to create that life. You are inactive in church. You probably have a lot of creative ideas about doing things in the church, but never any realistic plans for bringing these ideas to past. Your faith is dead because it is not coupled with works.

In the book of Romans 8:5 it tells us, *"Those who are dominated by the sinful nature think about sinful things, but those who are controlled by the Holy Spirit think about things that please the Spirit."* If your thoughts are of sinful things and/or you indulge in watching, reading and listening to sinful things or you talk about them, then you are still dominated by your sinful nature and are yet the enemy of The LORD. As long as you remain addicted to fantasy, you are unable to ever excel in the call of Yahweh on your life. To answer His call will require labor – which you hate. It will require discipline – which you lack. It will require concentration – which you are incapable of. It will require sacrifice – which you are unwilling to give. And it will require giving control over to and trusting Him – which you cannot even conceive or achieve!

The Worship Portrait

When I consider the importance of the mind, I understand that this is even one of the more detrimental spirits of sexual perversion, if not **THE MOST detrimental**. This spirit of fantasy causes you to meditate on those things that are offensive to The Father and destructive to your spirit. The Bible lets us know that the person who meditates on the Word of The LORD day and night, is the person that will be empowered with obedience and will therefore enjoy Yah's blessings *(Josh 1:8, Ps 1:2-3)*.

How can you meditate on perversion, or anything that is contrary to Righteousness, and meditate on the Holy Word of The LORD God at the same time? It is not possible! Your Christian walk is so heavily controlled by what goes into your mind. Undeniably, what you think about is definitely affected by what you see and hear. It is by the renewing of your mind that you are transformed into the express image of Christ – into a living epistle. The mind is where the battle between Holiness and evil is fought within you. If satan wins in the mind, he wins altogether! Just think about your walk with Christ and the times you have sinned. How many times have you sinned without first thinking about it?

If you are bound by this spirit, you are constantly feeding your flesh, your eyes and your ears with carnality and things that are offensive to Yahweh. You are constantly meditating on things contrary to His nature of Holiness. Your entire mind is corrupt and perverse and so is your spirit. You are perverse in your thinking concerning the things of The LORD. Instead of accepting Him as He is, for Who He is, you attempt to make Him fit into your mental image of *what He should be*.

You do likewise with His Kingdom and His ways. When you do worship, *if you do worship*, it is not done to please The LORD. It is done so that you can fulfill whatever fantasy you have concocted in your mind about what worship *should be*. Therefore, you are a selfish worshiper that cares nothing for how your worship affects The Father. You only do it to satisfy the craving that is created when you fantasize and dream your dreams of being a great wonder in the church. Truthfully, you are helplessly bound in all areas of your walk with God, until you determine to use His mighty weapons to cast down imaginations, tear down the strong holds in your mind and bring every thought captive into obedience to Christ *(2 Cor 10:4-5)*. Remember, the essential goal of this spirit is to corrupt your mind, in order that it might contaminate your heart.

"^{15}To the pure, all things are pure, but to those who are corrupted and do not believe, nothing is pure. In fact, both their minds and consciences are corrupted. (Titus 1:15)"

"^{19}For out of the heart come evil thoughts—murder, adultery, sexual immorality, theft, false testimony, slander. (Mat 15:15)"

"^{8}Blessed are the pure in heart, for they will see God. (Mat 5:8)"

Ah yes, "Blessed are the pure in heart, for they will SEE God." And here the real motive of this spirit is revealed – to forever change how you SEE. Think about it; once you see a person naked, you never look at them the same way again. Once you SEE someone a certain way, it is very difficult to go back to how you saw them before. What you *saw*, can forever affect what you *see*. What you see, affects your perception and your perception of something can overrule the actuality of it. And this is what the spirit of sexual fantasy wants to steal from you – your accurate perception of good and evil. This spirit wants to strip you of your ability to discern truth and prevent you from ever being able to SEE Yahweh God.

Insights from Dr. Intimacy

Reclaiming Your Spiritual Vision

Mark 8:22-26 *"²²When they arrived at Bethsaida, some people brought a blind man to Jesus, and they begged him to touch the man and heal him. ²³Jesus took the blind man by the hand and led him out of the village. Then, spitting on the man's eyes, he laid his hands on him and asked, "Can you see anything now?" ²⁴The man looked around. "Yes," he said, "I see people, but I can't see them very clearly. They look like trees walking around." ²⁵Then Jesus placed his hands on the man's eyes again, and his eyes were opened. His sight was completely restored, and he could see everything clearly. ²⁶Jesus sent him away, saying, "Don't go back into the village on your way home."*

After reading the profiles in this chapter, I was blown away. Living under the influence of the spirit of fantasy for the greater part of my life, I was disturbed to see myself in the lines of the text. As I read on, I felt almost helpless, saying to The LORD, *"So how does one get delivered from this? And more importantly, how is the damage repaired?"* The Holy Spirit immediately impressed the story of this blind man upon my spirit and said that the answer could be found therein.

Remember that the spirit of fantasy wants to steal your vision. In this passage of scripture, we have a man who had no vision. He wanted to see again, but there was a process that he had to go through. This healing was not like many of the "instantaneous healings" that Yeshua often performed. Nor does the scripture make mention of Him casting out any demon. This man had to go through a process to reclaim his vision.

1. *"...some people brought a blind man to Jesus, and they begged him to touch the man and heal him."* The preparation for the process to begin was the intercession of those that recognized his lack of vision. It was the people who loved him that brought the blind man to Yeshua. Just as a blind man fumbling his way down a busy city street, you have to understand that once you become spiritually blind, everyone who

has spiritual sight can see and recognize your lack of vision. When you are blind, it is impossible for you to be aware of what it is that you cannot see. The state of delusion that you come under through the oppression of the spirit of fantasy can cause you to be unaware of what you are blind to, and you will need the help of those who have sight to lead you to the place of healing. Do not resist the help of your loved ones. Reading this book is already part of that process. I wrote this book because I love you. By writing this book, I have become one of the people that are bringing you to Yeshua, in order that you might receive your sight.

2. *"²Jesus took the blind man by the hand and led him out of the village."* The next part of the process entailed the blind man getting away from familiar people, places and things. Remember that this spirit has used external influences to impart perverse images to your mind. In order to reclaim your vision, you first need to get out of the environment that corrupted you to begin with. Separation and consecration is going to be necessary. If you have to get rid of every TV and computer in your house; if you need to let your spouse have all of your bank and credit cards; if you need to withdraw membership from organizations; lose unsavory friends; change your phone number and email address; move to another place... **Whatever it takes** – you are going to have to separate yourself from what corrupted your mind.

3. *"...Then, spitting on the man's eyes..."* The third part of this process required the man to get cleansed. Yeshua spit in his eyes. In other words, He took water from His mouth – *the mouth of God out of which the Word of Life flows* – and He washed the filth and death from the man's eyes that had caused him to lose his sight. *"²⁶...holy and clean, washed by the cleansing of God's word. (Eph 5:26b)"* This clause of Ephesians teaches you that it is the Word of Yahweh that washes you and makes you clean. You are going to have to put The Word in you like never before. It is furthermore important that YOU **READ** the Bible for yourself. Yeshua spit **directly** onto the man's eyes. The Word of Yah, the water from His mouth that cleanses, **must make direct contact with your eyes**. It is not enough for you to listen to it on CD or to hear

someone else preach it. You must wash your eyes by using those eyes to read scripture. I cannot iterate it enough; **it is critically important for you to SEE the Word of God**. You should write scriptures on index cards and carry them around with you everywhere. Post written scriptures (not typed, *written* by your own hand, which forces you to SEE the words as they are formed on the paper) inside of your car; on your bathroom mirror; write them on your hand; put them on the wall in front of your bed; any and everywhere that they will be VISIBLE to you, and READ THEM ALL THROUGHOUT THE DAY.

4. *"...he laid his hands on him..."* Next, Yeshua touched the man. It is going to take a touch from The LORD for you to get delivered from this issue. Remember that this spirit trains you to detach yourself from people, preventing you from forming authentic connections. In order for someone to touch you, you have to be close enough for the person to reach you. Are you close enough to The Father for Him to touch you? Do not think that reading the scripture alone will be enough. You are going to have to stay close and intimate with The LORD during this entire process, in order to get your healing – *and for the rest of your life in order to remain healed!* <u>Intimate worship is the key</u>.

5. *"...and asked, "Can you see anything now?" The man looked around. "Yes," he said, "I see people, but I can't see them very clearly."* Honest evaluation of the progress you have made is very necessary. After going through the process up until this point, the man had definitely received a partial healing, but the process was not complete. I am sure after being blind for so many years, seeing anything was exciting to him and was better than seeing nothing at all. However, The LORD desires for your vision to be **completely restored**. If the man had walked away before the process was complete, he would have spent the rest of his days not being able to *see things clearly*. Even with partial blindness, you will be a dysfunctional part of the Body of Christ. You need to let the Holy Spirit ask you the questions that will keep you in a FULL state of awareness about where you are at in the process of your deliverance. Let the people around you and your

communication with The Father reveal to you whether or not you are really seeing clearly.

6. "They look like trees walking around." A tree is just as alive as a human being. However, trees are rooted creations that are designed to remain stationary. People, on the other hand, are beings that were created to move freely, from place to place. Without the clear vision that you need to have – that clear spiritual discernment – you will confuse that which should remain stationary, with that which was designed to move in and out. As you walk outside, a tree may first be *before* you and then it is *behind* you. Yet, it is not the tree that has moved; it is you that has moved. There are things in life that you need to pass by. You cannot get attached to inanimate, stationary things that are incapable of moving forward with you. No matter how much you love them; there are those things that are designed to be rooted and stationary in a certain place or season of your life that cannot move with you, when it is time for you to progress on to the next phase of growth. People on the other hand, move freely in and out of your life. They are going in one direction and you in another. You often have no control over their comings and goings, and they may pass by you or even choose to go backwards. Change can be intimidating, and often times your own fear causes you to begin to see people, places and things, as other than what they actually are. But alas, the blind man became aware of his confused sight! Awareness is the key. Finally you realize that you have been seeing people like trees, thinking they would stay in the same place forever. And trees (the stable things in life that make you feel rooted and sheltered) like people, thinking that those things could move with you.

7. "Then Jesus placed his hands on the man's eyes again..." The next part of the process was for the man to "not see". It had already been clearly established that he was not seeing clearly. It was then necessary for the man to stop using the eyes that were not working properly. People that are partially blind often wear dark shades to prevent them from using their partial vision. This is because partial vision can be more dangerous than complete blindness. It is better to not see at all, than to see with distorted vision that misguides you, leading you into danger that you are not even aware of. The brain is so dependent on sight that it will heavily rely on even the distorted images of partial vision, thus training the eye to continue to see in an ineffectual way. Yeshua covered the man's eyes, so he would not be able to see at all. You are going to have to go into a quiet place of complete dependency on God for a short season. *"[8]...but though his eyes were opened, he could see nothing... [9]And he was unable to see for three days, and he neither ate nor drank [anything]. (Acts 9:8-9)"* I believe that just as this text in Acts prescribes; a three day shut-in and total fast would be the next step in this process. Blindness is a type of isolation, and you need to completely isolate yourself from everyone, including your spouse if you are married, for three days as The LORD retrains your eyes to see effectively and with full functionality. He needs to reset your vision and restore right perception so that this will happen, **"...and his eyes were opened. His sight was completely restored, and he could see everything clearly."**

8. **"Don't go back into the village on your way home."** Lastly, once your sight is restored, you have to use wisdom about how you live. Do not go back to the people, places and things that you had to separate yourself from, in order to get delivered! Yeshua told the man to go home. Do not even go *through* the village – in other words, do not even walk through temptation. Go and get your life in order! Once your sight is restored, your first reaction will be teary-eyed joy and thanksgiving. However, once you begin to look at your life clearly, your next reaction may be despair and a feeling of being overwhelmed. You have to understand that your life has gotten messy since you went blind. Everything is chaotic and disorganized and dirty. Your relationships, your home, your finances, your body... everything has suffered due to your lack of sight. And now you will be able to clearly see what your illness has really caused. It will make you want to run back to the things that gave you the comfort of escape. You will want to go back to the village, back to the place where you had your false sense of control. It is going to be very important to walk circumspectly and live a consecrated life from this point forward. Do not allow yourself to even

come in contact with the people, places and things that will tempt you to give up your vision again.

This is the Holy Spirit's 8 step program, for anyone that is addicted to pornography, prostitution, day-dreaming, romance novels, fairy tales, fantasy, visualization... any type of stronghold of fantasy, delusion, distracted, wandering thoughts or mental defect of any kind, sexual or otherwise. If you really want to be able to SEE The LORD and life clearly again, this prescription will work for you. So let's recap:

Eight Steps to Deliverance from the Spirit of Fantasy

1. Let the people who are interceding for you, help you. Remember that they can see; you can't! Let them lead you to the resources that will connect you to The Healer.

2. Move away from the people, places and things that are keeping you bound and corrupting your mind. By any means necessary, you must get away from evil and distractions.

3. Read the Bible as much as you possibly can. You must SEE it so that your eyes can get washed of the filth and poison that blinded you.

4. Draw close to The LORD and let Him draw close to you. He needs to touch you in a special way, in order for you to really get healed.

5. Asking accurate questions, and looking at the lives of others to help you evaluate your progress, is essential. Don't get up from the surgeon's table before the procedure is finished. Stay the course until it is a complete deliverance.

6. Become aware of things that you have been confused about. Remember that this spirit is after your spiritual sight; your accurate perception of things. You cannot correct a problem that you are not aware of.

7. After you have done all of the above, emphasis on AFTER, plan a complete 3-day shut in and total fast. This will be a time that you have **absolutely no contact** with the outside world whatsoever, including even Christian media (such as preached messages or books.) Just you, The Father, His Word and a journal. This 3-day period of "not seeing" will be used to reset your vision and put the last piece in place for restoring right perception.

8. After this 3-day shut in, do not make contact with anyone unnecessarily. Don't call or visit anyone. Don't text or email anyone. Go home and get your life in order. You should limit your interaction to dealing with just the people that live in your house, your immediate family and necessary work activity. Everything will look different to you, and it will take time for you to get used to your new sight. Enjoy the process, take it in slowly, be very aware and avoid entangling yourself with temptation. The Holy Spirit will give you wisdom about who to re-connect with – *how, when and to what degree*. Just follow His lead!

I would love to have some written testimonies from some of you who use this process. Tell me your story and your results. Write me at drintimacy@drintimacy.com. *This is my personal email. No one else will read it, unless you want me to share your story.* **Thank you for sharing!**

Chapter 14

Rape (Sexual Abuse)

"Our enemies rape the women and young girls in Jerusalem and throughout the towns of Judah." (Lam 5:11)

*"But if any man think that he behaveth himself uncomely toward his virgin, **if she pass the flower of her age**, and need so require, let him do what he will, he sinneth not: let them marry." (1 Cor 7:36 KJV)*

Some Biblical References

Gen 34: 1-5; Lev 18:10; Lam 5:11; 1 Sam 13:1, Judges 19:22-30; Eze 22:11; 1 Cor 7:36

The Definition

Rape – the unlawful compelling of a person through physical force or duress to have sexual intercourse.

Molestation - to make indecent sexual advances toward another.

Pedophilia – the condition of being sexually attracted to children.

The Assignment

A person who rapes or sexually abuses others has a bloodthirsty lust for power. Rape is not just about sexual lust. Rape is about control and power over others. It is about taking, through violence and manipulation, what does not belong to you; destroying the hope and innocence of your victim; turning them into your property; having them eventually duplicate your actions. The spirit of rape wants to seize, subdue and conquer its victim. It wants to fill you with pride as you destroy others under its influence. **The ultimate assignment is to give you the perception that you are equal with Yahweh, preventing you from ever worshiping Him.**

The Practical Understanding

If you are now or have ever been bound by this spirit, I want you to rest assured that this offense is no less susceptible to the washing and cleansing of The Blood of Yeshua than any other sin. The Blood of The Lamb is able to thoroughly cleanse us of all sins, even those that are called detestable and are considered an abomination. This book is not being written to single any one out, to judge anyone or make anyone feel bad – including you. Society at large may try to make you feel as if there is no hope for you and that you are the lowest form of life on the planet. However, The Father is seeking you out, to heal you and cleanse you. He already knew every choice you would make when He formed you in your mother's womb, and He knew what you would suffer.

Studies have proven that sex offenders are the most unlikely category of criminals to be rehabilitated. This is true but not because you are unable to be rehabilitated. The reason that rehabilitation is so hard for you is because of the depths of self-condemnation that you experience. Even if others forgive you, you are seldom able to forgive yourself. Often times, the depth of guilt experienced by people who are bound by this spirit prevent them from ever being healed. This means that, like so many of the other spirits of sexual perversion, this one too makes you feel trapped – caught in a never ending and deadly cycle. Yet, if you are willing to open your heart to the love, healing and forgiveness of Jesus Christ, our Lord Yeshua, you will become a new person. You do not have to live like this one more day!

Having said that, let's take an honest look at what rape literally consists of. The more common, legal term used in place of the word rape is *sexual assault*. This is because for an act to be defined as rape there has to be forced penetration using the male organ. However, whether referred to using the term 'rape' or the term 'sexual assault', we are dealing with the same spirit. For the purposes of this book, I will use these terms interchangeably.

The most obvious form of rape is when a woman is forcibly penetrated by a man. However, people are often sexually assaulted by being penetrated with objects other than the penis, such as sticks, bottles, guns and so on. Also, penetrating someone with your hands is a form of sexual assault. Any type of forced penetration, whether vaginal, oral or anal would fall into this category. This includes the violation of a male in any of the above forms. This is the obvious manifestation of physical rape, but there are some gray areas too.

One of those gray areas is statutory rape. This is a case where the sex is fully consensual between both parties, but one of the parties is not of legal consenting age. Legal consenting age for sexual intercourse in most states is 16. This means that if any person over the age of 16, has intercourse with a person under the age of 16, that person can be convicted of statutory rape. Statutory rape is not consistent with a biblical view. In biblical times, once a girl and boy completed puberty, no matter what age that occurred at, they were legally able to get married *(have sex)*. Of course in Bible days, puberty occurred at a much later age than it does in this century. Also, there was a much higher regard for marriage and sex in those times. Righteous people did not have sex unless they planned on spending their lives together as husband and wife. Today that is not so.

I believe the statutory rape law was designed to protect youth from promiscuous behavior and from being taken advantage of by older persons that would manipulate them into having sex. It is a good law, however according to what we are studying in this book; statutory rape does not necessarily belong in this category. A perpetrator of statutory rape could fall under the lust category. This is especially true, if you are significantly older and long for sex with teenage girls. You may also belong in the fornication category, depending on the circumstances under which the sex occurred. For instance, maybe you were a 17 year old boy that had sex with your 15 year old girlfriend.

The main thing to understand here is that the spirit of rape is about force and control. If sex is fully consensual, between two sound-minded people that have reached puberty and desire to have sex, regardless of any age difference, the necessary element that constitutes rape is missing. The only case of statutory rape that would appropriately fall under this category is that which occurs under circumstances of child molestation, which we will discuss a bit further down in this chapter.

Here is another issue that comes up sometimes. Can a husband rape a wife? According to a biblical understanding of marriage, the answer is no. According to an understanding of how the spirit of rape operates, the answer is yes. Once married, the husband's body belongs to the wife and the wife's body belongs to the husband *(1 Cor 7:4)*. However, if you had a spirit of rape working in you before you got married, it can still be working in you after you get married. Men who watch pornography or practice sex with prostitutes often "rape" their wives – in a spiritual sense. A woman knows when you are not really there when you enter into her. Yet from a literal biblical viewpoint, this cannot be defined as rape. It could instead be referred to as emotional abuse or even physical abuse, if the husband physically overpowers his wife and forces himself on her against her will.

Then there is one more gray area, which is coerced sex. Force and coercion are different. Force has to do with physically subduing someone. Coercion has to do with mentally subduing someone. Legally, coercion is a very gray area of rape that is hard to get a conviction on. But it is not a complicated matter biblically. If a person is mentally challenged, they cannot realistically consent to sex. Such coercion is easily defined as rape. However, for people that function at full mental capacity, consent is consent – whether it is excited, aroused consent or pressured, duress consent. If you are old enough to fully understand what is happening to you, and you have the ability and option to get up and walk away or scream for help and you choose not to; you have not been raped.

There are cases where people are drugged by people they know, and then taken advantage of sexually in that intoxicated state. If you are drugged or intoxicated with alcohol **unknowingly**, and completely lose sense of what is happening to you or lose consciousness; it can be considered rape when you are subjected to sexual activity in that state. However, if you become intoxicated willingly, by using drugs or alcohol, and are still conscious, even if you become unaware of what is happening to you, you cannot consider any sexual activity under those circumstances as rape. You knew the situation you were putting yourself in and chose that outcome for yourself by default! If you can claim you did not know what you were doing because you were intoxicated, why cannot the perpetrator use the same defense?

When sexually active, post-pubescent people get together and get intoxicated, sexual activity is the likely outcome. Wake up and stop pretending to be the victim here! I think it is really important for me to address this because there are women and men who engage in sexual activity with someone, and then after experiencing regret or embarrassment, claim that they were raped. This is a very wicked thing to do. A rape conviction will negatively impact someone's life until the day they die. They will be viewed in society as a **SEX-OFFENDER**, a title that <u>CAN NEVER BE ERASED</u>. Sex offenders are the modern day lepers of society. And that is no wonder to me – with consensual sex so readily available and so easy to attain, only a true deviant would "steal" it from someone.

So don't you dare, ever falsely accuse someone of raping you! For in doing so, you will be in direct violation of the Ten Commandments. Rape, although a disgraceful act, is not addressed in the Ten Commandments. However, bearing false witness is! I believe that in Yahweh's eyes, a false witness is even worse than a rapist. If you have ever done this, go back to everyone you told this lie to and make it right. If the conviction was public, then make your apology public. Do whatever you have to in order to right this wrong! You will die under a curse if you do not! *Ok, moving on from that warning...*

I have only addressed coercion from the perspective of the person that claims to have been coerced. Let me now address the person that initiates coerced, pressured or intoxicated sexual activity. Even is a person is irresponsible for getting themselves into a compromising situation, you are still accountable for coercion. If you pressure a person into having sex, have sex with someone knowing that they seem uncomfortable about it or have sex with a person that is knowingly intoxicated, you are definitely operating under the influence of the spirit of rape. You are willfully taking advantage of someone. You are overpowering them mentally and emotionally. You are taking something away from that person, without any intent to compensate them for what you are taking. These characteristics denote what the spirit of rape is really all about.

This leads me into addressing molestation and pedophilia, acts that both belong in this category. Molestation, otherwise referred to as sexual harassment or sexual abuse, can be defined as *"inappropriate or unwanted sexual advances"*. We often think of children when we hear the terms *molestation* or *sexual abuse*. Molestation does often refer to the inappropriate sexual advancement toward a child, but it can happen to an adult as well. If you are dating someone and make unwanted sexual advances toward that person, you have molested them. If you make unwanted sexual gestures toward anyone – slapping their butt, feeling their breast, sexual movements with your body, making contact with their crotch, kissing or hugging them against their will, exposing to them any part of your body that is normally covered, blowing kisses – all of this behavior is sexual harassment.

If you make unwelcomed sexual remarks toward a co-worker, colleague, boss, employee, congregant, friend or family member – even making a sexual comment toward a beautiful stranger that makes him or her feel uncomfortable, you have molested that person. After reading everything in this book up to this point, you should have a very sound understanding of the weighty significance of sexuality. Flippant sexual remarks and corrupt playful gestures are inexcusable. There is NO PLACE for such behavior in the life of someone who wants to be a true disciple of Christ *(Eph 5)*. Furthermore, even these more subtle forms of sexual harassment, make the victim feel unclean and violated. And for you as the perpetrator, it can open the door to the more serious forms of sexual abuse, such as rape or child molestation.

Let's talk about child molestation and pedophilia before we move on to the profiles. Molestation has already been defined. Pedophilia is not an act, but is instead a mental state that leads to acts of molestation and sexual abuse against children. It is the state of being sexually attracted to a child. Even though humans are legally considered children until the age of 18, pedophilia in its truest form is attraction to children that have not yet reached puberty or those who are in the early stages of puberty. Although perhaps still a child legally according to age, as early as two years past the onset of puberty (six years at most), the body reaches physical adulthood. A child as young as 11 years old can have a fully mature body.

Nonetheless, people should govern their sexual affairs with child sex laws in mind. I am only attempting to separate the natural from the spiritual in this book, not condone sex with minors who look grown. At any rate, by law physical appearance does not matter, but spiritually it cannot be defined as pedophilia for someone to be attracted to what they perceive to be an adult body. As a pedophile you are above all else, attracted to a child's innocence, purity and vulnerability. Such qualities are only *apparent* in children before puberty is complete.

I say all of this to help you define accurately whether or not the spirit of pedophilia is influencing you. Next, I want to make it absolutely clear some of the physical manifestations of pedophilia that you may have overlooked. **If you can catch the subtle warning signs, it is not too late to prevent yourself from violating an innocent child with your perversion.** So please take note of the following signs of pedophilia.

If you enjoy seeing children naked; if you feel sexual arousal when seeing a child naked or when looking at a baby's genitals; if you make sexual jokes about a child; if you make mention of how you think a child will perform sexually when they get older; if you have mental images of sexual contact with a child; if you have feelings of "being in love" with a child; if you feel possessive or jealous over a child spending time with others or having a girlfriend or boyfriend; if you crave affectionate physical contact with children *(such as them sitting on your lap, kissing you, sleeping with you or hugging you)*; if you have urges to expose yourself nude or partially nude to a child; if you have a longing to bathe a child or go swimming with a child; if you purposefully leave the door open when you are changing clothes or using the bathroom when a child is around; if you reward a child for spending time with you *(such as with candy, money or an enjoyable activity)*; if you feel your time with a child is secretive or feel guilty about it: these are all signs of pedophilia.

Also, if you entertain child pornography that is an obvious sign. But here is one that is not so obvious – if you know of the availability of child porn or underage human trafficking victims and feel no sense of conviction about it, or fail to report it to authorities – that is also a sign! Acceptance of sin is always the first step toward participation in it.

As you have just read, the spirit of rape operates on a wide spectrum of manifestations. I wanted to take time to evaluate all of these manifestations because I want you to be able to recognize this as an issue in your life, no matter where you may land on this spectrum. It is also important for those of us that have been a victim of the spirit of rape to recognize such. People that are victims of sexual abuse often abuse others, and that is why it is so important for you to acknowledge any abuse that has occurred in your life. Maybe reading this practical breakdown of rape has brought it to your attention for the first time ever that you were sexually abused. Do not brush it off. Confront it, talk about it, pray about it and close every door that was opened through it.

THIS IS A PERSONAL PLEA TO EVERY PERSON READING THIS RIGHT NOW. PLEASE PRINT OUT THE PARAGRAPH ON THE SIGNS OF A PEDOPHILE AND CAREFULLY EVALUATE EVERYONE AROUND YOU. DO NOT TURN A BLIND EYE TO THE VIOLATION OF A CHILD; YOUR CHILD OR ANYONE ELSE'S. WATCH YOUR SPOUSES AND LOVERS; WATCH YOUR TEENAGE CHILDREN AND RELATIVES AND NEIGHBORS AND TEACHERS AND EVERYONE! THE LATEST STATISTICS SAY THAT 7 OUT OF 10 CHILDREN ARE MOLESTED IN THIS COUNTRY. WE HAVE GOT TO BRING THOSE NUMBERS WAY DOWN, ESPECIALLY IN THE CHURCH. IT IS GOING TO HAVE TO START WITH US GETTING EDUCATED ON WHAT TO LOOK FOR AND BEING COMMITTED TO DOING SOMETHING ABOUT IT WHEN WE SEE IT. AS A VICTIM MYSELF, I AM MAKNG THIS HEART FELT PLEA ON BEHALF OF EVERY CHILD ON THE PLANET. EVERYONE SHOULD HAVE THE RIGHT TO CHOOSE WHEN THEY BECOME SEXUALLY ACTIVE!!!

The Personality Profile

If rape is your strongman, you are a bully who takes advantage of those that are too weak to defend themselves. You force yourself into positions of authority that you did not earn and then abuse that authority. You are like an animal, sexually abusing others to "mark your territory" and claim possession of others. You want someone to belong to you because you have so often in your life felt as if you did not belong. You are trying to create a regime in which you are in power. In your regime people must be afraid or unwilling to reject you, in order that you might finally experience acceptance.

Rapist and pedophiles are manipulative, lonely people. Being "alone" is a temporal state of being; whereas being "lonely" is a set state of mind. You can be around people and still be lonely and that is typically how you feel. Just like committers of incest, you have experienced severe rejection in your lifetime. Your intention, especially true for pedophiles, is not to hurt your victim. You just want to steal back the acceptance that you were denied. You were starved for love, affection, affirmation and nurturing as a child, and you want to be compensated for that loss. You are just taking what you feel should have rightfully been yours in the first place.

Children make easy targets because they are so naïve, loving, kind, trusting and forgiving. Not every pedophile violently rapes their victims. You may, or may not use violence and rape. For the most part, you would rather them come willingly because the aim is not to hurt your victim, but is instead to experience what you consider "love". However, if the victim is being uncooperative, a situation can easily turn into a violent rape. An uncooperative victim causes you to experience rejection all over again. In your mind, you are just trying to show this person love, and they are rejecting your love. It makes you very angry. Pedophiles have an emotional attachment to their victims and are usually aiming to develop a "relationship" outside of the sexual abuse.

Not every person that sexually abuses children is a true pedophile. You could be a rapist that just happens to prefer child victims. A rapist has no emotional attachment to the victim. Some rapists are actually disgusted at the thought of pedophilia and look down on child molesters. They see this as a show of having no real power and lacking the element of resistance that would allow them to conquer and subdue the victim. However, if you are a rapist that violates children, the age of your victim is incidental. A younger-aged victim may simply be your preference for carrying out your acts of violence, yet you will not have the characteristics of an authentic pedophile.

Pedophiles and rapist are both after a sense of control, but the need is different. A pedophile wants a friend and a lover. Pedophiles rarely see their victims as *victims*. But as a pure rapist, you have lost all hope that love exists. You do not want a friend or a lover. You do not believe in love anymore. You became angry and bitter because of all of the pain that you suffered. You gave up hope at some point in your life and stopped caring. All you want now is revenge and control. You want to make someone a victim. You want to subdue and destroy the hope in others that no longer lives in you.

If you have become oppressed by this spirit, you were abused at some point in your life. You want to avenge yourself for the hardships and abuses that you have suffered in your lifetime. In your past, someone made you feel weak and helpless. They took control away from you, and now you desperately want to experience the sensation of control. You are often times just overwhelmed by the urge to be in control. These compulsions are what usually drive you to rape. You are addicted to the sense of control that you feel when you sexually abuse others. Mixing the euphoria that you feel when in control, with the ecstasy of an orgasm, is a powerful cocktail of addictive hormonal releases and positive emotions.

Regardless as to whether you are a pedophile or a rapist, someone violated you and now you want to redeem yourself by doing the same thing to another. Two different methods are used to accomplish this, depending on how this spirit manifests itself in your life. As a pedophile you want to control using charismatic manipulation and mental power. As a rapist you want to control using physical strength and intimidating violence. In both cases, the goal is to control someone else the same way that you yourself were controlled. In controlling your victim, you are attempting to force them to restore to you what has been taken.

Regardless of how you approach it, you are never satisfied after committing your acts of sexual perversion. What was taken from you can never be restored to you, in the way that you are trying to reclaim it. No matter how many victims you may sexually abuse, the void in your soul is never filled. When the reality of the offenses you have committed come to your conscious awareness, the addictive, powerful high that you felt dissipates. You again feel weak and helpless and also ashamed. After you victimize others, you feel the exact same way that you did when you yourself were violated and abused in your past – *except even worse.*

The abuse that you suffered in the past could have been sexual in nature but that does not have to be the case. Any act of abuse makes one feel powerless and weak. You could have been bullied or picked on in school. Perhaps you were abandoned or neglected by your parents. A relative may have physically abused you or you may have been sexually abused. No matter what type of abuse it was that you suffered, the end result was this spirit of sexual abuse entering into your life. You are after a sense of fulfillment and acceptance, but the guilt that follows your acts of perversion serves only to drive you further into degradation, isolation and deviance.

Socially, you are a sneaky, eerie type of person. You give people a "weird feeling". You may be very withdrawn, or you could be extremely outgoing. It depends on the depth of deception that you are in. In any event, you have a short temper and are easily frazzled. If you are the outgoing type, more common amongst rapist, then you want to be forthrightly in control of everything. Usually, your guilt is so deeply buried within you that you cannot even comprehend or acknowledge that you have done something wrong. In this case, you are a cocky and arrogant person. You have an intimidating demeanor about you that makes others leery about challenging you.

Especially true for pedophiles, you are a nervous person who is easily *spooked*. It is that deep sense of guilt that keeps you feeling this way. You are more likely to be the withdrawn type, but you too want to be in control. You accomplish this craftily and subtly through manipulation. Secretly, you take great pleasure in your ability to fool and control people. However in the midst of your pleasure, guilt is ever looming over you and you are depressed. You try to stop what you are doing, but the guiltier you feel, the more helpless you feel. It only facilitates your sexual sins because that sense of helplessness causes you to continually and desperately seek out empowerment and control through molestation.

With the right upbringing, you are likely to have a high-paying job due to your keen intelligence. You are more inclined to have jobs that enable you to work alone. You do not like being in situations where you have to work as part of a team, unless you can be the leader of the team. Politics, ministry, teaching, coaching – any job that gives you authority or leadership over others is very appealing to you. If you cannot be in authority over others, then you certainly want to maintain authority over yourself. You are rebellious in nature and thus prefer to do field work or work from home. A career in computer programming or graphic design, are examples of what would appeal to you.

It is likely that you have diagnosed emotional problems such as schizophrenia or bi-polar disorder, just for example. I am not suggesting or even hinting that a diagnosis of a mental disorder indicates demonic infestation or a spirit of rape. What I am trying to iterate is that the way this spirit manifests itself in your life often takes on the form of known mental and emotional disorders. This is especially true for those that are bound by sexual fantasy. If you are the rapist type, you probably enjoy a high level of physical fitness. Your physical strength is very important for you to maintain your power. If a pedophile, your intellectual fitness is extremely important to you, which means you probably read a lot of educational books and view informative programs.

The spirit of rape is not likely to enter into a person's life past puberty. The seeds for this spirit were planted early on in your life, when you were unable to accurately process the right and wrong use of authority and power. If this spirit entered into your life in your later years, it was due to exposure to it through a sexual tie, a soul tie or media sources. If you had sex with someone, voluntarily or through rape, that had this spirit operating in their lives, it could have been passed to you at that time. If you developed a soul tie to a rapists or pedophile, this spirit could have accessed you through such a relationship. Weak people often develop soul ties with rapists and pedophiles because they are so charismatic and very skillful at using their intelligence to hide their deviance. As a matter of fact, you are probably well-liked by others and respected.

Another way this spirit enters into your life is through media exposure – pornography. Pornography promotes sexual violence and often displays violent images of sexual intercourse. Child pornography is readily available and inducts many an unsuspecting person into the community of rapists and pedophiles. Demonic spirits can enter directly into you through media exposure. It was written earlier, and is worth repeating, that the five senses are the gateways to your soul. A gateway is an opening through which something enters in. Your five senses are openings through which demonic spirits can enter into your soul. Nothing about watching pornography is innocent. Those spirits can enter into you and cause you to do things that never before even entered your imagination, including rape and child molestation.

Rape may not be your strongman even if you commit these acts. It might be sexual lust or sexual fantasy, which both greatly foster acts of rape and pedophilia. You should be remembering to use your notes to help you determine this. It is important that you understand which spirits are driving you and which one is in control. This will help you in the deliverance process. Also, the spirit of pride is always operative in a rapist. Pride, violence and sexual lust combined will make a rapist out of you every time. So beware!

The Churchgoer Profile

Some of the most notorious pedophiles and rapists in history have been either satan worshipers or atheists. Rapists are angry, bitter people often angry even at whoever they perceive god to be. Commonly, this is the case because you were a victim of this type of crime at some point in your own life. Having said that though, there are plenty of churchgoers that operate under the influence of this spirit, both spiritually and naturally. The prevalence of the spirits of incest and sexual fantasy in the church world is one of the reasons you can expect to find rapists in the church.

If you were a victim of sexual abuse in your lifetime, you have been left not being able to trust people or God. You are rebellious at home and rebellious in the church. You are angry and bitter. You feel dejected, dirty and worthless. It is very hard for you to receive Yeshua's love and to believe that His promises are for you. No matter how much people minister to you, nor how much love they try to show you; you are always discouraged, down and depressed. But beware victims because you are the most likely people to become victimizers! That is how this spirit is able to maintain such a strong presence.

The number of people that have been victimized is a huge factor in why the spirit of rape can be found operating in so many churches. Even if you never become a victimizer in the literal sense, in a spiritual sense you are highly likely to be operating under this spirit without realizing it. If you are a churchgoer that is bound by this spirit, but without the physical manifestations thereof, it will manifest itself in your life by causing you to try and operate as if you are Yahweh. You see yourself as a god in your own right. You gravitate toward positions of leadership, which means you are either a leader in the church or pursuing to become one. You actually expect to be worshiped. You do not see it this way, but that is the truth of the matter. You force weaker Believers to worship you instead of The Most High, the same way that natural pedophiles and rapist force weaker persons to have sex with them.

You try to manipulate other Believers into your way of thinking. You are highly defensive and take it very personally if they do not agree with you. You will surround yourself with young, immature Christians that are easily controlled. You most often times will have an entourage of *"yes"* men and women around you, who agree with everything you say and do. You are a prime candidate for satan to use to start new cults. Occultism is all about mind control, deception and empowerment of the leader. Likewise, that is what this spirit is all about, and that is what you are all about.

Just like a rapist utterly violates a person's rights and tries to steal from them, you do the same thing amongst other Believers. You are constantly speaking into the lives of others, trying to control everything they do. You want your voice to be the loudest voice that others hear. You will of course be drawn to youth ministry. You will also gravitate toward singles ministry, recovery ministry, marriage ministry – or any of which is likely to draw in the most broken, weak and vulnerable people. These are the people that you are looking to take advantage of. You will "fix all their problems" and then have them pledge their loyalty to you.

Because you oppose submission to authority and want to create your own kingdom, you are inclined to leave the church and start your own ministry. When you leave, you will take with you all of those that you have brought under your power. With this spiritual rapist persona, you will pirate people of their spiritual value and worth. You are an intimidating leader that is subject to quickly "putting people in their place". You enjoy humiliating people. Anything that will depower people, and keep them in need of your leadership is likely to be a vice that you use against them. You strip people naked with your words, and then reward them with accolades to try and make them forget about it.

If you are reading this and find that you match this profile, even if only 50% so – I warn you that it will not take as much as you think to cross the line into the physical manifestations of this spirit. Please get some help right away! It is advisable for you to step down from leadership for a time to allow healing and cleansing to take place.

You do not have to tell people why you are stepping down; nor should you concern yourself with what they think about it. Do not let your fear of other people's opinions send your soul to hell! You need a professional, spiritual counselor and team of anointed intercessors to help you get thoroughly delivered. If you don't do this, you will soon find yourself involved in regrettable behavior and you will eventually be found out. Everything done in the dark, will come to the light.

The Worship Portrait

"Our enemies rape the women and young girls in Jerusalem and throughout the towns of Judah." (Lam 5:11)

As seen in this scripture, rape is often an act of war. Still, in many war-ridden countries today, the women are raped as part of the tyranny of warfare. It is important to understand that the root driving force behind the spirit of rape is PRIDE. Rape is not about physical pleasure. It is about much more than just sexual lust; it is a bloodthirsty lust for power. The spirit of rape is a spirit that wants to violently seize, subdue, conquer and destroy.

The reason that rape is used as an act of war is, first and foremost, raping the women of your enemies strips the men of their manhood. It is the ultimate act of debasement for a man to watch his woman get raped. The next purpose for raping women is to leave "your mark" on them. You make an everlasting impact on a person once you rape them. You put your seed in them and that person, in a sense, becomes yours. Often times, after stripping women of their value and subduing them through acts of rape, the women are held as slaves. Most women after experiencing such humiliation will not ever try to escape. They become completely destroyed inside.

One of the greatest conquerors in the Bible was the king of Babylon. In the book of Isaiah there is a passage of scripture that talks about the destruction of the king of Babylon. The ruler of Babylon, in this text, is actually a high order of spiritual wickedness that operated through the different Babylonian kings, rather than a particular ruler that is being referenced. This spirit is believed by scholars to be a prototype for satan himself, and the following text is often thought to be referring to the literal kings of Babylon and satan interchangeably. In chapter 14 it reads:

"*[6]You struck the people with endless blows of rage and held the nations in your angry grip with unrelenting tyranny... [13]For you said to yourself, 'I will ascend to heaven and set my throne above God's stars. I will preside on the mountain of the gods far away in the north. [14]I will climb to the highest heavens and be like the Most High."*

I share all of this to help you understand that under the influence of this spirit, you are being driven by a bloodthirsty and prideful lust for power. You are a deceived individual with a distorted understanding of Yahweh and His Kingdom. With you perceiving yourself equal to The Creator in many ways, any type of relationship with Him will be dysfunctional. No one will worship someone or something that they perceive to be inferior to or equal to themselves. There is nothing to say about your intimacy with The LORD, because you have none. You are incapable of experiencing true intimacy in any relationship, including a relationship with God.

What is worse than that is the judgment that will come upon you, if you don't repent. Shedding innocent blood, *(remember the blood of covenant that is released during sexual activity)* is one of the seven things that The LORD hates. There are very few times that the word "hate" is associated with the character of The Father. When this word is used, it speaks of His strong disgust and utter intolerance for such things and those involved in them. He wants nothing to do with an unrepentant heart that is laden with the traits of the spirit of rape.

"*[15]Therefore his calamity shall come suddenly; Suddenly he shall be broken without remedy. [16]These six things the LORD hates, Yes, seven are an abomination to Him: [17]A proud look, A lying tongue, Hands that shed innocent blood, [18]A heart that devises wicked plans, Feet that are swift in running to evil, [19]A false witness who speaks lies, And one who sows discord among brethren." (Proverbs 6:15-19)*

Insights from Dr. Intimacy

The Unsung Victims of Sexual Abuse

Being raped or molested is a terrible experience for anyone to have to go through. I know what it is like to be both raped and molested. I know what it is like to have a pedophile living in the home with you. I know what it feels like to be violated and robbed of what is rightfully and sacredly yours. I know what it is like to be tricked, lied to and betrayed by someone you love. I know what it is like to experience the fear that your victimizer will kill you when he is finished. Yes, I know what it feels like. I have experienced it more than once or even twice.

The nightmares do not soon go away. You remember the look in their eyes, the smell of their breath and the touch of their skin. You remember the press of their body on yours. You remember the fear, the panic and the helplessness. It seems that you cannot get over the disgust of it. You try to wash it away, but you never feel quite clean. You become worthless and dirty in your own eyes, and you feel as if that can never be changed. You remember the confusion and the anger that follows. The anger stays with you and sometimes turns into bitterness. The distrust lingers on and on until you are completely bound by it. You have been robbed and violated and even the thief himself cannot return to you what has been stolen.

As terrible as it is to be sexually violated, one of the most devastating and pivotal experiences of my life was not my own molestation. I was able to handle my own violation much better than I dealt with the day my older sister was raped. Her molestation had been occurring for nearly a year before then, but on that particular afternoon it escalated to sexual assault. I was only seven years old at the time. At that age, I had no conscious memory of the molestation and rape in my earlier years because I had blocked it all out. Therefore, I had no understanding of what sex or "penetration" was.

Her abuser always used to send me downstairs to "watch my baby sister". As long as I agreed to stay downstairs, I was rewarded with video game time. He informed me that he and my old sister would be "working on her singing" and could not be disturbed. He would watch me walk down stairs, the door would then be closed, the music would go loud and I would go off to fantasy land with my video games – none the wiser to what was really happening.

I started to get curious about these "practice sessions" when I noticed how miserable my sister always was afterward. My sister loved to sing. I couldn't understand why she was so miserable after "singing with Daddy". I asked, but she would never tell me. Then she began to ask me to stay and "practice" with them. I tried to persist with my stepdad, but he gave me two options: 1) Go downstairs and enjoy my developing video game addiction. *Or,* 2) Come upstairs and get whipped with a horse whip. *"Hmmm... Let's see – video games, or horse whip?"*

Nonetheless, my sister's escalating panic was becoming more and more apparent to me. She asked me to knock on the door during the "sessions" and say the baby was crying. I did my best. Sometimes I had to do something to make my little sister cry, in order to have an excuse to come upstairs. But every time I did, his threats grew fiercer. I had seen him use that whip on my sister – I was sure I wanted no part of it!

The last time one of these "sessions" occurred, my sister was extremely panicked beforehand. I had never seen her so stressed about "practicing". I guess she had a premonition, that God-given women's intuition that no woman can escape. She begged me to stay upstairs, but after a year of asking her why she hated practicing so much and not getting an adequate answer, I just couldn't risk it. If there is one moment in my life I could take back; if given the option to change just one decision from my past, it would be that one. I would take a licking from that horse whip every day, for the rest of my life, to spare what happened to me and my sister that night.

As I sat downstairs playing the video games, I was interrupted by the sound of Dad leaving the house. I asked him where he was going, but he just abruptly walked out saying he'd be back. I ran upstairs to ask my sister where he was going. She was in great distress. She kept saying, "He did it. I can't believe he did it. Laneen, he did it."

"Did what?" I asked in total confusion.

"He put it in me. He penetrated me!" She cried.

"What? Put what in you?" I asked.

"He tied me up and put it in me!!! His thang." I knew what a 'thang' was. That was our slang terminology for the word 'penis'. I heard what she was saying, but I couldn't comprehend it. As I looked at her with a blank stare of disbelief she said, "You don't believe me? C'mere. Let me show you!" At that point she took me into our parent's bedroom and showed me the bed and made me put my hand in the wet spot on the bed.

I still didn't understand what she was saying. *My little heart that loved my Daddy so much, the Daddy that I had prayed and prayed for after my own biological father walked out on me...* I just couldn't wrap my mind around it, or I *refused* to. My sister began to cry hysterically and she begged me to tell Mom, saying that Mom would believe me but would not believe her. All I could think about was the horse whip. If he did *"whatever he did to her"*, what would he do to me? I did not have the courage to get involved. I was so afraid and confused.

I will never forget how my sister stormed off in anger when I said I wouldn't tell Mom. I will never forget that look of utter abandonment and fear that consumed her very essence. A thick, black layer of failure and self-loathing came over me at that moment that I have not been able to shake to this day. I have spent much of my life being labeled as quite the "trouble-maker", due to my need to protect the innocent and heavily guard "my duty" to do so. It has often times manifested in rebellion against authority and put me in situations trying to help people that I have not been at all equipped or called to help.

That experience changed my whole life and my sister's as well. Neither of us were ever the same. It is painful going through the details of this story, but I need to paint a graphic enough picture for you to understand how the experience deformed my self-perception and laid the ground work for life-long issues with my sense of self-worth. My dominating thoughts became re-directed toward my hatred of self and it totally reshaped the course of my life. I always thought that if I could just help enough people, if I could stand up against enough abusive authority – it would make up for that moment of failure that had defined me for so long. Only as of about one year ago, was it even revealed to me why I have been so strong-willed and rebellious throughout my life. And I still, even to this day, have to fight the urges to "make up for failing my sister". It is a lot better, but I can't emphatically say that I am completely whole in this area.

You should understand that the person who is directly violated is not the only victim of sexual abuse. From that moment everything that I knew about life changed. My Mom went into a depression and I have never seen her fully restored. My older sister was destroyed. She left home at 16, got married at 18, only to be divorced a few years later. I lost the Daddy that I had prayed for and my younger sister lost him as well. She grew up angry and bitter that he was not in her life, never knowing the real reason he was gone. The stress caused my body to breakdown and I was stricken with Lupus, just a year later. Even years later in my own marriage, it affected me as a wife.

I love my stepdad. I have forgiven him. However, when I confronted him as an adult about how he hurt me, he screamed at me saying that he did nothing to me and owed me no apology. He took away my sister's right to sexual purity and tried to take away my right to grieve about it. That hurt as badly as the injustice from my childhood did and has prevented us from having a close relationship, to this day. He said I was trying to "condemn" him for something that God had already forgiven him of. But that is not the case. ***"Daddy, if you ever read this, I just wanted to know that you understood that you hurt me too with your actions; and I wanted to know that you were sorry for doing so."*** That is all I wanted, and still want to this day because when a person is remorseful, it is some assurance against them repeating the offense in the future. Without remorse, it is way too likely to happen again, or is at least a great fear in the minds of those that would be affected if it did.

If you have already committed this offense, I beg of you that you get help at once. You have, and will continue to destroy so many lives by allowing this spirit to operate through you. Not only are you hurting the persons you victimize, but you will also be responsible for victimizing everyone connected to them. Father God loves you and will forgive you. He understands why you behave the way that you do, and He wants to help you. He knows that you are hurting and that you yourself were victimized so badly. Although what was taken from you as a child can never be given back to you, Yahweh can restore all that is missing within you. The Bible says that *"He will restore the years (Joel 2:25)..."* He wants to heal you and set you free and restore <u>all</u> back to you. Please do not hurt anyone else. Just give The LORD a chance. He loves you.

And by the way, after you have been helped, don't forget to go back and apologize to **<u>EVERYONE</u>** that was affected by your actions, as many times as is needed, to express full remorse!

Chapter 15

Bestiality

"A man must never defile himself by having sexual intercourse with an animal, and a woman must never present herself to a male animal in order to have intercourse with it; this is a terrible perversion." (Leviticus 18:23)

Some Biblical References

Leviticus 18:23, 20:15-16, Eze 23:20; Dan 5; Rev 13

The Definition

Sexual intercourse or any type of sexual contact with an animal.

The Assignment

Bestiality is a perversion against the order of nature that is dark and disturbed. To become one, with that which you were given dominion over, is to show hatred for your authority, your honor and your prestige. To hate what you are and become like what you are better than, is what this spirit will cause you to do. **This spirit is assigned to completely darken your understanding of your identity as a human being or your likeness to The Creator. It wants to draw you completely away from Yahweh God. It aims to take you to the point of no return.**

The Practical Understanding

There is not really too much to say about this perversion because the literal manifestation of it needs little explanation, but for the sake of thoroughness I will outline some of the physical acts of bestiality. Any type of sexual involvement with an animal is a form of bestiality. This would include intercourse vaginally or anally. It would include oral contact, whether you are using your mouth on the animal's genitals or you are allowing an animal to lick your genitals, which is a common form of bestiality. It would also include any type of fondling of the animal, sexual abuse of the animal or use of the animal's body to sexually stimulate yourself *(such as placing your dog on your lap and gyrating sexually with its body heat and movements as a stimulant).*

It is a practice of some male homosexuals to allow small rodents, such as gerbils and lab mice, to crawl into their rectums and bring them to orgasm. This, or anything like it, is a form of bestiality. Also, experiencing sexual arousal, while intentionally watching animals have sex, is an act of bestiality. This includes pornography that involves sexual contact with animals. One more subtle act of bestiality is "animal fantasy" before or during sex. This is using mental images of animals having sex with each other, or sexual contact with you, to stimulate yourself sexually. Using those images to then have sex in animal-like positions, with the intent to emulate animal sex, falls under these acts as well.

What the act itself entails does not require a lot of discussion. However, the question of 'why' must be answered. Why bestiality? What is the appeal? How does it enter in to a person's life and heart? This spirit can enter into your life through a generational curse. It can enter in through sexual lust or a hatred for The LORD. Exposure to satanism and occultism can also bring this spirit on. Having an unnaturally hateful person in your life, at a vulnerable time, can also create an opening for this spirit. Of course, exposure to bestiality through a relative, friend or mentor as a child can introduce it to your life as well. And as with any demonic spirit, having sex with a person who suffers this oppression can inflict you.

The Personality Profile

The personality profile on bestiality is not complex. Once bestiality becomes your strongman, you will be inherently evil with no desire to repent or be restored back to normalcy. You will have no natural love within you for people, not even your parents or children. You will haphazardly hurt others without remorse. You will even get to the point of shunning humanity altogether because after a while, you will lose your identity as a human being. You will lack natural affection, and even the most basic moral principles and human values will be foreign to you. You will have no regard for other's feelings or appreciation for what others may try to do for you.

You have no goals, no dreams and no ambitions. You are likely to be heavily addicted to drugs, alcohol and porn. You are a violent person that argues or fights easily. A relationship with you is impossible. You are incapable of loving anyone or showing affection. You cannot love anyone because you do not even love yourself. You experience a lot of self-loathing and are likely to abuse your body through an activity such as self-inflicted cuts. If you can tolerate to be around another human being long enough to have sex with them, you will act out other sexually deviant behavior such as sadism, masochism or rape. As far as what you do with your life, it all depends on how much you got accomplished before this spirit really took over you. If it was late enough in life for you to get a good start on things, then you may do well. If this spirit enters into your life at an early age and really takes over though, you will get nothing accomplished. You will probably be poor and unaccomplished in all things.

As this spirit takes over your life more, you will become a mean and hateful person, who is mentally warped. You will have no respect for people, The Creator or any of His creation. You will not care about the environment or starving children in Africa. You just will not care ***period***. Your only care, if you have one at all, will be for the animals you connect with, which you may literally worship.

The Churchgoer Profile

The spirit of bestiality can truly take you to the point of no return. As a matter of fact, if bestiality is your strongman, you would probably never even pick up a book like this. It is highly unlikely that a person truly bound by this spirit would ever step foot in a Christian church or have anything to do with a Loving Creator. However, I must still include this section because I can't assume that there is no one at all in church that is seriously bound by this spirit. Furthermore, though you may be operating under this spirit, I can still appeal to you if it is not yet your strongman.

If you are churchgoer that is operating under the influence of bestiality, half of the time you do not even want to be bothered with religion. When you do attend church though, you have trouble fitting in and lack a sense of belonging and connectedness. You are ashamed about the way you feel toward The LORD at times; too ashamed to let anyone else know about it. Because many church people are so judgmental, if you have ever tried to confide in anyone, you were probably ridiculed and judged and pushed that much further into isolation. Yet, it is hard for other churchgoers to understand how someone could be so unnaturally disconnected from Yahweh. For this reason, you will not enjoy fellowshipping with the saints and avoid church functions and gatherings.

You are very uncomfortable during service, especially during worship and prayer. You will never voluntarily go to the altar. During the preached Word, you feel incapable of comprehending what is being taught. You have a very warped and unnatural interpretation of scripture and the Heavenly Kingdom. You are anxious to leave service and get out of the presence of deliverance. You prefer a dead-like, quiet church with a routine religious service that ends quickly. You are infested with demons that have little tolerance for being in a service.

You have no desire for a higher calling in ministry. You do not want to serve in any capacity in the church. You do not care about the salvation of lost souls. You often times sit in service and wonder what you are doing there. You are not even sure if you really believe in God at all. You feel like a foreigner in a foreign land. You cannot identify with others in the church and have no sense of who you are. It bothers you to see other happy, smiling saints. You will challenge the messages of faith because you do not want others to believe what you cannot embrace. This is all due to your inability to identify and be one with The Father.

If you see any signs of this spirit operating in your relationship with The LORD, bind it now and seek out prayer from someone who is seasoned and mature in love. If you do not soon get delivered, you probably never will!

The Worship Portrait

The spirit of bestiality is empowered by the insatiable lust of the flesh that is in the world. The Bible calls this sin a *"terrible perversion"*. What is so terrible about this sin though? Most people just find the thought of it detestable, but what really makes this sin so terrible is how inordinate and unnatural it is. Having sex with animals is a common practice in many satanic cults and that gives evidence to this spirit's assignment.

Man was created to worship The LORD – to fellowship with and have communion with Him. That is why we are the only creatures on earth created in His likeness and His image *(Gen 1:27)*. Any type of sexual perversion is a deviation from The Creator's intended purpose for mankind and is against His nature, but having sex with an animal is as far away from the natural order of creation as one can possibly get. We were created to have dominion over the animals of the earth, not to submit to them and become one with them through intercourse and sexual contact!

Anyone <u>sold out</u> to the spirit of bestiality utterly hates The Father and has no relationship with Him at all, aside from their hatred of Him. However, if you are a Believer that is not totally sold out to this spirit, but have fallen victim to it to some degree, whether physically or just spiritually, your relationship with The LORD is distorted in specific ways. You have a "love-hate" relationship with Yahweh, but you can't go on like this forever. You are lukewarm most of the time, and if a change is not made, He will spew you out of His mouth *(Rev 3:16)*.

Similar to the spirit of homosexuality, this spirit also affects your ability to produce spiritually and blinds you to your identity in Christ. However, this spirit goes a step further and distorts your identity as a human being altogether. The Word of The LORD says that man was created with a glory that is just a little lower than that of the angels *(Ps 8:5)*. To have sex with an animal prevents you from being able to even identify with humanity, and therefore almost hopelessly thwarts your hopes of ever being one with The Creator and Your Savior or taking on His nature. *(You likely are already sexually involved with animals or soon will be.)*

Yahweh is Love, but your love has grown cold. You worship the creation rather than The Creator and take on the nature of the beast. Just as there can be no greater deviation in nature from having sex with your spouse to that of having sex with an animal; so there can be no greater deviation in spirit from worshiping Yahweh God, to willfully worshiping satan. That is why this act is called *"a terrible perversion"*. This spirit's aim is to create in you a totally sold out satan worshiper.

If you are reading this book and bestiality is your strongman, maybe you just picked it up out of curiosity, or maybe the power of the Holy Spirit overcame you. Whatever the reason is, you are in a good place having this book in your hands. The fact that you have continued to read it shows that you do still care somewhere deep in your heart. The part of you that longs for your true Creator is crying out for deliverance, and if you want it, you can have it starting today – starting even right now! Please do not let the conviction that you feel pass away from you. If it does, you may never get another chance, as The LORD will eventually turn you over to a reprobate mind.

People that are involved in acts of bestiality are just too ashamed to admit it most of the times, which means that you refuse to seek help. You are even ashamed before The LORD, although He already knows what you are doing. Do not let the spirit of guilt and condemnation cause you to perish. Conviction comes from the Holy Spirit of Yeshua, but condemnation and guilt come from satan. Conviction motivates and moves you to pursue liberation, while condemnation paralyzes you in a prison of shame. The enemy wants you to feel too ashamed to seek out deliverance, but do not be fooled. Your Father still loves you and He wants to help you.

Do not wait until it is too late! Go to the epilogue on page 303 and find out how to become Born Again, and then continue to read this book. Find someone you trust or even a clergyman that you do not know, to confide in. Repent before Yahweh in the name of Yeshua and get prayer. He can and will break this stronghold off of your life! If you want me to pray for you, you can send me a message by email at drintimacy@drintimacy.com.

Insights from Dr. Intimacy

The Desensitization of Society

Although I had some exposure to this sin through school friends, I did not even really know what the word 'bestiality' meant growing up. Manifestations began when I got into a relationship with a domestic abuser in my twenties. His unnatural hatred for all of existence is the opening that made the impact. This man was extremely abusive and extremely hateful. He had six daughters, and his five year old he particularly hated. He would frequently say to me, *"I can't stand that f*%king, b#%tch!"* I could not understand how someone could hate their own child so much. He hated old people, white people, children, animals, babies, his own parents and siblings – he just hated everyone and everything – including me and my son. He especially hated anything that had to do with church or God.

We lived together during our relationship, and during that time I brought two cats home. It was then that I first began to fantasize about acts of bestiality. I began to strongly desire to watch animals have sex and found myself to be sexually stimulated by this activity. I also at times, had fantasies about my cats and emulated their sexual behavior during intercourse. I had four cats, prior to these two, and had never experienced any sexual stimulation or fantasies, thus I am certain that it was my connection to this man that brought forth this manifestation in my life.

Thankfully, what I have mentioned is as deep as it got in terms of the actual physical manifestations of bestiality in my life. These happenings occurred many years ago, and I think what helped temper the temptation was society's view at large concerning bestiality and animal cruelty. Even as the atheist that I was at that time, I was disgusted at thoughts of having sex with animals and disturbed by my enjoyment watching them engage in intercourse. However, I can say that the identity issues, bouts with mental illness, such as multiple personality disorder, and an unusual ability to hate people stayed with me for many years – even after I became Born Again.

Today, things in society have changed. Imagine a world where you can flick through the channels and see acts of bestiality depicted on local TV, in a non-threatening and even appealing way? A world where bestiality can be seen in a movie or one where it is readily available to view on-line? Actually, you don't have to *imagine* it because that is the world that we currently live in.

Not so many years ago, a popular actor played a scene in a comedy movie where he fell in love with and had sex with a donkey. There are websites that you can go to that are solely dedicated to bestiality porn. NBC has a special that aired, containing a scene where a man has sex with a pig. And the worse one of all – a very popular TV show geared toward teen-agers, whose plot basically revolves around werewolves who get involved in relationships with "regular humans". You can even see subtle forms of bestiality in cartoons, where human characters fall in love with an animal or vice versa.

It may all seem innocent. *C'mon, what's a little bestiality in the media in the name of good, down home, mind-numbing entertainment? Right?* Wrong! Twenty-five years ago, seeing homosexuality depicted in mainstream entertainment threads was radical – *risqué* at best. Today however, you can find homosexuals and their agenda proudly displayed in every media venue that is available for our entertainment.

The media was strategically used to desensitize society and numb its disdain toward homosexuality. A little joke here; a quick glimpse there; a tear-jerker TV drama over here… Little by little, mainstream society became "comfortable" with seeing homosexuality. How common was it in your childhood to see two gays displaying affection in public? What heterosexual Christian could have ever imagined that the government would legalize gay marriage? Are we headed in the same direction with the desensitization of society toward bestiality? Can we expect 25 years from now to see a man proudly fingering his dog in the park, or expect to hear a priest say *"I now pronounce you man and beast"*?

That probably sounds ludicrous to you, but it may not be as far-fetched as it seems. On December 1, 2011, the Federal government, the Senate specifically, passed a bill legalizing bestiality in the military! If the leaders of our country have become that desensitized to the act of bestiality, what will the rest of the country do? How will the media respond? What will happen to the children that will be exposed at a younger and younger age? It is really something to think about because the bottom line is this, with so many people being angry or bitter toward God, this spirit could easily manifest itself prevalently in society, in the very near future. *A little joke here; a quick glimpse there; a tear-jerker TV drama over here... Little by little...*

2 Timothy 3:1-5, NLT

"[1] You should know this, Timothy, that in the last days there will be very difficult times. [2] For people will love only themselves and their money. They will be boastful and proud, scoffing at God, disobedient to their parents, and ungrateful. They will consider nothing sacred. [3] They will be unloving and unforgiving; they will slander others and have no self-control. They will be cruel and hate what is good. [4] They will betray their friends, be reckless, be puffed up with pride, and love pleasure rather than God. [5] They will act religious, but they will reject the power that could make them godly. Stay away from people like that!"

Chapter 16

Promiscuity

"Why spill the water of your springs in public, having sex with just anyone?" (Prov 5:16)

Some Biblical References

Duet 22: 21; Prov 2:16, 5:15-23 6:24, 7:5, 23:27; Sol 8:9; Eze 16:25-36, 23:19-29; Hos 1:2; Mat 7:6, 10:16, 1 Rom 13:13; Thes 5:6

The Definition

Lacking discrimination or selectivity, especially when referring to a number of different sexual partners.

The Assignment

A promiscuous person is typically one that has sex with many different partners. Most of these sexual encounters take place in non-committed, aimless relationships that only serve to provide temporary pleasure in the flesh. Although temporary in the flesh, the works of promiscuity can be everlasting in the realms of the spirit and soul! While promiscuity is not an actual spirit of sexual perversion, it effectively assists spirits of perversion. **Its assignment is to assist other demon spirits (sexual demons as well as other types) in gaining access to your life. Ultimately, it is assigned to scatter, deplete, distract and confuse you.**

The Practical Understanding

Before we learn about the last spirit of sexual perversion, which is sexual lust, let's discuss promiscuity. When promiscuity is prevalently operative, sexual lust will usually be greatly facilitated. You should keep this in mind as you read the next chapter. But promiscuity is about much more than just empowering lust, so let's get an understanding of promiscuity and how it works.

Promiscuity cannot in and of itself be the sexual strongman, nor is it an actual *act* of sexual perversion. Promiscuity is a spirit that acts as an assistant to other demon spirits. Promiscuity is not assigned to any one spirit in particular. It will work with any of the other spirits of sexual perversion that may be operating in your life. There are, of course, some acts of sexual perversion that are less likely to use the aid of promiscuity, such as the act of incest, which induces you to focus on just one person. Then, there are some acts of sexual perversion that cannot be effective without the aid of promiscuity, such as prostitution, in which case you will have sex with scores of people. In most cases though, no matter which spirit of sexual perversion is your strongman, promiscuity is going to be operating in your life to at least some degree.

The moment you move on to your second sexual partner, unless your spouse has died and you have remarried, promiscuity has entered your life. You were truly created to have sex with only one partner in your lifetime, and therefore having even just two partners has already altered The Creator's perfect design. Yet, promiscuity will not stop at just two sexual partners in a lifetime. Promiscuity's assignment, when working alongside a spirit of sexual perversion, is to cause you to commit acts of sexual sin with as many different partners as possible.

Once promiscuity can find an opportunity to operate in your life, its job is to open the door for other demons so that those spirits may build new strongholds of influence around you. The Bible teaches us that the act of sex causes two people to become one *(1 Cor 6:16)*. You are literally joining yourself together with whomever you commit acts of sexual perversion with. This brings forth the understanding that when you commit an act of perversion with someone, any spirit that oppresses that person, then has access to you through your connection with him or her. In this way, exponentially more spirits of sexual perversion can gain access to you. You may not actually become "possessed" or "infested" with every demon that is associated with your sexual partners. Those spirits, will however, have access to your sphere of influence. Once they have that access, it can be just a matter of time before you commit a new act of perversion and possibly become indwelt by those demons.

Something that we have not talked about yet is the fact that the names that have been listed for these spirits of sexual perversion are just **categorical headings**. There is not *a* spirit of prostitution operating in the earth, or *just one* spirit of homosexuality responsible for all acts of that kind. For each heading or title name that you have been taught, as representing different acts of sexual perversion, there are innumerable spirits that operate in the earth bringing forth the manifestations of those acts. Each of these innumerable spirits is attempting to carry out the specifications of the assignment that is listed under its category.

Furthermore, each spirit will operate within the limitations or greatness of its power because there are different levels of power among demons. *(We can read about this in the Bible in Ephesians 6:12 and Matthew 12:45.)* In actuality, it is possible for you to have two, three or even more spirits of the same kind operating in you all at once, each functioning with a characteristic rank of power. Mark 5:9 and 16:9 respectively read: *"[5:9]Then Jesus demanded, 'What is your name?' And he replied, 'My name is Legion, because there are many of us inside this man.'" "[16:9]After Jesus rose from the dead early on Sunday morning, the first person who saw him was Mary Magdalene, the woman from whom he had cast out seven demons."*

I tell you this to help you understand that promiscuity will not only open doors to spirits and acts of sexual perversion you have never committed before, but that it can also enable spirits of sexual perversion that are already operating in your life to manifest themselves more strongly. For instance, I already had a presence of the spirit of prostitution operating in my life as early as age fourteen. It was not a very strong presence though, and had only been able to manifest itself through those less blatant acts of prostitution.

However, after making sexual contact with a street prostitute, the spirit of prostitution gained a much stronger presence in my life. The sexual connection that I made with the street prostitute gave more powerful spirits of prostitution entranceway into my sphere of influence. Those new and more powerful spirits began to work along with the spirits that were already present, thereby increasing the effectiveness of the overall assignment. Consequently, I went from just dancing on stage as a stripper, to fulfilling "off-stage request", to making plans to go out of town to work a street corner in Atlanta. Thankfully I never fulfilled those plans, but this is how promiscuity works in your life.

The Personality Profile

Even though promiscuity is not an actual act of sexual perversion and is only an assisting spirit, it is a very dangerous spirit. Just think of all of the demons you are exposing yourself to when you have sex with different people. You are opening the door to every demon of perversion that is associated with the person you have sex or sexual contact with. This means that if you are strictly heterosexual, and then have sex with someone who is homosexual – homosexuality now has a doorway of influence in your life. You may then see that act manifest at some later time. What makes it so bad is that it is not only spirits of sexual perversion that gain entrance into your life through sexual contact. ANY type of demon that is operating in the life of the person you connect with will now have access to you. It could be a spirit of anger, hatred, addiction, manipulation, witchcraft or otherwise. A demon of any kind can enter into your sphere of influence through the workings of promiscuity, causing you to take on that spirit's nature.

Have you ever done something that was really uncharacteristic for you and just asked yourself the question, *"Where did that come from? Why in the world did I do that?"* A lot of times these are the workings of demon spirits that have been transferred into your life from someone you had sex with. I started smoking cigarettes when I was fifteen, just months after being in an on-going sexual relationship with a guy that smoked, even though I had always hated cigarettes. I started selling drugs shortly after getting into an on-going sexual relationship with a guy who sold drugs. I began to crave violence after being in a sexual relationship with a man who loved death and murder. The list could go on and on. Through our sexual contact, I picked up their demons and the character flaws associated with those demons.

It having already been established that two people actually become one through sex; you have to understand that you are not only receiving spirits, but losing them as well. That is why promiscuity can bring about emptiness and confusion in your life. You are allowing to enter into the space around you, influences that were not before present – and losing the presence of familiar spirits that you have become accustomed to and dependent on. Think of it in the way that professional athletes are traded between teams. Demons negotiate with one another for access to you!

Also, sexual contact can create a soul tie. When that happens – *and it almost always does* – you become not only one body, but also one soul. The soul being defined as the mind, will and emotions; understand that you are exchanging thoughts, desires and feelings with your sexual partner. The soul tie that is created during sex does not automatically cut itself off at the end of the session. It is a "tie". Until that soul tie is broken, there will be a continual exchange from soul-to-soul, regardless of time and space.

You are losing your individuality and unique identity with every person you have sex with! Having sex with different people is like taking different jigsaw puzzles and mixing the pieces of them all together. Let's say for example, you and every person you have sex with are each represented by a 5,000 piece jigsaw puzzle. Now think of approximately how many people you have had sex with. Now think of mixing all of those different puzzles together. Now imagine trying to sort them out; imagine the despair of trying to make sense of the jumbled mess that lay before you!

Bear in mind also that if the people you have had sex with, have already had sex with others, then they were already jumbled up when you met them. And the people they had sex with may have been jumbled up already too. **Oh my LORD**, what chaos and confusion this causes. Your entire soul will eventually consists of the fragmented pieces of the many wounded, wicked and dysfunctional people that you have had sexual contact with. You will not even possess all of your own fragments anymore, and yet you will contain a multitude of fragmented mess whose owners cannot be identified.

That is why if you have promiscuity operating in your life, you are suffering from an identity crisis. One of the most common non-sexual spirits that you are going to see in conjunction with promiscuity is confusion. Because confusion is in your life, you cannot really define who you are. You really do not know what you are or what you want to be. And this is especially true if you became promiscuous at a young age because when you are young, you have not yet had a chance to fully develop accurate thinking processes, emotional stability or defined desires. You have not even yet been established as an individual, as opposed to being defined as someone's son or daughter. You have not *discovered* yourself in The Creator, nor have you had a chance to perfect and polish who you are.

With this being the case, the effects of promiscuity can lock you into a place of indefinite immaturity. You can spend your entire life with a stunted mentality and uncontrolled, childish emotions and desires. Promiscuity takes its assignment as an assisting spirit very seriously, and you better take it seriously too. You are losing your ability to think, feel and want independently of others more and more, every time you have sex with someone who is not your spouse. You are losing yourself. You are becoming more mentally confused each time you connect with someone.

One of the most detrimental impacts of promiscuity is that the effects of its workings in your life extend long beyond the sexual experience. Referring back to the example of the jigsaw puzzles – you can stop mixing new puzzles into the jumbled mess. However, that is not going to cause the ones that have already been mixed together to automatically sort themselves out. The pieces of your soul will still be scattered across the earth, and you will not know what in you is really you or really a fragment of someone else. The demons and habits that you pick up through the workings of promiscuity will stay with you for years, maybe even for life.

Promiscuity manifests itself as a personality type and not an actual act, and therefore I cannot list all of the personality traits. Pinpointing the personality traits of promiscuity is not so easy. A promiscuous person has the traits of many different human souls and demons. The influence of this spirit in your life could really manifest itself in an endless number of ways. This is a picture of such complex confusion that only the Holy Spirit will be able to sort you out and put you back together. Only by allowing The Father to come in and make you whole once again, and restore you back to His image and likeness, can you be healed and redefined as an individual.

The Churchgoer Profile

Promiscuity is going to have essentially the same effect on your personality both in the church and out of the church. For this reason, we will discuss more of the common character flaws associated with this spirit in this section, as they relate to your experience as a Believer. The spirit of promiscuity will have no particular or direct bearing on your likelihood to be a regular church attendee. Instead, it will simply manifest in your characteristics the same was, whether you attend church or not. The only difference that will be noticed is that the person who is not a professing Christian will display more *obvious acts of sin* than the person who is a Believer.

If you are a sexually active person that has sex with more than one partner, the fact that promiscuity is operating in your life is obvious. But just as is the case with each of the other demons we have discussed, this spirit can still work in your life even if you are not committing any **acts** of sexual perversion. Because it is not an act, the spirit of promiscuity often manifests itself as this seemingly harmless, fun-loving personality type that is often ignored. In the absence of sexual activity, or as a Believer that is having sex only with your spouse, you may not consider this spirit to be a threat to you. However, promiscuity is about more than just sex with different people.

Just look again at the definition, *"Lacking discrimination or selectivity..."* If you are a person that never really has a favorite anything; if you instead of choosing one, take them all; if you are in love with someone new or adopt a new person to be your "pet-project" every month; if one week this show is your favorite and the next week it is another show; if you change friends often, or if you just do not care who you hang out with; if you feel a need to be a part of everyone and everything; if you get explosively passionate about every new venture you take on and then fizzle out: you have a spirit of promiscuity operating in your life.

Being choosy about whom you let into your circle of association is important, in and out of Christ, but as a Believer selectivity is even more important. We are often warned, in the Bible, of the dangers of false prophets and doctrines *(2 Pet 2:1-3)*. We are also admonished to separate ourselves from other churchgoers that are not walking uprightly before The LORD. We are furthermore, strictly charged to sanctify ourselves from the world *(2 Cor 6:17)*. Promiscuity will hinder your ability to fulfill any of these mandates.

There are a number of different ways that spirits can gain access to your life. Sex is only one of those ways. Promiscuity does not have to work only through sexual relationships. It can work through friendships, fellowships, teachings, the media and activities. Promiscuity wants you to expose and passionately connect yourself to as many different things, people and entities as possible. Maximum exposure yields the greatest opportunity for new demonic influences to enter your life.

Promiscuity is going to affect your prayer life, your study of the Word and your intimate worship. It drives you to connect with things and people so often that you are left with no quality time for Yah. Not spending that quality time with Him is going to leave you confused about His true call on your life. In church and in life in general, you are going to be truly indecisive about almost everything. You are not going to be sure if you want to sing or dance or usher or even be in church at all. You will be unsure if you are called to be an evangelist or a teacher or a pastor. Not being able to make a decision about what is, and what is not, for you in terms of ministry work, will keep you all over the church trying to do everything. You will be totally misplaced and completely ineffective in the work of The Kingdom.

Having an indiscriminate nature is also going to leave you open to believe just about anything. You are highly susceptible to false teachings. And with no time to study the Bible for yourself, you will probably never know that you have been duped. The influence of this spirit will furthermore stifle your ability to discern spirits. You will accept just about anything or anyone – anything goes with you, and everyone is *OK*. You are not able to watch and pray when this spirit is operative in your life because you are too busy trying to be a part of everything and everyone. You have to be in the mix of everything. You can never miss anything. Even when you have no real purpose for being involved in what is going on, you feel compelled to be there. You cannot effectively see the picture, when you are always a part of the picture.

You are one of the churchgoers, leaders included, that have to always be at someone else's church or have someone else at your church. You are constantly running and gunning and talking about the need to preach out or *'fellowship'*. That's *if* you even have a church that you regularly attend. There is a good likelihood that you are a church-hopper, moving from church to church, from week to week – desperately trying to find "the place" where you feel connected. All of the seeking and church-hopping will become a hindrance to authentic spiritual growth. Gathering together is important, but it should never come before your intimate relationship with The Father!

The dangers of this assisting spirit are very real. The most common personality trait for you, in and out of church is **CONFUSION**. This spirit's greatest assignment is to ultimately bring about confusion in your life and keep you aimlessly busy and distracted. Examine yourself and make sure promiscuity is not in your life.

The Worship Portrait

There is not much to say here. The worship portrait of a person operating under the influence of promiscuity could be summed up in just one single word – DISTRACTION. You are too distracted by all of the energy of other souls and spirits, going on within you and around you, to stay focused long enough to get a breakthrough in worship. You feel disconnected when you "try" to worship, as if your prayers are not going through. Your mind is all over the place. You are thinking about a phone call you need to make, what you will cook for dinner, the service you were at last night... anything at all except being present in that quiet moment with The LORD.

As a matter of fact, *"stillness"* is an enemy to you. You do not know how to function in quiet places. You have to make a call or have the TV on or the internet open or the radio playing – something; anything to make noise. The scattered, fragmented condition of your soul becomes painfully obvious when everything is still around you, and therefore you deny quietness a place in your life. Another thing that makes having a real worship experience impossible for you is the difficulty you have crying. Brokenness and contriteness of heart is a necessary element of deep, meaningful worship. But nothing is really meaningful to you; nothing is sacred to you. You are involved in too many things to really grasp the value of any of them. Your own experiences are not even meaningful to you. You cannot even stay focused on your pain long enough to cry about it. Some joke, experience, movie scene or motivational quote will pop into your mind and break your concentration. The next thing you know, you will be laughing out loud, instead of weeping before The Father.

You lack control over your mind. It darts all over the place like a sparrow or a fly. Intimacy is a deliberate choice. It takes conscious effort to make it special. Because worshipping Yahweh does not give you any immediate gratification of connection, the mental focus that is necessary to labor in worship before Him will always escape you. More than likely, you will end up getting a good nap when you lay before Him. Then you will wake up, just like you went to sleep – CONFUSED!

Insights from Dr. Intimacy

The Number One Cause of Divorce is Marriage

Promiscuity was a serious stronghold in my life, and it really effectively executed its assignment. There were a lot of openings for promiscuity to gain access to my sphere of influence. However, I think what really allowed promiscuity to operate at maximum capacity were the wounds of rejection that infected me. When a person experiences rejection, they begin to feel desperate to connect with anyone and anything. This was certainly the case with me, from as far back as pre-school. Rejection was prevalent throughout my childhood and really escalated when I got sick. By the time I started having sex, I just wanted to be a part of anything or anyone that wanted to be a part of me.

For a long time, I just did not care anymore. I was so confused about who I was and why I was alive. I was just a mess. I cannot even describe to you how worthless and used up I felt when it was all said and done. I did not know that I was giving a part of myself away every time I had sex. I did not know what was happening to me, but I knew that I felt very scattered and empty. I felt all warped and twisted inside. I could not even begin to fathom the remote possibility of me ever being whole again. How could all of the missing and scattered pieces ever be reclaimed?

I am saddened that I did not have an answer to that question before I got married in 1999. I had sex with so many people before I got married. The revelation that I am about to share with you could have very well saved me from becoming a wife, when I was not really available to do so. It is unfortunate that so many sincere Christians get married, with the best of intentions, but perish due to the lack of knowledge that I am about to share with you: **The number one cause of divorce is marriage!** *Marriage at the wrong time, for the wrong reasons, under the wrong circumstances – a marriage that is doomed long before the couple says "I do".*

The marriage that I am speaking of that is the number one cause of divorce, is the one that takes place between two people who are already tied to, and in covenant with another (*or others*). It has been discussed thoroughly in this book how sex creates a blood covenant between the partners that engage in it. And surely, I have expressed it clearly enough, in the chapter on fornication, that marriage begins with sex, not a ceremony. There are many, many scriptural references to prove this – more than I am even willing to share here in this brief article. But let's look at one story that hits the nail right on the head.

"²¹Finally, Jacob said to Laban, Give me my wife (fiancée), for my time is completed, so that I may take her to me. ²²And Laban gathered together all the men of the place and made a feast [with drinking]. ²³But when night came, he took Leah his daughter and brought her to [Jacob], who had intercourse with her. ²⁵But in the morning [Jacob saw his wife, and] behold, it was Leah! And he said to Laban, What is this you have done to me? Did I not work for you [all those seven years] for Rachel? Why then have you deceived and cheated and thrown me down [like this]? ²⁶And Laban said, It is not permitted in our country to give the younger [in marriage] before the elder. ²⁷Finish the [wedding feast] week [for Leah]; then we will give you [Rachel] also.... (Genesis 31:21-23, 25-27)"

Here we can clearly see that Jacob ended up with a wife that he did not intend to have. He paid a dowry for Rachel, but that did not make her his wife. They held a wedding ceremony for him and Rachel as his fiancée, but that still did not make her his wife. Regardless of the ceremony held, the money paid or even Jacob's great love and desire for Rachel – it is Leah that became his wife that night! When he had intercourse with Leah, they became married. If you continue to read on in the story, a week later Jacob is allowed to have intercourse also with Rachel. It is not until that happens that she "officially" becomes his wife.

Having intercourse is what constitutes a marriage, in the eyes of The Father. All of the licenses and ceremonies and wedding vows and rings that we make such a fuss over in this country, do definitely enhance the experience. However, in essence, they are man-made customs that have nothing to do with what The Creator honors as a marriage. Bearing this in mind, how many people in this country go through the wedding ceremony process as virgins? I do not have any specific statistical data, but I saw one study that suggested only around five percent. However, if we tighten the guidelines on what it really means to be a virgin, according to everything we have learned in this book – a person that has had no sexual contact **AT ALL** – the percentage might drop down to .0001%!

But even by the broadest definition, most people are walking down the aisle to get married, when they have already been married multiple times, without ever getting one single divorce! It is no wonder why 90% of all marriages are affected by adultery. According to what we have learned about marriage in The LORD's eyes, almost 100% of marriages **begin in adultery** – so of course it will manifest at some later time. Then let's take into consideration all of the soul-ties created through promiscuity. In most cases, soul ties to every person the bride and groom has had sex with before each other *(and even other people that they just got really close to)*, still exist. How in the world can anyone expect a marriage to thrive, when starting off under these circumstances?

Is this article making sense to you yet? Number one, both parties of an engaged couple are already married to other people. Number two, neither of them knows who it is that they are really marrying because the person that they are engaged to is merely a collection of fragmented souls. The <u>actual person</u> that belongs in that body that they are so attracted to, is scattered across the face of the earth, like ashes in the sea! If I had known when I got married, what I know now – I never would have taken those vows. I did not even know who I was standing at the altar that day. It is only now, after experiencing the trauma of divorce, that I finally understand why my marriage was so unhealthy.

I was devastated when I realized that my husband and I would be getting a divorce. I was so confused and angry. *How could this happen to two good Christian people?* After the divorce was finalized, I was obsessed with getting an understanding. I knew that I did not want to spend the rest of my life as a single woman, but certainly I did not want to find myself in another unhealthy marriage. I asked Yahweh to show me how to prepare for marriage the **right way this time**, and what you are about to read is part of what He shared with me. So please, take this to heart when considering if *you* are ready for marriage or even available to get married in the first place!

Break All Soul Ties Before Getting Engaged

A soul tie is created in the soul, not in the spirit or the flesh. This is important to understand because your soul is your mind, will and emotions. A soul tie has nothing to do with your body or your spirit. A soul tie is when you are intellectually, desirably and/or emotionally dependent upon a person, place or thing, as a source of stability, security or fulfillment. You read correctly – *you can be soul-tied to places and things* too, not just people.

A soul tie cannot be broken by prayer alone, and you cannot "cast it out". Pleading The Blood of Jesus won't get it done either because it is not a spirit you are dealing with. To break a *soul tie*, you have to do some *soul searching*. You need to discover why your soul has become dependent on who or what it is tied to. You must go all the way back to the season of your life in which the tie was created and evaluate what void was being filled or need being met or stability was created through the tie.

Understand that a "tie" anchors you and can give you a false sense of security. Thus, once you discover exactly what benefit the soul tie is providing for you, you have to replace it with something else. Find wholesome relationships or activities that provide those same benefits, without becoming dependent on them. Let The LORD alone be the anchor for your soul. Let Him provide your stability because the only legal soul tie in The Kingdom, is the one that should exist between husband and wife *(Eph 5:21-33)*. If your soul is already tied to other people and things when you get married, how will you effectively become one with your spouse?

As you break all soul ties in your life through *"the discovery and replacement method"*, and spend adequate time in The Father's presence, allowing Him to reveal your purpose to you – He will begin to rebuild the scattered pieces of your soul. In the Potter's House He will remake you, and you shall be whole again. This should be a **COMPLETE** work before you even get engaged because before this process is complete, you really have no idea who you even are. The person that is finally revealed, when wholeness is fulfilled in your life, may not be pleased with the person that the "scattered, false you" chose for a mate!

<u>Divorce All Previous Spouses</u>

We know that sex creates a marriage, but just as a reminder from chapter 2 of the book: It is more specifically the blood exchange that occurs during intercourse that creates the marriage covenant. Remember that the blood is exchanged during each sexual encounter, whether the people involved are virgins or not. Before Yeshua died on the cross on our behalf, sexual blood covenants were everlasting. They could only be broken by death and thus even if you gave your spouse divorce papers, you were still in covenant. The divorce papers gave you the right to not be obligated to live and care for each other any longer. However, those papers did nothing to break the sexual blood covenant that had been made. Nothing on paper can ever break, change, correct or rectify something that has been established in the spirit.

Just as a soul tie has nothing to do with the spirit, a sexual blood covenant has nothing to do with the soul. Paperwork – divorce papers – appease your intellect. They trick your mind into thinking that you are no longer in covenant with your spouse. Yet, if according to the Bible paperwork cannot marry you, then nor can it un-marry you! It took partaking of each other's bodies and blood to make that covenant, and it is going to take partaking of The Body and The Blood of The New Covenant to break it.

*"²²And as they were eating, Jesus took bread, blessed and broke it, and gave it to them and said, "Take, eat; this is My body." ²³Then He took the cup, and when He had given thanks He gave it to them, and they all drank from it. ²⁴And He said to them, **"This is My blood of the new covenant**, which is shed for many. (Mark 14:22-24, NKJV)"*

If you recall in chapter 2, we learned about the parallel between sex and the practice of communion. With that understanding, it is much simpler to break a sexual blood covenant than you might think. To break all sexual blood covenants and **TRULY DIVORCE** all previous spouses, you need to take a dedicated communion. It need only be done in brokenness of spirit and contriteness of heart, as a Born Again Believer in Yeshua The Messiah (Jesus Christ), as Your Lord and Savior; with understanding of its purpose, and faith in its power and effectiveness. You do not need to fast, plead, beg, call out everyone's name or anything complex such as these things.

The Blood of Yeshua was shed to **COMPLETELY ERADICATE** all of our sins and give us a New Covenant. That Blood has not lost its power and there is no blood covenant in existence that can stand against the Blood of the Lamb of God, Who takes away our sins and fixes our mistakes. Performing this communion, in repentance and in faith, will make you a spiritual virgin, who is truly available to enter into a wholesome, adultery-free marriage. Refresh your understanding, by reading chapter two again. And when the time comes, make sure your spouse-to-be applies this same principle, so that he or she will be divorced and available too!

Chapter 17

Sexual Lust (Lasciviousness)

"For all that is in the world, the lust of the flesh, and the lust of the eyes, and the pride of life, is not of the Father, but is of the world." (1 John 2:16)

*"Now the works of the flesh are manifest, which are these; Adultery, fornication, uncleanness, **lasciviousness**," (Gal 5:19 KJV)*

Some Biblical References

Gen 6:11; Ex 34:15; Num 11:4; Job 22:24, 31:1, 31:11; Psalm 68:30, 81:12; Prov 6:25, 11:6, 27:20; Isa 57:5, 57:8; Jer 2:24, 2:34, 13:27, 51:39, Eze 16:30, 16:36, 20:30, 21:16, 23:8, 23:11, 23:17, 23:20; Hos 7:4; Nah 3:4; Mat 5:28-29; Rom 1:27-31, 7:8, 13:13; 1 Cor 7:9, 10:6-8; Gal 5:16-21; Eph 4:22; Col 3:5; 1 Thes 4:4-5; Heb 13:5; James 1:14-15, 4:2; 1 Pet 1:4-6, 4:3; 2 Pet 1:4, 2:3, 2:10, 2:14; 1 John 2:16-17

The Definition

Lust – A desire for that which is unrighteous or detrimental; the willingness to break laws of Righteousness, in order to get what you want.

Sexual lust – Craving, longing, or desire to achieve sexual gratification through acts of sexual perversion.

Lasciviousness – Extreme sexual lust; sexual lust completely unbridled and totally unrestrained; the insatiableness of lust that will drive one to create endless new ways to commit sexual perversion. All acts of sexual perversion that are not mentioned by name, within the assessments, fall under the category of lasciviousness *(i.e. orgies, sadism, masochism, sex with demons, etcetera.)*

The Assignment

Lust causes you to desire to have or do something that you know you shouldn't. It is also the willingness to do something that you know is wrong, in order to acquire a legitimate need or want. Lust can quickly take an otherwise innocent situation and turn it into something wicked. **This spirit is assigned to make you feel a complete loss of control over your mind, body and soul; one desperately driven to satisfy the nature of your flesh. It is assigned to totally consume you, until you completely give in to the heart of satan. It will breed in you total hostility for Righteousness, making you a slave to sin, resulting in separation from The LORD and spiritual death!**

The Practical Understanding

Have you been unable to identify your strongman as of yet? Maybe you have seen yourself in several of these assessments, but you have not yet been able to pinpoint exactly which spirit of perversion is really dominating in you. It is probably because sexual lust is your strongman. Sexual lust, although a very strong spirit, is one that cannot be easily identified as the strongman because it does not operate with its own unique identifying *act* of perversion.

Before I explain why this is, let me make sure there is no confusion concerning the difference between sexual lust and sexual impulse. Sexual impulse is the physical urge to be sexually gratified and is not in and of itself a sin. Almost every human being was created by The Creator to experience sexual urges, at some point in their life. The spirit of sexual lust goes beyond just the natural, inbred urge to be sexually gratified. Sexual lust occurs when you actually begin to desire acts of sexual perversion, in order to fulfill your natural sexual urges. You must exercise discipline to prevent sexual impulses from turning into sexual lust.

Lust, whether sexual or otherwise, is a sin in its own right. Just the fact that lust is present in one's heart, is evidence that evil and sin resides within that person. The Bible says that lust is not of The Father but of the world *(1 John 2:16)*. Lust is not just a desire for something. It is a desire for something that is evil and contrary to Holiness and Righteousness; it is the desire to do something wrong, to get something right. The reason that sexual lust is not easily identified is because the sensation of lust itself is not an actual **act** of sexual perversion. The spirit of sexual lust must work through the manifestations of some other spirit of perversion, in order for an actual **act** of sin in the flesh to take place. This is what makes sexual lust so difficult to identify as the strongman.

If sexual lust is your strongman, you are dealing with the greater stronghold of *"lust of the flesh"* that is in the world. Sexual lust is just another manifestation of that greater demon of lust in general that operates within the entire earth. If this is the dominating sexual spirit in your life, it may be the case that no particular act of sexual sin is your weakness. Sexual lust drives you to seek out sexual gratification in whatever vice is available to you at that time – whether it is fornication, masturbation, bestiality, incest or otherwise. It does not matter. You just want to satisfy that craving.

The spirit of sexual lust can drive you to commit any act of sexual perversion. You might have a favorite act of sexual perversion. You may even turn your nose up at other acts, but you have to understand that lust just wants the craving to be satisfied. If, at the time lust consumes you, your preferable act of sexual perversion cannot be fulfilled for some reason, you will settle for whatever other act is available. This includes even acts you swore you would never commit. Sexual lust will drive you to do things that you never dreamed you would do.

Sexual lust is the spirit that causes you to have sex with the ugliest person you know, even though you are not attracted to them. It is the spirit that will cause you to commit homosexuality, even though you have always been homophobic. It is the spirit that will cause you to cheat on your spouse, even though your marriage is solid and your spouse the person that you really want to be with. Lust will cause you to do **anything, anywhere, anytime** without **any thought** of the consequences that may follow.

Have you committed acts of sexual perversion that are not listed in the assessments? Acts such as sex with dead people, orgies, multiple partners in one night, swinging, sex with demons or masochism? These acts do not each have their own individual category because the Bible does not expressly describe them. Because lust is never satisfied, the world will never cease to think of new ways to pervert intimacy, and so the Bible just sums it all up with one word – *lasciviousness*. Whatever you are into, that may have not yet been named, is implemented by the spirit of sexual lust. **Sexual lust is your strongman.**

If sexual lust has already gotten to the stage of lasciviousness in your life, you are in a great level of bondage, and it is unlikely that you would even be reading this book (*unless you thought you might get some new ideas)!* Lasciviousness is an INSANE LUST, and only a sane and sound mind can consciously choose to accept Yeshua as LORD and servitude to The Father.[6] To put it plainly, **LASCIVIOUSNESS IS EXTREME LUST.** It is lust completely unrestrained and totally out of control. Most people involved in acts of lasciviousness have been exposed to satanism, occultism or witchcraft. This exposure may have been intentional and obvious *(i.e. voodoo, spells, incantations, calling on demonic powers)*, or intentional but out of ignorance *(i.e. horoscopes, physics, deceptive religious group, mind control, manipulation)*. Either way, lasciviousness only occurs in your life when you have, with extreme prejudice and hostility, alienated yourself from The LORD. You have intentionally rebelled and pledged allegiance to satan – if not by your words, certainly by your actions!

In the case of lasciviousness or otherwise, sexual lust makes your flesh burn. This spirit can actually convince you that you are going to literally die if you do not do something to satisfy the craving immediately. It makes you restless. It takes over your mind and your body all at once. It is an ambushing spirit that likes to attack you

---

[6] If this does describe you, and you are somehow, by the Mercies of The Almighty God reading this book, I beg of you to accept Yeshua (Jesus) as your Lord and Savior right now. You can turn to page 303 to find out how, or just pray to re-dedicate yourself to Him, if you once knew Him but then turned away. He must be seeking after you to have given you the fortitude to read this book. Please open the door of your heart for Him.

suddenly. It will lie dormant and then suddenly attack you at a time that you feel unprepared to deal with it. It will then incite some act of sexual perversion, in order that your lusting can be satisfied. Sexual lust often works through sexual fantasy. This is because the desires of lust are most easily fostered and empowered through sexual fantasy.

In any case, the other spirits of sexual perversion cannot operate in your life without the partnership of lust. The <u>desire</u> to commit the act of sin is what finally causes most people to fall. However, it is important to note that *'sexual lust'* is only one type of lust. James 1:14 reads, *"But every person is tempted when he is drawn away, enticed and baited by his own evil desire (lust, passions)."* Every sin, whether it be lying, stealing, cussing, hating or fornicating, is birthed out of our own different types of lust – greed *(lust for more)*, gluttony *(lust for food)*, jealousy *(lust for attention)*, hatred *(lust for death and murder)*, gossip *(lust for destruction)*, loneliness *(lust for companionship)*, stealing *(lust for provision or material possessions)* and so on, and so forth... The point is simply this: *'lust'* and *'sin'* are two synonymous and interchangeable words. The definition of lust is NOT *'sexual sin'*. The definition of lust is *'the desire for unrighteousness; the willingness to break The Law'*.

The reason that I am defining what lust is and what it is NOT is because it is important to understand that **NOT EVERY SEXUAL SIN, IS BIRTHED OUT OF SEXUAL LUST**. For instance, some people commit acts of sexual perversion and do not at all desire the act itself and/or get no enjoyment out of it. If this is the case, it is the desperate need to fill an emotional void that drives you to commit acts of sexual perversion, without sexual lust being present. There are times when couples, through mishandling love, express sexually what they share with one another. This type of sexual sin is no more the product of sexual lust, than a person stealing food to feed their children is the product of greed. It is important to know and discern the difference because it helps you determine whether or not sexual lust is your strongman.

The Personality Profile

If sexual lust is the dominate spirit of sexual perversion operating in your life then you are undoubtedly an impatient, restless, greedy, desperate, untrustworthy, selfish and envious person. These traits are manifested because if sexual lust is present in your life, other manifestations of lust are present as well. You are restless and anxious to satisfy your lust. The deception here though, is that **lust can never be satisfied**. Lust is **ALL** that is in the world. This whole world's system is founded in lust, and it always wants immediate gratification, and it will never be satiated!

Therefore, if the spirit of sexual lust binds you, you will certainly be a greedy, impatient individual that is never satisfied and is always restlessly trying to fulfill your desires. You are so desperate to satisfy your lust that you will beg, borrow or steal. As was stated previously, this spirit makes you feel as if you absolutely cannot survive unless the craving is satisfied. That sense of "a need to survive" creates a feeling of desperation within you, and you cannot be trusted. You cannot be trusted because you will do anything to satisfy your own desperate, greedy cravings.

Your mindset is all about the first law of nature – **Self Preservation**. This means that lust breeds selfishness in you. You do not care who you have to hurt or let down or hinder, in order to satisfy your lust. It could be your children, your friends, your family, your employer or anyone else. Anyone or anything that is standing in the way of you satisfying your lust is going to be crushed. You are loyal to no one because lust is a slave driver; you are allowed to serve only it. You can be unreliable because of this and do not make a dependable friend to people.

This does not mean that you will not have friends; it means that you cannot be depended on to keep your word because you are so easily taken in another direction when lust calls. Lust is a covetous spirit, and thus you are an envious person. You are never satisfied with what you have and always want what someone else has. Lust makes you think that you must have what they have, and drives you to go after it. But no matter how much you have, you always want more. **YOU ARE NEVER SATISFIED.**

Sexual lust literally makes your flesh burn, and that is why the Apostle Paul says in the Bible that it is better to marry than to burn with lust *(1 Cor 7:9)*. Paul was not encouraging people to just find any old *Tom, Dick* and *Harry* – or any *Sue, Jane* or *Mary*; but he knew how dangerous this spirit of sexual lust is. Most of these other spirits that we have discussed take over your life somewhat slowly. You can see what is happening with the other spirits and regain control, before it is too late. However, this is not so with lust. Lust blind sides you. You never know that it is coming, and by the time you realize it, it is often times too late to fight it. Sexual lust will cause your life to spiral out of control so fast that you will not even be able to remember exactly how and when it happened. You will just know that you are now lost in blinding darkness and trapped within your own evil desires and the consequences thereof.

Lust is all that is in the world. Lust is the spirit of the world. Lust is the soul of satan.

The Churchgoer Profile

Sexual lust is the most likely spirit of sexual perversion to be the strongman of a Born Again Believer. This is because, more than any other spirit, sexual lust plays on your natural inclination toward sexual desire. Every other spirit of sexual perversion operates out of some spiritual void or emotional wound within you. As you get closer to Yahweh and the voids are filled, those spirits no longer have a place to reside; they are cast down and become inoperative. But the demon of sexual lust is an opportunist. It thrives on desires that were naturally given to you by The Creator that *will never go away*. Therefore, lust will always have a channel through which to operate in the church.

Lust does not care if you go to church or not. It is going to try to take advantage of your urges, needs and desires. If you are a truly Born Again Believer, I must warn you that the weaker you are spiritually and the more carnally minded – the more likely you are to be dragged into sexual sin by this spirit. As a true Christian, lust cannot **utterly <u>control</u>** your life because you have Yeshua's Spirit. **<u>With His Spirit in you, it is impossible for lust to be the overall dominating spirit of your entire life.</u>** Nonetheless, it can be the dominating spirit, as far as sexual sin is concerned. If you are really struggling with the spirit of sexual lust as a Christian, it would come as a surprise to me if you are not actually *acting out* some other sin of sexual perversion. It could be fornication, homosexuality or even perversely motivated sex with your spouse. It could be any of the acts that have been discussed.

Lust is a powerful spirit and is usually able to manifest itself in some sexually perverse *act of sin in the flesh*. If you were to tell the truth, you would have to admit that you are often times struck by sexual lust even during church services and personal devotional time. During your pursuit of intimacy with The LORD, you become extremely susceptible to this spirit because of the parallel between natural sex and spiritual worship. Because often times your spirit is already perverted to begin with, you do not know how to separate the two. You become very vulnerable when attempting to worship. It is worth repeating to say that **sexual lust is an ambushing and opportunistic spirit**. It waits until your own natural sexual urges are stirred and then attacks!

Not only during attempted worship, but sexual lust will attack during a situation that is as innocent as washing your genitals while taking a shower. You are performing a necessary function, and the next thing you know, a sexual urge arises. The urge itself is not bad, but if sexual lust is operative in your life, it will seize that opportunity and consume you with burning in your flesh, inciting masturbation. A sister in church may be kneeling at the altar for prayer and her breasts become exposed, causing a stir in your body. That stir is not wrong, but lust will attempt to seize that moment and turn it into a sexual fantasy. Maybe some perverse person on your job touches your butt one day and walks away. Lust will have you to follow after the person and commit adultery. This is the way lust works and because humans are creatures of habit that tend to do things the same way all the time, lust becomes very familiar with the scenarios that will easily trip you up!

If you are operating under the spirit of lust, you will always try to find some excuse to fulfill your evil desires. You are good at twisting the Word of Scripture into something that will support the fulfillment of your lust. You are very opinionated and are blinded by lust from the truth. You are impatient and lack faith. You always want immediate answers and immediate gratification. You will not be able to <u>maintain</u> a close personal walk with The Father because your lust always drags you into sin, which separates you from Him. You are seldom at peace because you are always restless about having your desires met right away. At times, when you are winning the battle, you may be very spiritual and fruitful. But when you are losing, you will see a stark difference in your personality. You ride a spiritual roller coaster and lack stability in your walk with Yahweh, due to the frequency of falling into sin when consumed by lust.

You are greedy for position and prestige in the church. You are the one that preaches for filthy lucre and manipulates people for your own personal gain. You are a dangerous person to put into leadership positions because you are greedy and selfish. You lead according to what will cause you to prosper and to your own benefit. You have no concern for the needs of the people. You may covet the gifts or positions of others, due to envy because you are never satisfied with what you have. You are often gifted but seldom anointed. The anointing is only given to those whom The LORD can trust, and those operating in lust cannot be trusted. You are desperate to satisfy your own desires. Even if your desire is concerning some ministerial pursuit, it is still not according to Yah's will because your motives are not Righteous. Since it is not The Father's will, His blessing is not on it, and you will move in desperation, severely compromising the principles and Word of The LORD, in order to fulfill your lustful pursuits.

So much more could be said about how the spirit of lust manifests itself in the life of a churchgoer. It could actually manifest itself according to any profile previously listed because it can operate through any of the other spirits of perversion. Every Believer, no matter how mature or sincere in his or her Christian walk, is susceptible to the attacks of this spirit. Why? Because we all experience spiritual lows and walk carnally after the flesh, at times. If sexual lust is your worship strongman, I must warn you that you have quite a battle on your hands. But I can encourage you at the same time, by reminding you that the Spirit of Victory is living in you! Yet, you should not take this situation lightly because you are in a very dangerous place.

As a Believer, sexual lust wants to do much more than just cause you to commit acts of sexual perversion. You already learned that sexual lust is actually under the authority of that stronger demonic *ruler of lust*. Ultimately, it is this stronger *ruler of the darkness* that is in the world that aims to control you. When lust is in your heart, it causes you to desire things that are against Yahweh's Righteousness. You can truly love The LORD and really want to serve Him and yet struggle with some really evil desires. You may not always act out these desires, but the fact that they are present within you, is evidence that evil still resides in your heart. This means that the bottom line of the churchgoer profile, for those of you operating under the influence of the spirit of lust is this: **You will not bear the fruit of the Spirit of The LORD, but will instead manifest the works of the flesh.**

The Worship Portrait

Lust is the foundation of every sin on earth that has ever been committed or ever will be committed. *"But every man is tempted, when he is drawn away of his own lust, and enticed.* **Then when lust hath conceived, it bringeth forth sin:** *and sin, when it is finished, bringeth forth death. (James 1:14-15, KJV)"* Satan lusted after Yahweh's throne and Power in Heaven, and it caused him to sin. Eve lusted after the forbidden fruit in the garden, and it caused her to sin. Cain lusted after Abel's relationship with The Creator, and thus he sinned. **Sin begins and ends with lust.**

As was already mentioned, lust is the spirit of world. Therefore, **if lust completely dominates you or has gotten so out of hand that is has become lasciviousness**, you are not truly a *Born Again* Believer in Yeshua. You may be a religious churchgoer, but you are not a **Born Again Believer**. Or, the case may be that you are a completely backslidden, reprobate *former* Believer, but you are certainly not a Christian at all. You cannot be a true child of The LORD and be **dominated** by the spirit of satan. *"...If anyone loves the world, love for The Father is not in him. (1 John 2:15a, AMP)"*

This may sound harsh to you, if you have been considering yourself to be a Christian, but if any type of lust **controls and dominates** your life; you are not of God the Father and do not at all have His Spirit. The above scripture, and many others in the Bible, substantiate this truth. You belong to satan and are not a part of the covenant of reconciliation that was established in the Blood of Yeshua. Your eternity will be spent with your father the devil, *if* you do not repent wholeheartedly and let Yeshua clean your spirit. Please do not be offended by this statement, but instead examine yourself truly, and read the Holy Word of God, in order that you may see yourself in the Light of His truth. Yah can cleanse you and save you, but you must be aware of your **utter NEED** for His intervention!

I have to say that first because you cannot worship Yahweh God the Creator, even in the most dysfunctional way, if you are not yet Born Again. If you are a true Believer in Yeshua as The Resurrected Lord, the more you yield to The Father and delight yourself in Him, by meditating on and studying His Word, the more your desires will change. If you continue to give into lust, by failing to exercise discipline and self-control, by failing to build up your spirit man in the things of The Kingdom; you will be led into more acts of sin. Sin causes separation from The LORD and separation from Him leads to death. Lust wants you to be totally separated from Your Creator; to be sold out to the pleasures of this world and die spiritually. It wants you to be totally consumed mind, body and spirit, with the pleasures of this world and desperately driven to fulfill your evil desires.

Lust is always aiming to become lasciviousness within us, and lasciviousness often times takes people to the point of no return. This is because lust is the spirit of the world, and satan is the spirit of the world. Satan hates The LORD, and if you continue to indulge in lust, you will come to hate Him as well. We can look into the Bible and find two instances of lasciviousness taking a people to the point of no return.

"²And many will follow their immoral ways and lascivious doings...⁵And He spared not the ancient world... when He brought a flood upon the world of ungodly [people]. (2 Pet 2:2a, 5a, c, AMP)"

In these phrases of scripture, the Bible talks about the flood in the days of Noah. What was going on in those days? Lasciviousness had taken over. People were having sex with demons. Sexual lust had gotten completely out of control, and it was said of that people *"⁵Now The Lord observed the extent of the people's wickedness, and he saw that all their thoughts were consistently and totally evil. (Gen 6:5)"* The Creator then destroyed every wicked person on the earth because they loved lust but hated Him. Then again we see Him destroy an entire geographical location that was inhabited by a lascivious people.

"⁷[The wicked are sentenced to suffer] just as Sodom and Gomorrah and the adjacent towns – which likewise gave themselves over to impurity and indulged in unnatural vice and sensual perversity — (they) are laid out [in plain sight] as an exhibit of perpetual punishment [to warn] of everlasting fire. (Jude 1:7)" The Lord said of these people, *"...the shriek [of the sins] of Sodom and Gomorrah is great and their sin is exceedingly grievous. (Gen 18:20b)"* AMP

If you read the entire story that the above two scriptures are making reference to, which can be found in Genesis chapter 19, you will see that these people were unnaturally wicked in their sexually perverse acts. Just as the people in Noah's day, they too desired to have sex with spirit beings. They had no regard or reverence for The LORD God or His Holy beings. In both of these instances, lasciviousness had taken the people beyond the point of no return, and the end result for them was eternal damnation. This is Yah's response to dominating lust. This is what sexual lust wants to do to you!

I believe that sexual lust is the most detrimental spirit to your worship and intimacy with The LORD; more than any of the other spirits of sexual perversion, for the following reasons:

1) You can be whole in Christ and still be confronted with and fall into sexual lust.

2) It can lead you into all other acts of sexual perversion.

3) It takes advantage of your natural desires and everyday needs.

4) It can so quickly take over your life.

5) It can never be permanently shut out because of how it comes in; discipline and self-control must be exercised every day.

6) It can lead you into bondage to a greater stronghold of the ruler of lust, which is the spirit of the world and the soul satan.

Lust can overtake you with lasciviousness and doom you to eternal damnation and separation from The Father, where you will never know intimacy with Him again! *"...Then when lust hath conceived, it bringeth forth sin: and sin, when it is finished, bringeth forth death."* If you lust, you will eventually die...

Insights from Dr. Intimacy

Three Steps to Disempowering Lust in Your Life!

I hope in all that you have read in the spiritual assessment chapters that you have not lost sight of the main point: **The devil wants to steal your worship**. No matter what your sexual vice may be, the enemy is after your worship. I have spoken throughout the book about how these spirits pervert your worship experience with The LORD. But the ultimate goal of satan is not just to pervert your worship; he wants to completely *steal* your worship from Yah. That is what lust is really aiming to accomplish, to altogether destroy worship in your heart.

You can have no consistent intimacy with The Creator when lust inhabits your heart. Because lust can show itself in fleeting manifestations, you may experience some awesome moments of intimacy and worship with Yahweh. But they will be just that – *moments* that will get fewer and further in between. Yet, there is not anyone that does not have a personal experience with sexual lust. Lust is more than just a generational curse; it is a mankind curse. If you are a human being, lust runs in your family! So how can you remedy that? What can you do to protect your worship from the enemy that wants to steal it? What can you do to really have the upper hand on this spirit?

If we can understand how something operates, we can find an effective way to combat it. Since lust takes advantage of needs, desires and urges – let's examine what those words really mean and search out answers in scripture that will enable us to win the battle over sexual lust.

✳✳✳

Need → Desire → Urge

Need - something that you have to have: **Desire** - something that you want to have: **Urge** - something that you are quickened to have.

✳✳✳

Determining what legitimate **NEEDS** are, and sufficient ways to fulfill those needs, is the first step to disempowering lust in your life. **A need is something that is absolutely essential to your very survival. A need is something that you will literally die without**. It's not something that you *feel like* you will die without; it's something that you would *actually* die without. As human beings we only have a few basic needs: air, water, food, clothing, shelter and possibly medicine. Anything not listed here, IS NOT A NEED!

Understanding the difference between *sufficiency* in meeting a need and *abundance* in meeting a need, is important as well. A need can be sufficiently met by the most readily available, least expensive resource. For example, uncontaminated water is a need that can be *sufficiently* met by turning on the average sink faucet. Purified, super-oxygenated water from Mount Everest is NOT a need. That is instead, an *abundant* way to meet a basic need, which means having that particular type of water is a *desire*. If you have limited income and yet insist that expensive, bottled water flown in from a far region is a *need*, lust can overtake you. The basic need for water can give way to thoughts of stealing bottled water that you cannot afford.

To prevent lust from taking advantage of your needs, learn to be content with little. This does not mean that you should not envision living abundantly. However, envisioning an abundant life – in faith that The LORD is going to do exceeding, abundantly above all you ask or think and that He has given you power to get wealth – should not breed discontentment within you. Faith never breeds discontentment; **discontentment is always a product of lust at work in your heart.**

Therefore, your <u>greatest NEED</u> should always be the need for Righteousness. Lustful *"needs"* can never be satisfied, but your need for Righteousness can be! *"**Blessed and fortunate and happy and spiritually prosperous (in that state in which the born-again child of God enjoys His favor and salvation) are those who <u>hunger</u> and <u>thirst</u> for righteousness (uprightness and right standing with God), for they shall be <u>completely satisfied</u>! (Mat 5:6, AMP)**"* For those natural needs of the flesh that have to be fulfilled, always remember that lust is never necessary to satisfy the needs of the saints. *"**And this same God who takes care of me <u>will supply all your needs</u> from his glorious riches, which have been given to us in Christ Jesus. (Phil 4:19, NLT)**"*

<u>**A DESIRE is something that, for an extended period of time, you really want to have**</u>. Some desires could even be classified as *"secondary needs"* because although you can *survive* without certain things, you cannot *thrive* without them. Things that we desire will usually have a long-term, positive impact on the quality of life that we live. A desire that is a secondary need would be things such as: purified air, enriched water, organic food, a clean, safe, adequately spacious place to live, well-fitting, clean, stylish clothes, medical and dental care, a reliable automobile, a loving spouse, trustworthy friends, intimacy, etcetera. This would be a very long list if completely compiled. The general gist is that desires that can be classified as *secondary needs* make you thrive in life and more effective at living.

Then there are desires that do not fall anywhere within the margins of a need: a sports car, a mansion, an oxygen chamber in your bedroom, a one million dollar wardrobe, a trip around the world, marrying a rich king or supermodel, hot steamy sex five times a day... I think you get the point. Deciphering between desires that represent secondary needs and those birthed out of pure greed is the next step in disempowering lust in your life. I iterate again that I am not an "anti-abundance" preacher. I believe that we should have the riches of this world, as children of The Most High God who owns everything. But learning to differentiate between abundance and secondary needs is very important. Too many people are in debt and lusting after filthy lucre for lack of an ability to note the difference! The absence of secondary needs can shorten your life span, but so can the presence of greedy ones. There are so many "things" to desire in life. You do not have enough years available to live that you might experience every pleasurable thing that there is to experience. The constant pursuit of pleasure will lead to a selfish, purposeless, wasted life that is spent up too soon.

Remember that lust cannot be satisfied and thus will drive you to want EVERYTHING. Therefore, your foremost desires should be for the things of The LORD. *"But his delight and desire are in the law of the Lord, and on His law (the precepts, the instructions, the teachings of God) he habitually meditates (ponders and studies) by day and by night." (Ps 1:2, AMP)"* *"I desire to do your will, my God; your law is within my heart. (Ps 40:8)"* Your desire for Righteousness is the one desire that lust can never take advantage of. If you focus on desiring the things of Yahweh, Psalm 37:4 will surely be fulfilled in your life: *"Delight yourself also in the Lord, and He will give you the desires and secret petitions of your heart. (AMP)"*

An URGE is a sudden quickening; a conscious, unprovoked prompting to have or do something. Urges are fleeting, temporary desires that create moments and memories. An urge can feel much like a need because it can be quite overwhelming when it hits. But urges are not needs, and ungodly urges have to be tempered through discipline. An urge to get drunk, masturbate or steal something are examples of ungodly urges that must be cast down. Sometimes an urge can be good; a quickening is what the Bible calls it. You may have a sudden urge to clean or exercise or do something nice for a friend. Urges like this should be indulged and enjoyed immediately, when possible!

Often times an urge can be neutral – meaning that it is neither good nor bad and that your response to it is what is going to determine what it becomes. For example, a sudden sexual impulse is an urge. If you are married, the urge itself is neutral. But what if your spouse is not available? If you fulfill that urge through means that do not involve your spouse, you have allowed lust the victory. If you put that urge on ice until you are with your spouse and can engage in pure intimacy, Righteousness has won! Here is another example. You may have a sudden urge to eat ice-cream. If you are not fasting or dieting and have the funds available to purchase the treat, you have guilt-free liberty to eat and enjoy the ice-cream. But if you buy a quadruple scoop sundae, with triple fudge, double whipped cream and extra everything else, lust has beat you. That is 4500 calories worth of pure gluttony!

An urge is probably the best friend of lust. Urges come suddenly and catch you off-guard. The third and final step to disempowering lust in your life is tempering your urges. Walking after the Spirit consistently; living, moving and having your being in Him; is the necessary element to direct your urges toward Righteousness. Urges rise up out of your sub-conscious mind. Urges are not pre-meditated, and therefore you do not have **direct control** over your urges. However, you do have indirect control over them, by virtue of what you submit to in between urges. Submitting yourself to the Spirit of The Living God and allowing your entire being to be filled with His Righteousness will produce quickenings of empowerment. An evil urge cannot rise up out of your subconscious, if nothing evil is in your subconscious. And a neutral urge will always give way to Righteousness, when good fruit is produced in you through the power of the Holy Spirit.

While you are in the process of being cleansed and transformed, ungodly urges will continue to rise up within you. When they do come, immediately take authority over them, and ask the Holy Spirit to fulfill these scriptures in you: *"Behold, I have longed after thy precepts: <u>quicken</u> me in thy righteousness (give me an urge to pursue righteousness). (Ps 119:40, KJV)" "But if the Spirit of him that raised up Jesus from the dead dwell in you, he that raised up Christ from the* *dead shall also <u>quicken</u> your mortal bodies by his Spirit that dwelleth in you (Rom 8:11, KJV)"*

In conclusion, just like great intimacy between husband and wife begins long before the couple ever hits the bed, so does good spiritual intimacy with The Father begin long before you hit your knees. In order to **PROTECT YOUR WORSHIP** from being stolen by the enemy, you are going to have to live a lifestyle that cuts off the life source of lust. Live as if your flesh is dead and thus prevent lust the opportunity to ambush you through your needs, desires and urges. Dead flesh cannot be used!

1. Don't let lust take advantage of "false needs". Understand what a true need is, and how to meet it sufficiently; knowing that The LORD *will supply all of your needs. Be content in all circumstances, even with little. Let your greatest need be your hunger and thirst for Righteousness.*

2. Don't allow desires to become greedy and lustful. Believe and work toward abundance, but be grateful for what you already have, knowing that more will be added to you through pureness of heart. Let your greatest desire be for living uprightly before The LORD *and having His Word in your heart.*

3. Urges can only be effectively controlled by how you live in between them. Your urges will align themselves and yield to whatever you fill your heart and soul with. When evil urges come, cast them down immediately and ask the Holy Spirit to quicken you toward Righteousness.

Romans 8:1-14, Amplified

"¹THEREFORE, [there is] now no condemnation (no adjudging guilty of wrong) for those who are in Christ Jesus, who live [and] walk not after the dictates of the flesh, but after the dictates of the Spirit. ²For the law of the Spirit of life [which is] in Christ Jesus [the law of our new being] has freed me from the law of sin and of death .³For God has done what the Law could not do, [its power] being weakened by the flesh [the entire nature of man without the Holy Spirit]. Sending His own Son in the guise of sinful flesh and as an offering for sin, [God] condemned sin

in the flesh [subdued, overcame, deprived it of its power over all who accept that sacrifice], [4]So that the righteous and just requirement of the Law might be fully met in us who live and move not in the ways of the flesh but in the ways of the Spirit [our lives governed not by the standards and according to the dictates of the flesh, but controlled by the Holy Spirit]. [5]For those who are according to the flesh and are controlled by its unholy desires set their minds on and pursue those things which gratify the flesh, but those who are according to the Spirit and are controlled by the desires of the Spirit set their minds on and seek those things which gratify the [Holy] Spirit. [6]Now the mind of the flesh [which is sense and reason without the Holy Spirit] is death [death that [comprises all the miseries arising from sin, both here and hereafter]. But the mind of the [Holy] Spirit is life and [soul] peace [both now and forever]. [7][That is] because the mind of the flesh [with its carnal thoughts and purposes] is hostile to God, for it does not submit itself to God's Law; indeed it cannot. [8]So then those who are living the life of the flesh [catering to the appetites and impulses of their carnal nature] cannot please or satisfy God, or be acceptable to Him." [9]But you are not living the life of the flesh, you are living the life of the Spirit, if the [Holy] Spirit of God [really] dwells within you [directs and controls you]. But if anyone does not possess the [Holy] Spirit of Christ, he is none of His [he does not belong to Christ, is not truly a child of God]. [10]But if Christ lives in you, [then although] your [natural] body is dead by reason of sin and guilt, the spirit is alive because of [the] righteousness [that He imputes to you]. [11]And if the Spirit of Him Who raised up Jesus from the dead dwells in you, [then] He Who raised up Christ Jesus from the dead will also restore to life your mortal (short-lived, perishable) bodies through His Spirit Who dwells in you. [12]So then, brethren, we are debtors, but not to the flesh [we are not obligated to our carnal nature], to live [a life ruled by the standards set up by the dictates] of the flesh. [13]For if you live according to [the dictates of] the flesh, you will surely die. But if through the power of the [Holy] Spirit you are [habitually] putting to death (making extinct, deadening) the [evil] deeds prompted by the body, you shall [really and genuinely] live forever. [14]For all who are led by the Spirit of God are sons of God."

Chapter 18

Incubus and Succubus – Sex Demons of the Night

Some people think they are a myth, but for those afflicted by these demons they are all too real. Learn what incubi are and how to get victory over them.

It seems that people are really hungry for understanding of and deliverance from this particular issue. It may be one of the most perplexing sexual afflictions faced by Believers. I once suffered from these attacks myself, so I know how disturbing they can be. As a sold-out, devout, consecrated, prayer warrior for The Kingdom, I was still at times accosted by these demons at night. Like many Christians who suffer these attacks, I thought I was the only one. I did not understand what I was going through or why I was going through it.

I probably would have continued to suffer in silence had it not been for the loud cry for help, made by those visiting my blog. I heard stories that brought me to tears and some that just left me scratching my head but still had no substantial insight to share. Yet, as more and more people came to me desperate for help on this issue, I knew that Yahweh was mandating me to get an understanding and bring forth a Word of deliverance, for those in need. That is why I am so glad to be able to share this information with you. It has already helped a lot of people. I pray that it will help many more.

(You can read about other people's experiences with these spirits on my blog at http://drintimacy.wordpress.com on the dedicated page entitled, with the same title as this chapter. There are many comments on the page, and you can leave one as well, if you'd like to.)

What Are They?

According to *Meriam-WebsterCollegiate.com,* the definition for these two spirits are as shown below:

<u>Incubus</u>: An evil spirit that lies on persons in their sleep; *especially* one that has sexual intercourse with women while they are sleeping.

<u>Succubus</u>: A demon assuming female form to have sexual intercourse with men in their sleep.

These are just basic, secular definitions of these two spirits, which are also commonly referred to as "sex demons", "night demons" or "spirit husbands and spirit wives". These demons are primarily spirits of sexual perversion. Whenever we are talking about demons, always remember not to put too much merit into the common names that they are called by. Spirits go by many names; even God and satan are identified by numerous names and titles in the Bible. Night demons are no more than spirits of lust. They are a powerful, high-ranking class of demon.

Do They Really Exist?

"¹And it came to pass, when men began to multiply on the face of the earth, and daughters were born unto them, ²That the sons of God saw the daughters of men that they were fair; and they took them wives of all which they chose."

The above scripture is from Genesis chapter 6. We looked at this scripture earlier in chapter 3 of this book and learned that its literal interpretation is that demon spirits had intercourse with human women. Maybe you are wondering how it is possible for demon spirits to have intercourse with humans. Throughout the Bible there is plenty of evidence that spirits can take on some type of physical form and function as the creature whose form they take on.

The one called satan, who is a spirit, took on the physical form of a serpent and spoke to Eve *(Rev 12:9, Gen 3:1-4)*. We see another case where The LORD and some angels also took on physical forms and functioned as human beings. If you read in Genesis, all of chapter 18 and chapter 19 through verses 23 *(I suggest the New Living Translation for better understanding),* you will find proof of this. In the text, The LORD, and two angels, manifest themselves as human beings. They actually talk, eat, rest, walk, have their feet washed and even sleep.

Herein is the biblical proof that spirits can manifest themselves in physical form. There are other scriptures that make reference to this point as well. Thus, there is no question in my mind as to whether or not these spirits do indeed exist. As a matter-of-fact, I know by virtue of my own personal experience that they do exist. The encounters that people share about sex demons are actual experiences, as opposed to *"schizophrenic episodes"*, which is how doctors try to invalidate these experiences.

People are sometimes mystified by these spirits, not knowing how to determine if they are actually being plagued by *incubi (plural for incubus and succubus)*. However, whether or not you are being attacked by these spirits is usually pretty obvious. They manifest themselves to your conscious mind and cause you to experience all of the stimulation and physical feelings that take place during intercourse or sexual contact with a physical person. The demons most often reveal themselves to people during the nighttime hours but can manifest themselves at any time of the day. Many people claim to actually see spirit bodies that come and subject them to various sexual acts. These spirits are often violent and will attack you – beating, choking and restraining you. They may even disturb things in your home and break things. Think of them as you would an extremely abusive sex partner or rapist, and you will start to get a picture of what these spirits are all about.

Another effect these spirits have on people is causing **overwhelming** sexual urges in the body. You will know that you are being attacked by demons, if the sexual urges are so strong that they completely take over your mind, even to the extent that you may feel a little insane or tormented. This can happen at any time but tends to be most common when you are lying down. You cannot think about anything else, and it seems like nothing you do to make the urges go away works *(i.e. a cold shower, involving yourself in another activity, shifting positions, etcetera...)*. It seems that the only relief for the urge is to have an orgasm, by any means necessary. Sometimes you will have an orgasm spontaneously, which will be stronger than usual.

If you have these types of urges, THEY ARE NOT NORMAL. Now please understand that I am not saying that every powerful sexual urge in the body is due to a demonic manifestation. Strong sexual urges can be purely hormonal or just good old-fashioned arousal, at the thought of enjoying intercourse with your lover. *(This was discussed at the end of chapter 4 in the "Insights from Dr. Intimacy" section.)* Nonetheless, when sexual urges come on suddenly; without warning at times that seem inappropriate; without any external stimuli, and you simply cannot control them without having an intense tormenting battle – that is when you know they are demonic.

This class of demon is also responsible for sex dreams. In these dreams, you will be engaged in sexual contact or intercourse. Or, it could be a non-sexual dream, during which your body has a spontaneous orgasm. Another, much less obvious, manifestation is nightmares – *realistic, graphic, heart-stopping nightmares* that rob you of sleep and cause you to awaken frightened. Just as is the case with sexual urges, not every sexual dream, sleep-time orgasm or nightmare is a result of an incubi attack. Incubi attacks are very "realistic" and impressionable experiences that will make a weighty impact to you emotionally and spiritually. They are experiences that **deeply disturb**; not something that you get up, brush off and forget about. Such dreams, when induced by demons, also tend to come in cluster attacks, as opposed to scattered, isolated incidences.

What is Their Purpose?

"⁴In those days, and even afterward, giants lived on the earth, for whenever the sons of God had intercourse with human women, they gave birth to children who became the heroes mentioned in legends of old."

Looking at Genesis chapter 6 once again, we learn that the assignment of these demons is to impregnate you. In the above scripture, we learn that when these demons had sex with the women, the women became pregnant and gave birth to abnormal children – children that were perversions of nature. Incubus and succubus are the same class of demon that operated in those times, only now they are looking to impregnate you with spiritual perversion.

Once the spirits get you sexually aroused or subdue you through violence, you will let your conscious guards and defenses down. They are then able to plant their evil in your subconscious mind, where it will go unnoticed for a season of time. Similar to carbon monoxide, though unnoticed, it is actively causing major damage. It can likewise be compared to the way a girl who is being molested gives herself over to the control of her abuser. Once his seed is inside, she does not know where it goes or what it does, but it could be actively changing her in major ways. She may have conceived a child or even contracted an STD, but she will not know it for quite some time.

Remembering again the analogy of the abusive boyfriend or rapist, know that these spirits want to control you, subdue you and make you feel worthless. Although they are skilled at causing extreme sexual pleasure, they make you feel miserable in every other way. The ecstasy that you experience with these spirits is usually exceedingly more intense than most natural sex and is highly addictive. Because of the pleasure your body experiences, you are induced with guilt, which lowers your resistance even more. Just as your natural body is fatigued after intercourse, an encounter with an incubus or succubus spirit will usually leave you feeling emotionally and spiritually drained because they steal virtue from you. In place of what they steal, they impregnate you with their seeds of perversion and lust.

The purpose of them causing nightmares is to impregnate you with fear, therefore perverting your faith. One reason for this is that fear induces a desire to seek out comfort. Sexual activity, especially sexual fantasy and masturbation, brings about a temporary sense of false comfort. Therefore by inducing fear, these lust demons cause you to be that much more likely to commit sexually perverse acts. But even more so than that, *"without faith it is impossible to please God (Heb 11:6)"*. Which means, to pervert your faith, is to literally undermine your entire relationship with Yah and purpose for living.

If it is true that *"all things are possible to them that believe"*, as was stated by Yeshua in Mark 9:23, then the opposite is also true. Without faith, we cannot believe anything, which means we cannot accomplish anything because nothing is possible to us in our subconscious minds. People that are afflicted by these spirits will experience a tremendous amount of failure and may even feel "cursed" with bad luck. It is not bad luck – it is simply that your belief system has been perverted.

Where Do They Come From?

Remember, the main point is that night demons are simply spirits of sexual lust. Bearing that in mind, let's consider again what lust really is. We studied lust in great depth, in the previous chapter, but let me simplify it, even a little bit more. *1) Lust is a **desire** for illegal pleasure. 2) Lust is the **willingness** to meet a natural and legal need or desire, in an illicit or sinful way.* The bottom line is this: LUST IS SIN, and SIN IS DISOBEDIENCE TO YAHWEH'S LAW OF RIGHTEOUSNESS. This is what most people miss in the struggle for deliverance from night demons. There is some open door of disobedience in your life, if these spirits are still able to afflict your body.

Now for some people, to refer to these sexual lust demons as a "uniquely named spirit" *(such as incubus or spirit husband)* draws the person into a "victim mindset". There are so many people who love to be the victim. They do not want to participate in their own deliverance. They just want to continue to feel sorry for themselves and want you to feel sorry for them too: *"Oh these big, ol' bad incubus spirits rape me every night..."* I am not saying everyone is like this, but a lot of people who approach me about night demons are this way.

Truth be told though – NO spirit can "rape" you unless <u>you give them access</u> to your body. Except in a case where you are already literally ***in-dwelt*** by a demon, no demon can access your physical body unless you allow it to. The open door may not have anything to do with sexuality at all. **Any type of disobedience can give a demon access to your body** for its use. For people who are actively and willfully living in sexual sin, the open door is apparent. It is the people who are doing what they believe to be right before The LORD, but are yet still struggling with these spirits, that are the most perplexed. They do not understand why their tactics for deliverance are not working. This was the case with me.

To help bring more understanding, look at what the Bible says, *"All that is in the world is the lust of the flesh, the lust of the eye and the pride of life. (1 John 2:16)"* The term 'world' in this scripture means – *the sin nature of the flesh, and the carnal life, as being separated from submission to Yah's Holy Spirit and His Will*. Your flesh is a part of the world. The nature of your flesh is evil; it always has been and always will be! The open door can be *something you are not doing, in order to subdue the nature of your flesh (such as studying the Bible or praying more fervently)*, just as much as it could be *something that you are doing (active sin, compromising lifestyle)*. It could even be sin that only lives in your mind. Even if you do not act on a lustful desire, you have still sinned by virtue of the desire being in your heart. This, of course, does not mean just a fleeting thought of sin, but it means that somewhere in your heart you desire and are willing to carry out a sinful act – you give it *"thoughtful consideration"*.

If you are truly serious about getting delivered from night demons, then you are going to have to take accountability for not being in your place of authority over these spirits and allowing them access to you through your actions. You have to be willing to really examine your heart and your lifestyle, in the light of The Father's truth, and find that open door. Then slam that door shut for good; be free indeed, in the freedom of Christ Yeshua! Let me help you, by listing for you, these common but often overlooked doors for night demons.

Fornication - Fornication is a word that covers any type or act of perversion *(i.e. adultery, incest, homosexuality, etcetera…)* You relinquish your authority over sexual lust, when you willfully involve yourself with sexual perversion.

Masturbation - Masturbation is particularly inviting, when it comes to the invasion of night demons, because through masturbation you sin against your own body, and subject it to evil. You become a slave to sin through masturbation.

Pornography - Pornography is also particularly damaging when it comes to these attacks. Pornography is an act that specifically aims to contaminate your mind. The reason that these spirits come primarily at night is because your conscious mind shuts down when you are tired and when you are sleeping. It thus leaves you vulnerable to their control and weakens your resistance to evil. Whatever you fill your mind with during your waking hours, is what will reign over you while you sleep!

Unforgiveness/Bitterness - Unforgiveness cuts you off from The LORD's grace, and therefore His ultimate protection. Bitterness gives access to every demon of hell, to invade your temple and your life!

Carnality - Spending too much time doing *non-spiritual activities* – even if those activities are not sinful – can be very detrimental. Any activity which does not **purposefully and deliberately** build and edify your spirit, in the things of God, is a carnal activity. Remember, you are *vulnerable* in your mind during the night hours or times of fatigue. Your decision-making process is impaired during these times. That is when you must totally rely on the strength of your spirit man to keep you from evil. If you do not build your spirit man up, then it will not be strong enough to yield to the Holy Spirit and access His empowerment.

Fear/Doubt – Having fear and doubt in your life opens the door to these spirits because they thrive on fear and aim to increase fear in your life. They want you to be afraid because fear paralyzes you and robs you of your faith, which ultimately robs you of your relationship with Yahweh God and your purpose. It takes faith to believe in Him, in order to begin and maintain a relationship with Him.

Witchcraft - The Bible says that *"rebellion is as the sin of witchcraft (1 Sam 15:23, KJV)"*. Rebellion is another word for disobedience. Thus in all simplicity, witchcraft is to go against Yah's way, in order to do it your own way. There are many manifestations of witchcraft that are overlooked such as – *astrology, superstitions and chain letters.* An especially common but overlooked form of witchcraft is manipulation. Manipulating our children and spouses and others that are close to us is so common, and it leaves the door open for night demons to attack!

Sexual Abuse - Being molested or sexually abused opens doors in three ways. First, it often attaches spirits of perversion to the abused. Secondly, it subjects the abused to a mindset of victimization. In other words, you constantly see yourself as a victim. Remember, night demons are sexual aggressors and they want you to feel victimized. Thirdly, molestation is another doorway to fear in your life.

Verbal/Emotional Abuse - Remember that these spirits are likened to abusive spouses and rapists, meaning that being a victim of child or domestic abuse can definitely introduce these spirits into your life. Any abusive situation is a very comfortable environment for such demons.

Emotional Wounds – It bears repeating that these demons are taking advantage of weaknesses. Being wounded leaves you weak and therefore, leaves you vulnerable to these attacks. That is why it is so important to be healed.

Soul Ties - If you are soul-tied to someone or something or some place that causes you to be spiritually weak or that is subject to sexual perversion or fear; you have now created an open door for night demons. When your soul is tied, there is easy transfer to and from the person or thing that you are tied to.

Spiritual Warfare - The last thing that the Holy Spirit revealed to me is about spiritual warfare. Bearing in mind, once again, that night demons take advantage of the vulnerability factor; you have to remember that spiritual warfare causes spiritual weakness. You must be properly replenished in Word and in worship, after engaging in spiritual warfare – this is especially the case when you are warring specifically against spirits of sexual perversion!

The Dangers of Them

Some people think it is fun to be visited by these demons, while enjoying the intense sexual pleasure that they give. They are very skilled at causing you to feel ecstasy. They are very dangerous though, and the consequences of an encounter with them can be utterly detrimental to you spiritually, mentally and emotionally.

It is important to remember that one of the first keys to deliverance from anything is understanding your enemy! As I prayed and studied, not for *deliverance* but for *understanding* of my enemy, that is when I finally was able to receive the revelation of what I must do, in order to get total deliverance. Whether the incubus/succubus spirit lives "inside of you" or oppresses you from without, is not a major factor in how to go about deliverance. The process is still the same, although it may be a bit more intense and drawn out for someone who has many of these spirits and/or for someone who is literally "inhabited" or "indwelt" by them.

Keeping in the front of your mind that the purpose of incubi spirits is to impregnate you; the main factor of deliverance is to spiritually abort *(not literal, physical abortion)* that which they have successfully planted in you. The casting out or sending away of these spirits will do nothing to tear down the strongholds that they have already successfully built in your life! Therefore, after casting out, binding, rebuking, renouncing or sending away these sex spirits — do the same to all their offspring and seeds.

Sex demons want to impregnate you with fear, which will pervert your faith. They want to impregnate you with lust, which will cause you to desire evil things to satisfy and fulfill your soul. They want to impregnate you with different spirits of perversion, especially those of a sexual nature, so you will help their cause by committing sexually perverse acts with others and transfer their seeds. Lastly, they want to impregnate you with rebellion, which will lead to an interest in all forms of witchcraft. First it will be the more subtle forms — like manipulation for "good" reasons, horoscopes and superstitions. It will then escalate to more moderate forms — palm readings, communicating with stars, good luck charms and trinkets. Finally, it will develop into full-fledged satanism – communicating with the dead, calling for assistance from demon spirits and so much more. The assignment of every demon, ultimately, is to completely disconnect you from Yahweh God and see you eternally damned!

Steps to Deliverance

Disclaimer

*The views and opinions that I express concerning sex demons and their ability to impregnate someone, are strictly spiritual views. I am not a supporter of abortion, legal or otherwise. Furthermore, I would judge, according to the Holy Word of Scripture, the actions of any man or woman that would harm or murder their child, for any reason. It is a spiritual impregnation that I am referring to, and it should be dealt with through a spiritual abortion. Nothing should be physically done to anyone's body, in order to address an incubus issue! *

Seven Steps to Deliverance from Sex Demons

1) You must renounce not only the lust demons that have entered into your life, but you must also renounce their works. You need to **verbally** destroy and renounce and murder everything that they have conceived within you and caused you to give birth to. If you fail to do this, they will always have access to you. This is done through declaring the Blood of Yeshua (Jesus) and the Word of Scripture, out loud. Another important part of this renouncement is declaring your commitment to Christ and His ownership of your body, by taking a dedicated communion. *(If you are not yet a Born Again Believer or are unsure, please go to the epilogue on page 303, and make Yeshua your LORD and Savior. Communion is irrelevant, if you are not Born Again. If you need instructions on how to take communion, you can watch a video by visiting this link www.youtube.com/watch?v=ylqsbisOVio or read about it at this link http://crossingonline.org/taking-communion-at-home. Also, feel free to email me or blog me for questions.)*

2) Depending on your level of bondage and what you are involved in sexually, it may take some time and effort to get complete deliverance. It is likely that after step one, you will have other encounters. If you do have an encounter with a night demon – IMMEDIATELY ABORT WHAT THEY HAVE PLANTED IN YOU. Think of it as taking a "morning after pill". As in step one, this is all about verbal declaration of Yah's Word and denouncing their works through the power of the Blood of The Lamb.

3) DO NOT EVER LET AN ATTACK CARRY ON WITHOUT CHALLENGING THE SPIRITS! When an attack begins, say **verbally and out loud** something like, *"I know what you are and what you are here for, and I renounce you in the Power of the Blood of Yeshua! My body does not belong to you. It is the temple of the Holy Spirit, and I command you to leave me right now, in Yeshua's name! I do not receive your seed into me and will not give birth to your offspring of evil!"* As long as you don't have any *obvious* open doors in your life, this will usually and **immediately** bring under subjection any assault that takes place while you are awake. This includes those incredibly overwhelming sexual urges that come over you and cause you to have spontaneous orgasms or to commit an act of perversion, such as masturbation, pornography or fornication.

As a side note to this step: For sexual urges that are not demonic, a simple "mind over matter" approach is sufficient. Think about something else, or involve yourself in an activity that requires you to concentrate on what you are doing. Also – don't kid yourself! Don't expect this to work if you are still willfully watching pornography, horror films, listening to sex-filled secular music, watching soap operas, reading horoscopes or otherwise. Demons do not like to be <u>challenged</u>; they are seeking rest. You offer no challenge to them, if you live a willfully carnal and sinful lifestyle — you become a place of rest for them, and they ain't leaving (slang intended)!

4) For those attacks that occur while you are sleeping, apply the Blood of Yeshua to your mind, and renounce these spirits <u>before you lay down</u>. Purpose in your subconscious mind to wake up, if you start to have a sex dream or nightmare. When you wake up, IMMEDIATELY ABORT ANYTHING THAT THEY MAY HAVE PLANTED IN YOU! This is so important. You cannot let their seeds grow in you. KILL THE SEED, by pleading the Blood of Yeshua against it! And, **DO NOT REPEAT what you have dreamed about** to anyone at all *(unless briefly when in a counseling situation)*!!! This is *extremely* important. The demons want you to speak out the images from your sex dream because the power of life is in your tongue. Speaking it out gives birth to it. The words you say after an encounter can either give life to their seed or bring death to their seed, and that is why usually your first unction is to tell someone about it. Furthermore, don't rehearse the dream in your mind. Cast down the very thought of it from your conscious and subconscious mind. This is so important, *and remember this applies to nightmares as well.*

5) IT IS VERY, VERY IMPORTANT THAT YOU CONSECRATE YOURSELF! Every spirit must be cast out of your life and every door closed, as much as you are capable of doing. That means that you do not willfully involve yourself in anything at all that is sinful or ungodly. When you do fall or make a mistake, you must repent and get up quickly. Not that you will be perfect, no one is, but every sinful and carnal area of your life must be **CHALLENGED TO THE MAX**. This is especially true, when you are in the midst of a deliverance process. This means that you should *commit* to fasting and praying; but also *omit* every evil influence from your life — people, places, things, habits and ESPECIALLY the MEDIA.

6) Get and study the book, *"STDs: Sexually Transmitted Demons"* along with this one and of course The Holy Bible! If you are experiencing these attacks, it makes it apparent that you do not have a full understanding of sexual perversion and how to walk in total deliverance. Remember that any weakness in your life will allow these spirits in to attack. You need to have a **COMPLETE AND FULL** understanding of sexual intimacy, sexual activity and sexual perversion — what it is, the purpose for it and the remedy for unhealthy manifestations. You will learn this in these two books. No sexual stronghold will be able to stand in your life, once you learn and apply the principles in these two books, along with your personal Bible study notes. Furthermore, understanding these teachings will help you develop your intimate relationship with Yahweh and strengthen all of your relationships.

7) Lastly, I remind you once again that incubi are lust demons. Lust is a force that is ever-present in the earth realm and therefore is not something that you can say, *"I will never face this again."* Everyone is subject to the temptations and pressures of lust because it is the passion of satan's heart, and he is the prince of the world. Not everyone will fall victim, but everyone is subject! Even after you are delivered, anytime that you are spiritually weak it is possible – not likely but possible – for you to have an encounter with a night demon. If this does happen once you are delivered, just remember to implement the steps above, and watch your level of consecration *always*. You especially want to be mindful of the media that you expose yourself to, the people who you are around and any subtle forms of witchcraft that may be in your life *(like horoscopes or manipulation)*.

I know these steps will work because they worked for me, and I have received testimonials from other people that have gotten victory implementing these steps. To help you even further, if you feel that you need it, visit my YouTube page. I recorded a 12 video teaching series that is based on this chapter that you just read. It is very powerful, and I believe it will be very helpful as well. Here is the link to the first video, http://youtu.be/EW77CWne8B4.

Insights from Dr. Intimacy

Divorce the Devil – Get Away from Your Abuser!

I have been researching sex demons for about 10 years now. I initially thought it was a rather simple matter that could be addressed like any other stronghold. I have since gone on to understand that this issue is of grave significance and can be extremely complex. I use to favor the term "night demon" when referring to these spirits, although the most common names used for them are "incubus" and "succubus". There are some other names used as well, but none of those terms seem fitting to me any longer. In African cultures, these spirits are referred to as *"spirit spouses"* – *"spirit husband"* for an afflicted female; *"spirit wife"* for an afflicted male. These are the names that I now favor because I understand that they offer the most accurate natural comparison that can be made, in terms of how these spirits operate.

The most effective way to process what is happening to you, is to perceive this sexual demon as an abusive, jealous spouse. Remember what you have learned in this book about the marital covenant that is made through sex, and understand that these demons want to marry you. Satan is always intent on falsifying every experience that we were designed to have with Our Creator. As we were created to be one with Him and be His intimate bride, the devil concocted his own plan to make us one with him instead.

Through spirit spouses, the devil is aiming to make us his bride. And although the term *"spirit wife"* is used in association with men who are afflicted by these powerful lust demons, understand that demons are genderless. Satan is attempting to emulate, The Church being the wife of Christ, through these sex demons. He wants to make all people, male and female, his unified bride. Just as we are to be filled with the Holy Spirit of The Messiah, he aims to fill us with his spirit.

Satan is the driving force behind sex demons, trying to make himself your *"spirit husband"*, in place of Yeshua. When you think about a jealous, abusive spouse, you can understand that he wants to destroy every good relationship in your life. This is especially the case in a marriage or an attempt to get married. He wants to keep you financially poor, to prevent you from escaping. He wants to keep you isolated to hide the scars that he leaves on you. He is the epitome of domestic violence in your spiritual life!

I know that this particular affliction is frustrating and perplexing for those that must face it. You may feel desperate to learn as much as you can. There are some people that contact me and say, *"Oh you should really read this book about the demon named _____."* Or, *"Check out this preacher who teaches about the spirit of _____."* And people make other suggestions, such as these. However, you have to consider the **source** of knowledge of these teachers that many chase after. Many that teach in the name of "God" are not Believers in Yeshua, as Savior and Lord. They mix in pagan teachings and new age spiritualism, along with biblical principles. Some do believe, but are not equipped to teach on this subject. They lack the anointing to really make an impact with the teachings. Their words are dead. If you visit my YouTube page and watch my videos, you will find that there are hundreds of other videos on incubi. You will see some of them advertised right next to mine; some of them posted by satan worshipers!

Understanding your enemy is definitely a key element in deliverance and victory. However, research can become very distracting. Study can actually hinder implementation of what you have already learned. There is enough information in this book for you to get delivered from any sexual issue you have. You can study this book for the next several years, and learn something new each time you pick it up. This book is literally **The Encyclopedia of Christian Sexuality; God's Handbook on Sex Education**! It is more than enough to start with, and I don't suggest you move between this book and other teachings, until you have **finished this course**.

Unless you have a specific calling on your life to teach and minister in the area of demonology or sexual perversion, I discourage you from chasing after teachings on this topic. The devil would love to divert you away from the *real truth* that will make you free. This is the truth that you need to know: **DIVORCE YOUR SPIRIT HUSBAND**. Kill all of the children that you have borne with him. Move to a spiritual zip code where he can't find you. Get away from your abuser! Use what you have learned in this book, and focus on the most excellent way of all – **LOVE**. The most important thing that every Believer needs to be studying is LOVE – for God is LOVE. Hatred will bow in the presence of Love. Your abuser will not be able to find you, when you live in the Love of God. Chase Love, and the devil will flee. Chase love, and wisdom and deliverance will chase you! *Selah...*

Chapter 19

The Conclusion of the Matter

So much information; what to do with it all? This chapter will give you a jumpstart on the deliverance process so that you can begin to walk in victory every day.

Say this phrase very slowly and deliberately:
"DELIVERANCE IS A PROCESS, NOT AN EVENT."

This is extremely important to come to grips with. I know that you want to finish reading this book and run around in circles in the church screaming, "**I'M DELIVERED!!!**" and never fall again, but that is unlikely to happen. It took you a long time to get in the condition that you were in when you started reading this book, and it is going to take some time and processing to walk in newness. In the first edition of this book, I included an entire section on deliverance; over 100 pages worth of information. I realized though that many people, after reading over 200 pages of knowledge on sexual perversion, were only skimming through the deliverance section.

Thus, I removed that section and am currently editing it into a separate manuscript, which I will probably name *"Breaking the Bonds of Sexual Perversion!"* (Keep an eye on my website for the release of that book some time soon). The reason that I felt led to do this is that TRUE and TOTAL deliverance is a detailed process and a life-long journey. It is a topic that deserves its own platform. I implore you to get a copy of the book once it is released so that you can make the best possible use of all that you have learned in this book. In the mean-time though, I want to give you an overview of the deliverance process, as it has been revealed to me thus far, so that you will at least have something to get started with.

Triune Deliverance for the Spirit, Soul and Body

For years I kept getting "delivered" from things, only to find myself in bondage once again sometime afterward. I would find myself back at the altar for the same struggles over and over again. At times, I was so beat down and discouraged that I just wanted to quit. It really seemed like I was never going to win the battle. Unbeknownst to me at that time, I had not been getting **total** deliverance. I failed to understand the dynamics of an **absolute** deliverance.

Man is a triune being. We consist of spirit *(heart, essence, core)*, soul *(mind, will, emotions)* and body *(flesh, earthly, physical vessel)*. I was getting delivered in only one or two parts of my being at a time. For example, I would work on my spirit only or my body and soul only or my soul only, for example. The problem was that without a triune deliverance, there was always a part of me that was yet in bondage. This would eventually lead to overall bondage once again and a total sense of failure. Because I was receiving a partial deliverance, I would see a difference for a time, but it never lasted. Then the Holy Spirit revealed to me that in order to really be **TOTALLY AND COMPLETELY DELIVERED** from something, I must work on all three aspects of my person – spirit, soul and body – simultaneously.

I learned through that experience that it is very important to understand the fundamental make-up of humanity, before attempting to implement deliverance. So let me outline just a little bit about this. Your spirit is the true essence of who you are. It is the part of you that comes from Yahweh. This is the *"true" you*. Your soul consists of your intellect, desires and feelings. The soul is where all of your experiences and learning are processed and creates *your "personality"*. This is "the you that people meet". Your body is your physical vessel; literally your skin, hair, nails, bones, DNA – *you get the picture*. Your body is the house for your spirit and is the *"actual" you* that interacts with the physical world, using the five senses and physical chemical reactions.

Your physical brain processes facts that define *"actuality"*. Your soul produces the perception that defines your *"reality"*. However, it is your spirit that reveals *"undeniable truths"* to you. Your spirit steams live, information from the eternal realm – where the foundational principles of The Creator's TRUTH exists. Truth supersedes both fact and reality. The soul is responsible for creating unity and harmony in your being because it has access to both the physical and spiritual worlds. Since the soul is essentially the connector between those two realms, when initiating deliverance, you should begin in the *soul man*. In this way, you can most efficiently implement deliverance efforts that will affect your **entire triune being**.

After initially seeking deliverance in the soul man, you must not neglect to turn your attention to your *spirit man* and your *flesh man* as well. It is really a simultaneous relay of deliverance that is started off in the soul realm, when your desires begin to determine your course of action. You cannot get total deliverance in any one part of your being, without addressing the other parts as well. It becomes a cycle. As the soul is strengthened – it will enable the spirit to be strengthened – which will enable the body to be strengthened – which will then enable the soul to be strengthened even further, *and so on and so forth*. It is a cycle that will never end. Therefore, **absolute** deliverance is going to be **totally** dependent upon how well you balance out **the triune cycle** of the deliverance process, as is noted in the following scripture, *"[23]Now may the God of peace make you holy in every way, and may your whole spirit and soul and body be kept blameless until our Lord Jesus Christ comes again. (1 Thes 5:23, NLT)."*

So now that you understand that you must approach deliverance as the triune being that you are, we can explore some practical steps that can be taken in the quest for absolute deliverance. First, let me say this though; the word *'process'* is defined as *"a series of actions or operations conducing to an end"* (Merriam-WebsterCollegiate.com 12/05/2004). You do not just go to an anointed church service and come home **delivered** or recite a scripture every day for 30 days and get **delivered**. **DELIVERANCE IS A PROCESS, NOT AN EVENT.** It is a progressive work that once accomplished, must be maintained daily for the rest of your life. For this reason, as you read this part of the book and begin to go through the process that will be discussed, I do not want you to have any unrealistic expectations. Deliverance should definitely be approached with a sense of urgency, but should NOT be put on a timetable.

Do not go into this thinking that you must accomplish your goal within a certain amount of time. Instead, grasp hold of and understand the fact that in order for this to work, it has to be approached as a **total lifestyle change**. Do not focus on how fast or slow you are seeing results. <u>**Let your focus be on living a new life, for the rest of your life and forever transforming who you are.**</u> Furthermore, let your focus be toward the restoration of the *you* that Your Creator created you to be. It may seem discouraging at first and as if nothing is really changing, but there are changes occurring that you cannot yet discern. If you persevere and continue to pursue the Righteousness that is yours through Christ; one day suddenly, you will realize that you are no longer the same. You probably will not be able to pinpoint the exact day or hour that it happened, but you will know that you are a transformed person in The LORD, walking in newness of life!

What I want to share with you now is a synopsis of the 12 steps of deliverance that I write about, in the deliverance book I mentioned. Since we have already discussed approaching deliverance from a triune perspective, I categorize the process in this way as well. I do believe that the Holy Spirit has revealed the divine order of these 12 steps, and that is why I have numbered them. Ultimately though, you have to follow the course that the Holy Spirit sets for you specifically – allowing yourself to freely flow in Him, and work on all parts of your triune being simultaneously.

Each individual's needs are different. Their struggles are different. There are different levels of bondage and different degrees of relationship with The Father and knowledge of Yeshua and His Word. All of these factors, and some others as well, will have an effect on how you ensue *your process*. That is the wonderful thing about the Holy Spirit. He can customize a deliverance plan especially for you! These steps that I am going to outline should only serve as a **guideline** and not a rigid regimen. You never want to limit what The Father can do in your life. The Bible says that we only know in *part (1 Cor 13:9)*, and thus I can only share with you the *part* that I know. The Holy Spirit may want to reveal to you some things that He did not reveal to me, so it is important that you remain flexible and receptive to Him.

Deliverance for the Soul Man

Step 1 – Confession/Acknowledgement

The very first thing that you need to do is to acknowledge **within yourself** that you have a problem. This step is pretty straightforward and simple. This step is about being honest with yourself. You need to take a look at your life and evaluate the way you are living. Even though this step is *simple*, it may not be *easy*. It is hard to see who we really are sometimes.

Step 2 – Discovery

The second thing that needs to happen is the discovery of how demon spirits entered into your life. It is very important to take the time to evaluate the life events that led to your oppression. I have shared many of the stories that led to my dysfunction, and you can enjoy even more of my testimony in my other book, ***"STDs: Sexually Transmitted Demons"***. My list of reasons is very long... *But, guess what?* Everybody has a long list! Your list may be similar to mine, or it may be quite different, but **everyone has a list**. Discover what your list is because it is the things on that list that gives satan access to your life. No one turns out defective intentionally. Life events create openings, and this discovery process will give you the insight that you need to make sure those openings are closed forever. The four main entranceways for demons, and how you can close those entranceways are:

> **Generational curses** – These are demons passed through your family bloodline. Pray for the forgiveness of your family, even the dead ones. Renounce generational demons because they have no

right to afflict you, once you become a part of The LORD's family. Your bloodline has been changed!

Involuntary exposure – These are demons that you are exposed to *without choice*. This usually happens during childhood, but can happen on a job, through marriage or in any situation in which you do not have control over the environment. Renounce and bind these demons. Cover yourself in the Blood of Yeshua, and they will have to release you. They also have no right to afflict you.

Spiritual wounds – First you must make sure that you have implemented forgiveness and are free of bitterness. You must allow yourself to grieve. Grieving must be done in the presence of The Father, where you will be healed. Once healing has taken place, the demons will no longer have a place to reside within you. *(Read my article, "Have You Had a Good Cry Lately" http://drintimacy.wordpress.com/2011/12/13/have-you-had-a-good-cry-lately/).*

Voluntary exposure – This is when you make a **deliberate decision** to sin or put yourself in bad situations. This type of exposure gives satan the greatest access to your life because with voluntary exposure, **you invite him in**. This is also a form of witchcraft because you are deliberately rebelling against Yahweh. Ask for forgiveness, and make a commitment to change, in order to close the doors that you have opened through sin.

Step 3 – Renewing the mind

The mind must be renewed, in order for change to take place. Your mind is the **control center** of your being. The Bible tells us that we will be transformed, if we renew our minds *(Rom 12:2)*. Everything that you do begins with a thought. That is why, if you are planning on changing your behavior, you are going to have to start with changing the way that you think about things. You have to put the right things into your mind, and keep the wrong things out. Everything that you see, hear, touch, taste and smell has an impact on how you think. Renewing your mind in a way that will allow you to be transformed into the person that you want to become, is going to require you to keep your mind free of corruption. You can't watch sexual movies, listen to sexual songs, read sexual books, hang around sexual people, wear sexual clothes and expect to have pure thoughts! Don't kid yourself! Watch Christian programs, read your Bible, listen to Gospel music, go to church – *and this is especially important* – **Write, Read, Memorize** *and* **Recite** scriptures to strengthen your weaknesses!

Deliverance for the Spirit Man

Step 4 – Confession/Admittance

The first part of confession is between you and yourself. This second part of confession is **between you and God**. It is not enough to just "know" that you have a problem. Once you know, you need to confess your sins to Yahweh. The Bible says if you confess your sins to Him, He will be just and faithful to forgive you and cleanse you of all wickedness *(1 John 1:9)*. You can't be forgiven, if you don't first confess. And please, be real with Him when you make your confession. Don't beat around the bush and tell half-truths. He despises the pride that induces such false prayers. He already knows everything and is waiting to forgive and restore you, but you must be honest.

Step 5 – Penitence/Humility

The Bible says that Yahweh will not despise a contrite heart and a broken spirit *(Ps 51:17)*. This means that when you confess to Him, it needs to be done with brokenness and humility. Have you ever apologized to someone just because you were told to, but you weren't really sorry in your heart? That is what we do to The LORD sometimes! You WILL NOT experience deliverance, if you do not have brokenness and remorse for your sins. You have to really be sorrowful and willing to change. **TRUE REPENTANCE IS ALWAYS FOLLOWED BY CHANGE.**

Step 6 – Confession/Exposure

The first part of confession was between you and yourself; the second part was between you and Yah; this third part is **between you and other Believers**. You need to find another Christian, who is really living a clean life that won't gossip and knows how to pray. Let that person know about what is going on in your life. Telling someone else about your struggles is going to do two things: *1)* It is going to make you accountable for your actions; *2)* It will allow that person to be able to pray for you, in order to help strengthen you. **One of the main reasons people stay in bondage is because they have a victim mentality.** I love this quote: *"Life is 10% what happens to you and 90% how you respond to it!"* This is so true, so true, so true... Confess your faults to someone, and share with them your plans for change. Be accountable for your actions, as they pray for you. Cast down the victim mentality and **choose to be an overcomer!**

Step 7 – Forgiveness and Letting Go

DELIVERANCE CANNOT TAKE PLACE IF YOU REFUSE TO FORGIVE OTHERS because it will prevent The Father from healing you. It will also cause your heart to be hard and embittered, making it impossible for the Holy Spirit to work with it. Finally, it will deny you The LORD's forgiveness of your sins *(Mat 6:15, Luke 6:37)*, which will prevent you from connecting and fellowshipping with Him. If you want to be free – you are going to have to free other people. You have imprisoned people with your bitterness and unforgiveness. As long as you hold onto the past, your arms will be too full to embrace your future.

Step 8 – Spiritual Warfare: Putting on Your Spiritual Armor

This step is based on Ephesians 6:14: *"[10]A final word: Be strong in the Lord and in his mighty power. [11]Put on all of God's armor so that you will be able to stand firm against all strategies of the devil. [12]For we are not fighting against flesh-and-blood enemies, but against evil rulers and authorities of the unseen world, against mighty powers in this dark world, and against evil spirits in the heavenly places. [13]Therefore, put on every piece of God's armor so you will be able to resist the enemy in the* time of evil. Then after the battle you will still be standing firm. ¹⁴Stand your ground, putting on <u>the belt of truth</u> and <u>the body armor of God's righteousness</u>. ¹⁵<u>For shoes, put on the peace that comes from the Good News</u> so that you will be fully prepared. ¹⁶In addition to all of these, hold up <u>the shield of faith</u> to stop the fiery arrows of the devil. ¹⁷Put on <u>salvation as your helmet</u>... (Eph 6:10-17, NLT)" Your spiritual armor will be used to defend yourself from the attacks of the enemy:

The Belt of Truth for protecting yourself from the shame or guilt of your indecencies and sins, with the truth of The Father's Word concerning forgiveness and deliverance.

The Body Armor of Righteousness is for acquiring Righteousness through faith in Christ Yeshua, as your LORD and Savior, and thus covering your entire body in His protective Blood.

The Shoes of Peace will protect your feet with the truth and joy of the Gospel; knowing that you are a Born Again Believer; in a right place with Yahweh God and that He, through His Love for you, controls the outcome of your life. This will enable you to walk on the path of Righteousness, without hindrance, and stand on the battlefield without being moved.

The Shield of Faith will protect you from the fiery arrows of the enemy, which are specifically designed to attack you in your weak areas. Believing The LORD's Word is true, will assure you that Yahweh can keep you, even in your weaknesses.

The Helmet of Salvation is designed to protect your mind with the understanding that salvation is not a complete work until Yeshua returns, and will condition your mind to focus and endure until the end. "He who endures to the end, shall be saved. (Mat 10:22)"

Step 9 – Spiritual Warfare: Using Your Spiritual Weapons

This step is based on Ephesians 6:17 and 2 Corinthians 10:4. "...and take the sword of the Spirit, which is the word of God. (Eph 6:17b, NLT)" "For the weapons of our warfare are not physical [weapons of flesh and blood], but they are mighty before God for the overthrow and *destruction of strongholds, (2 Cor 10:4, AMP)"*. Yahweh has given us mighty weapons of attack that enable us to go after the enemy and defeat him:

The Sword of the Word is used for close combat. By speaking The LORD's Word, you can cut down every demonic influence in your life! Read it, study it, memorize it and become a skillful swordsman.

The Power of Praise can be used to confuse the enemy and render him defenseless. In his confusion, he will self-destruct and actually end up helping you, instead of hurting you! Praise ushers you into His presence *(Ps 100:4)* and when you are close to Him, He is close to you *(James 4:8)*. When you praise God, you bring Him right into your situation to defend you against satan.

Christian Fellowship can be used to come into agreement in prayer with other Believers or to absorb strength from the anointing of other Christian men and women, by just being in their presence, or through the laying on of hands. There is strength in numbers!

Praying and Fasting will be the most powerful weapon you have. Prayer is a direct link to The Father and is truly putting the battle in His hands. Fasting makes prayer more effective because it puts the flesh under subjection and makes you more submissive to the Holy Spirit, in order for Him to do the praying through you.

Taking Communion, which is partaking of The LORD's supper through the breaking of bread and the drinking of wine *(or juice)*, is the most powerful way to connect with Yeshua. It is the only way to **OBLITERATE** all sexual blood covenants and get a **COMPLETE SPIRITUAL DIVORCE** from all previous spouses and sex partners *(with their demons)*. Yeshua's Blood of the Covenant breaks all other covenants and connects you to Him intimately!!! *(Remember that we discussed communion in great detail in chapter 2 and at the end of chapter 16; re-read it to refresh your understanding of the power of communion.)*

Step 10 – Spiritual Warfare: Retreat and replenish

In every long war, there are times when the warriors must retreat and replenish themselves. It is important to step back from the warfare and just refresh your spirit in the pureness of worship, in Yahweh's presence. Don't burn yourself out. Even though it is called *"spiritual"* warfare, it still requires *"physical"* energy.

Deliverance for the Flesh Man

Step 11 – Discipline of the flesh

Deliverance in the flesh man is all about discipline. Most of us hate this word; I know that it was never one of my favorites *(smile)*. However, your flesh is really the least important entity in this process. Discipline is not so hard to achieve once you work through deliverance for the soul and the spirit. It is important to understand though that discipline is not *something that you **do***; it is a mindset and **_a nature_** *that you take on*. This is what you need to know about discipline:

> **Understanding Why Your Body Sins** is very important. You have to realize that your skin, muscles, hormones, bones, sex organs or any other parts of your body **CANNOT CONTROL YOU!** It is the sin nature of the flesh, which is the power of satan, that causes you to sin. The enemy is defeated; you can control your body through submitting to the Righteousness of Christ!
>
> **Understanding Self-Control** is the simple truth that discipline is all about self-control, **in subjection to the Holy Spirit**. Set small discipline goals for yourself *(i.e. five minutes of daily prayer; a three hour fast, twice a week; one scripture memorized daily)*, and pursue them consistently. At The Spirit's leading, slowly build on the foundation *(i.e. from five minutes to ten; from three hours to four, three times a week; from one scripture to two)*. Do not put too much emphasis on discipline, until you have implemented the steps for the spirit man and the soul man.

Step 12 – Walking after The Spirit

Once deliverance has taken place in your life, it must be maintained daily, by walking after The Spirit. Deliverance is not a once and for all deal. If you do not maintain it, you can lose it. Remember to protect the gateways to your mind. Keep them free of all contamination, corruption and sinful influences, by meditating on The LORD's Word constantly. This step is about how you live your life from day-to-day. It is about offering your body up as a living sacrifice to Yahweh God. It is about being a light in a dark world and not giving into the pressures of temptation. You have to be willing to be different; willing to stand out and do what Yeshua did when He was on the earth. Remember that people are always watching you, so you need to watch yourself!

With everything you do; every step you take; every word you speak; ask yourself... "Will this glorify God? Will this bless The God of Holiness?"

Four Fierce Obstacles You'll Face

I know that you are probably brimming with excitement by now. You are reading the last chapter of this book! You are full of the power of knowledge and ready to conquer the enemy of sexual perversion that has been afflicting you for so long. You are closer to victory now than you have ever been before. However, there are just a few more things that I want to let you know, before we wrap this up. Just the fact that you have read the book through to this last chapter shows your commitment and determination to get delivered, but there are many enemies to deliverance.

Other demonic spirits are going to try their hardest to prevent you from successfully completing this process. It is known by satan how important sexual purity and wholeness is to your spiritual development and enduring intimate relationship with Yahweh God. Thus, when he sees you trying to get free, he is going to work over time, often times sending his most powerful cohorts after you, to stop you from being liberated. I cannot list the name of every demon or vice the enemy might try to use against you, but I do want to at least highlight what I believe are the four most powerful enemies that you will face in the deliverance from sexual perversion, *(or any deliverance for that matter)*. They are as follows...

1. Loneliness

To be alone would mean that you are somewhere all by yourself. The word alone describes the state of your physical body being separated from other people. It can also denote a lack of interaction with other people, even though they may be nearby. However, loneliness is an internal condition. You can be in a room full of people and still experience loneliness. The truth that loneliness is an intrinsic condition is even indicated by the fact that we consider loneliness not to be a physical state of being, but instead an emotion. It can be just a temporary emotional condition, but it can also be a spirit that attacks you emotionally. In either case, loneliness is going to affect you emotionally, which means it is a condition not of the flesh but of the soul.

There are many emotions that can be detrimental to your walk with The Father and this deliverance process. This is true whether they are just sporadic emotional experiences or long-term demonic strongholds that manifest through certain emotions. Yet, I am emphasizing loneliness because **it is the deadliest of all of the emotions when it comes to deliverance from sexual perversion**. The lust for companionship can continually draw you back into perversion, or even keep you from ever leaving. In my own personal experience, this was definitely the case. There were so many times that I wanted to try, so many times that I began to walk the road of sexual purity, but loneliness was always the U-turn in the road.

The deception about using sexual perversion as a cure for loneliness is that I was trying to fix an internal problem, using an external remedy. It cannot be done. It was like trying to use a topical rub to heal a broken leg. The sex medicated me, but it did not cure me. When the medicine wore off, I was looking for another dose right away. I did not understand at that time of my life that only Yeshua can fill the loneliness void in a person's heart.

I do not think that there is anyone that does not feel lonely at times, but you need to be able to recognize when loneliness is no longer a fleeting emotional experience, but instead is a serious demonic stronghold. If you feel lonely the majority of the time, even feeling lonely when you are with other people, then you know that this is a stronghold in your life. If you are willing to engage in sinful activities, just to keep people around you so you will not have to be alone, you are bound by loneliness. If you are suffering from loneliness, it is partly because you do not like yourself and do not like to be in your own company.

The only – **THE ONE AND ONLY** – cure for loneliness, is to first of all, understand that Yeshua is the answer to your every need. Secondly, allow fellowship and oneness with Him to be your consuming desire. When your desire is for The LORD only, you will never feel lonely because He is always with you. As matter of fact, He lives right inside of you! That is why He says in the book of Hebrews 13:5 that He will never leave you or forsake you. Developing this type of understanding and desire for God is not going to happen overnight. It does take time. But if you recognize what the true remedy for loneliness is, you can pursue that remedy, instead of seeking out yet another *temporary loneliness pain killer*. Those pain killers never meet the expectation and lead to so much disappointment.

If you are suffering from loneliness, I know that it hurts, but you are going to have to keep fighting through the tears. *"Weeping may endure for a night but joy comes in the morning (Ps 30:5)"*. There is going to be a stage of this deliverance process when you are doing everything the book says you should be doing, and yet still not feel any better. But, keep on standing anyway. It will seem like you are going to be crushed under the pressure of loneliness, but persevere because as you do, you are going to draw closer to The Father and begin to enjoy the wholeness that only He can provide. There is no easy cure for loneliness, but the harder you seek Yahweh, the faster you will be healed. All of your spiritual armor and weapons will be needed, to help you win this battle with loneliness, but the best strategy for combating loneliness is to worship The King. That experience of intimacy with Him will obliterate any chance of loneliness being present in your life.

2. Anxiousness – Not Pacing Yourself

Anxiousness for deliverance will lead to frustration, and frustration will make you quit! Furthermore, not knowing how to pace yourself will put you on what I call *"the righteousness roller coaster"*. You will be *"Extraordinary Mega Christian"* one week, and the next week you will be *"Super Sin Sensation"*. You have to have balance in your life. This process is not a short-distance sprint, it is a long-distance marathon. <u>You need to map out a steady course and travel at a consistent pace</u>. You must take one step at a time, and rest along the way. I am not suggesting that you should not tenaciously and fervently pursue Righteousness. You certainly should. However, you should not be anxious about it. The Holy Spirit gave me a powerful one-liner that I say to myself when I begin to feel anxious. He said to me that **"Anxiousness is the enemy of preparation"**.

Anxiousness causes a chemical to be released in the body that interferes with mental clarity and focus. Thus for example, if you are anxious about taking the test, you are less likely to prepare well for it because you will be too nervous to concentrate on studying. Likewise, while you are so busy being anxious about deliverance, you will not be concentrating and focusing on what you need to do, in order to walk therein. Where there is anxiousness, there will be a deficit in preparation. So instead of being anxious, flow gracefully with the wind of the Holy Spirit. Do not put yourself on some rigorous deliverance regimen and be a slave driver over yourself, anxiously watching the clock to see if you have *arrived* yet. Such anxiousness will drive you nuts because the truth is that you will *be arriving* every day, for the rest of your life. No one truly *arrives,* until The Messiah our LORD *arrives* to take us home!

I have a personal testimony about deliverance from anxiousness. After I became Born Again, I used to really beat myself up over my personality flaws and some lingering sinful behaviors. I had so many personality flaws that I just could not stand myself. I would so often make these long, long lists of all of my faults. Making the lists would take hours sometimes. Then I would create these strict fasts and long consecrations to go on, determined to overcome ALL of my faults during that time. When I would initially implement the regimen, I would be really enthused about it. I would be really on fire and full of zeal. But, as I would anxiously check the calendar every day, wondering how much longer before I was going to see results, I would become frustrated.

The over exertion of energy that I expelled in the beginning, would leave me lethargic very quickly. It would not be long before I would abandon the assignment; slump into a defeated mindset; meditate on my failure and flaws until I got sick of myself; lose all of my strength and fall into sin and depression. I would then start the entire exhausting cycle all over again! The Father began to deal with me about this anxiousness. He told me to get off of the righteousness roller coaster, stop being anxious, stop creating these ridiculous regimens and to just **enjoy my relationship with Him**.

So I did just that. I did not make any more lists, but instead learned how to move in His Spirit. He knew when I should fast, when I should pray, when I should go to church and when I should stay home. I submitted to the Holy Spirit and stopped marking off the days. Sometime later, as I was reading through one of my old journals, I saw one of those lists. I read the list and was amazed to see that nearly every personality fault and area of sinful struggle I had written down had been changed! Yah did it, and I did not have to be anxious about it! I just made the right preparations, and He stepped in and made the changes. Now I know firsthand that The LORD does not need my anxiousness to get it done.

I simply learned how to pace myself. I repented for my daily failures, and I thanked Yeshua for my daily victories. The failures became fewer and the victories became more. Remember that you have been chosen to bear fruit that remains. The fruit of the Spirit is love, joy, peace, **<u>patience</u>**... Where there is anxiousness, there is not going to be the forbearance that comes with love; you will not have joy; you will not be at peace, and undoubtedly you will fall short on patience. **Relax!!!** You already know that victory is waiting *(it is not going anywhere, it is **waiting**)* for you, at the end of the road. Allow yourself to enjoy the journey as you travel there!

3. The Frustration of Failure

Another great enemy that you will face that brings about discouragement is failure. There are many failures in life, but I am talking specifically about you failing yourself. As far as this deliverance process is concerned, the failure that I am talking about is you falling into sin – failing to continually walk in uprightness. I can remember certain times going through this deliverance process; I used to feel so rotten when I messed up. There were many times that I just abandoned the entire pursuit because of one fall. What I did not understand then is that **falling is a natural part of learning how to walk**. We can learn this even from observing a baby. They fall many times when they are learning how to walk. Sometimes they cry, sometimes they get frustrated, but always they get up and keep on trying, until they master the skill of walking uprightly.

Spiritual growth works the same way. You will fall along the way. Part of what makes these falls so seemingly unbearable is *the struggle to achieve Holiness through your own works*. If you continue to engage in this struggle, frustration and discouragement will certainly set in. When you feel like it is **your responsibility to be Holy**, you cannot handle falling. What you do not understand is that <u>you need to fall</u>. The Bible tells us that *"…a righteous man falls seven times and rises again, but the wicked are overthrown by calamity (Pro 24:16, AMP)."*

Notice that the scripture says *a Righteous man falls*; not a wicked man but a Righteous man. Seven is the number of completion and perfection. The revelation of this scripture is that The LORD is going to allow you to fall as many times as it takes, for you to be perfected in this area of your life and completely delivered! The scripture we just read could have just as easily been translated as,

"Yahweh's chosen children will fall as many times as is necessary to be perfected, but each time they will get up, and in the end will remain standing surefooted on the path of Righteousness..."

It is not bad to fall. It is only a problem when you stay down. Only the wicked wallow in sin, making excuses as to why they cannot get up. That is why the scripture says that the wicked are overthrown by calamity. They do not get up. The very fact that you feel convicted about falling shows how Righteous you really are. Once the Holy Spirit begins to control your life, you cannot stand to stay in sin. You just want to get up as quickly as you can. If you were not giving your ear to the Holy Spirit, you would not even care.

Paul tells us that we all have sinned and fallen short of the glory of God *(Rom 3:23),* and he was not talking to wicked people when he said this. He was talking to Christians. We are all going to fall sometimes, but falling is often times the best way to learn and the very best way to ensure that once you are fully delivered, you never turn back to sin. So do not FOCUS on *'not falling'* or *'not sinning'*. Sin is unrighteousness, and therefore, if your focus is on *'not sinning'*, you are actually focusing on unrighteousness and the works of satan. Your constant meditation should be of The LORD. Therefore, let your focus be on building your relationship with Him and becoming one with Yeshua, and thus being consumed by His nature. As you pursue Righteousness and intimate relationship with The LORD, *'not sinning'* will be the natural, subsequent end result.

You cannot continue in sin, when you are one with The Father. Then too, no matter how uprightly you may be walking, your light is always going to show itself dim, in comparison to the Light of the Holy One. The closer you get to the mark, the more you realize how far away from it you really are. So if your focus is on *"never falling"* or *"trying to be perfect"*, you will surely be discouraged. Know too that *"...all things happen just as he decided long ago. (Eph 1:10)"* Even Yahweh allowing you to fall has been carefully designed by Him, to fulfill His ultimate will. Just imagine if He had not allowed me to fall seven times. Would I have been able to write this book? If this book has touched your life, it is only because of how I am being perfected through falling, in the areas that I have written about.

When you fall, do not be discouraged. Instead, receive The Father's forgiveness **quickly**; know that His grace is sufficient for you *(2 Cor 12:9)*; get up, and continue on in the pursuit of deliverance. Encourage yourself by thinking on The LORD's goodness in your life, the many blessings He has blessed you with and the progress that you have made so far. Meditate on the vision of you walking victoriously in deliverance. See the day that you fall in this area no more, and just praise God for it now. **Praising The Most High is the most awesome cure for discouragement.** It is an instant high for your soul that never gets old and will not leave you with a hangover! Discouragement will not stand a chance in the midst of your praise!

4. Disappointment with God

Finally, I believe that the number one enemy to the deliverance process is going to be another kind of discouragement. Discouragement can enter into our lives through many channels, but I believe that the most detrimental path is when we experience disappointment toward The LORD. When you feel like God has let you down, you are in a dangerous place spiritually. I do not know if you have ever felt this way toward The LORD. You may feel this way even now, or might in the future, so we need to talk about this because this will definitely sabotage the deliverance process.

First of all, let me say that I believe that it is a normal part of your spiritual development to feel disappointed with Yah. The Father often times does not do what we want Him to, and this can be upsetting. The Creator never makes any mistakes and always does what is best, but the Bible teaches us that His ways are higher than our ways and that we cannot understand His plans *(Isa 55:9)*. It takes a lot of spiritual maturity to understand and accept the Sovereignty of Yahweh God and until you do, you are going to feel let down when He does not do what you want Him to.

Yahweh is <u>The</u> Sovereign God. He can do whatever He wants to; whenever He wants to; however He wants to. He does not have to consult with anyone, and He is justified in all that He does – **POINT BLANK** *(Rom 11:34-36)*! That is not always easy to accept when you feel like you need Him to do something for you, and you know that He has the power to do it, but yet He does not do it. The LORD's unwillingness to answer certain prayers in your life is an even greater let down, when you are serving Him the best way that you can and giving Him your all. When you fall into this category, you sometimes feel like you *deserve* to have your prayers answered.

Why did that close loved one die, even though you prayed? Why did God allow you to be raped or abused? Why didn't you get the job or the house or the spouse or the money to go to college? These are legitimate needs and desires, and yet The LORD did not come through for you. It can be so bewildering. There are good reasons that these things happen, but most often times only The LORD Himself understands those reasons. Not understanding His reasons can leave you confused and disappointed.

The greatest danger in feeling disappointment toward The LORD is that if that disappointment is not resolved, it will lead to anger. So many people are angry and bitter toward Yahweh, and once you become angry at God, you are no longer interested in what will please Him. No one really wants to please someone who has hurt and angered them. That is why **<u>THIS DELIVERANCE PROCESS CAN BE COMPLETELY DEVASTATED THROUGH DISAPPOINTMENT TOWARD The Father</u>**. The entire process is centered on building a relationship with and pleasing Him. If you have no desire to please Him, you will not have the heart to continue on in this process. When you are angry at another person, you may often purposely try to inflict emotional pain upon that person, as vengeance. Pleasing the person is usually the last thing on your mind. In the same manner, you may try to hurt Your Creator by living sinfully, in order to 'get back at Him'.

I am going to say to you again that you need to understand that **<u>YAHWEH is Sovereign</u>**. All of creation is His; He made it, and He still holds the owner's certificate. I do not care how uprightly you are living; **YAHWEH DOES NOT OWE YOU ANYTHING**. Even your ability to walk uprightly, belongs to Him! Everything is His – *your service, prayers, worship* – whatever you consider yourself to be *"doing for The LORD"* all belongs to Him anyway. I do not care how many injustices or hardships you have suffered in your lifetime. **<u>The LORD owes you nothing!!!</u>**

You also have to realize that many of your prayers are not in line with His will. They do not fit His plan or help to fulfill His purposes. You need to understand this, in order to be able to accept His decisions. He loves you. He wants what is best for you, yet He also has an entire universe to manage – every life and happening on this planet affects the balance of the entire universe and all of time. That is a rather big job *(not for Him but certainly for us)*! So how can anyone be arrogant enough to think that they know what is best, more so than Elohim, The God Who Created All Things?

Your desires and your prayers are based on what you know about yourself, your family, your friends, your past, your ideas about the future, your living environment – in other words, *your prayers are based on what you want and your very limited knowledge of life and the world*. There are so many other factors to consider, so many things that you do not know. Yahweh has to operate based on what is best for all of creation; not based on what will make you happy! That is why we learn that His ways are higher than our ways and that no one can understand the scope of His great plan. He has a divine plan for creation, and your desires are not always conducive to the coming to pass of His perfect plan.

Suffering on earth is a part of what helps us to understand our need for The LORD, His goodness, satan's wickedness and why I AM is due all the glory, honor and praise. Therefore, we will all experience our share of suffering, but He will never allow you to suffer beyond what you can handle. Quite truly, the more you suffer, the more you can know that The Father has made you strong and placed a great mantle on your life. Understanding this, and seeking to love The LORD more, is the only thing that is going to heal you of the disappointment that comes when He does not answer your prayers or allows painful occurrences in your life. Sometimes the Holy Spirit will tell you *'why'*, but often times He will not. You have to learn to just trust Him. You have to be **willing** to let Him use your life to bring Him glory, no matter what that means. Yeshua suffered more than us all, but He never turned His back on The Father. He understood that His suffering brought The Father glory.

It is OK to feel disappointed, but it is not OK to become bitter toward Your King. You have to be certain that He loves you. The way that you can be certain of His love for you is simply by remembering that He gave His very own, one and only begotten Son to die, in order to save your life. Would you sacrifice one of your children to die a gruesome, painful death for someone who hates you and treats you badly? I know that I wouldn't! But Yahweh did it for you, so you know for sure that He does indeed love you. Sometimes you need to just stop trying to figure out *'why'*, and rest in His love for you and His Omniscient ability to successfully manage what He has created. Allow Him to comfort you, and you will be fine. This is how you can close the entranceway of disappointment.

Moving Forward in Freedom

Sexual sin is one of the hardest sins to be liberated from. It sometimes seems impossible that you will ever be able to be freed from these spirits. But now you know that it is not impossible and that <u>**you can walk in total liberty and victory!**</u> You have learned so much and are now so full of knowledge about living victoriously. But now that you have acquired and apprehended the knowledge, **YOU MUST APPLY IT**. I admonish you to remember the importance of a triune deliverance and working simultaneously on ALL of your being. The spirit, soul and body are all directly linked. What you do in one, will affect the others.

Also, please do not forget to be mindful of the fact that **DISCONTINUING AN ACT OF SIN PHYSICALLY, DOES NOT NECESSARILY MEAN THAT YOU ARE DELIVERED FROM THAT SPIRIT**. True and absolute deliverance must consist of these five manifestations:

1) No longer committing the physical acts.
2) No longer exhibiting the personality and spiritual characteristics.
3) No longer *struggling* with the temptation.
4) Being able to boldly share with others what The LORD has delivered you from.
5) Being hated and/or revered by demons of sexual perversion and those whom they operate through.

Consistently monitor your behavior, to be sure that these spirits are not still operating in your life. This is important because as you have already learned, satan's primary goal in introducing sexual sin was to distort our intimate relationship with The LORD. So, **get delivered from the spirit, not just the act**. I say this especially to you who are married and those of you who would consider yourselves to be sanctified. You may have been reading this book just so you could learn how to help others, but be sure that you yourself do not have these spirits operating in your life, interfering with your interactions with other Believers and your intimate relationship with The Father.

AND HERE IS A WARNING FOR EVERYONE: REGARDLESS OF WHERE WE ARE IN THIS PROCESS RIGHT NOW, WE ALL HAVE TO ALWAYS KEEP BEFORE US THE FACT THAT WE WILL NEVER BE FREE OF THE WARFARE BETWEEN OUR FLESH AND THE HOLY SPIRIT. DELIVERANCE, ONCE ACCOMPLISHED, MUST BE MAINTAINED DAILY. IT IS NOT A ONCE AND FOR ALL DEAL! WALK AFTER THE SPIRIT ALWAYS, AND DO NOT MAKE THE MISTAKE OF GETTING DELIVERED AND THEN FALLING ASLEEP. *WATCH AND PRAY CONSTANTLY, SO THAT YOU WILL NOT FALL INTO TEMPTATION AND BE ONCE AGAIN ENTANGLED WITH WHAT YOU HAVE BEEN DELIVERED FROM!* (MAT 26:41, Gal 5:1).

A Final Prayer

Now close your eyes as you read this prayer. *(I'm just kidding. You can't read and close your eyes at the same time! Laugh.)* Seriously though, read this prayer **out loud** and move further into your journey to victorious freedom and newness, knowing that the Spirit of Yeshua is with you!!!

Father Yahweh, I thank you for this book. I thank You LORD for providing a way through which I can see the Light of Your truth. I ask You LORD to forgive me for all of my sins, Father. Please allow Your Holy Spirit to lead me, as I commit myself to getting totally delivered from every spirit of sexual perversion that operates in my life. Expose and heal every entrance wound Father. Give me the boldness, desire, zeal and endurance to complete every step of this process, without leaving anything undone. I thank you now for your grace Father. I don't plan on sinning anymore but if I do fall, I commit to receive your forgiveness and get up immediately and continue to seek your face Yahweh. You know My LORD that my intimate relationship with You has been perverted because of these demons in my life. Please restore me back to proper intimacy with You oh LORD. I will give Your Name the praise always and with Your help will boldly tell of Your deliverance in my life, once it is complete, so that I may help others, even as Dr. Intimacy has helped me. In Yeshua's (Jesus') mighty name, I pray these things, in the power of Your Holy Spirit and know that because it is a prayer prayed according to Your will that every word of it is already answered and will be completely manifested in my life. Amen. HalleluYAH!

Epilogue

Start a New Life Today!

Being a Born Again Believer in Yeshua (Jesus), Resurrected Savior, Son of the Living God, is the prerequisite to deliverance!

So many wonderful truths have been presented throughout this book. However, the most wonderful truth of all is Yeshua (Jesus) the Messiah! Yahweh God saves, but the promises of redemption, deliverance and salvation only belong to Born Again Believers in His Son. If you are not Born Again, you will not be able to move forward in the deliverance process. You must be a Born Again Believer in Yeshua Ha-Mashiach, in order to truly live a life of freedom. The ultimate purpose and destiny of every human being is to be re-connected to the God that created them. The pathway to Yahweh God is through his Son Jesus Christ, or as He was originally named – Yeshua. The Bible says that the only way to have a relationship with The Father, whose name is Yahweh, is through His son Yeshua. So how do you become Born Again? You must: KNOW, BELIEVE, ACCEPT and SERVE.

First, you must **KNOW** who Yeshua is. Yeshua is the Holy and sinless Son of Yahweh God. He is the Messiah, The Savior of all humanity. The Bible teaches us that The Father and the Son are one, and so although Yeshua is the Son; He is God.

Second, you must **BELIEVE** the truth of the Gospel. Yeshua was born by the virgin Mary. She conceived Him by the Holy Spirit and not a man. Yeshua lived on the earth and performed great miracles as the Anointed One of God. He then willingly gave His life up, by being sacrificed on the cross. He shed His Blood for your sins. He died and after three days, He was risen from the dead. After being risen, He stayed on the earth for 40 days and then ascended back into heaven to sit on the throne at the right hand of The Father.

Third, you must **ACCEPT** Yeshua as your personal Savior and Messiah. In order to accept Yeshua as your personal Savior, you must confess out loud with your mouth what you KNOW about Him and what you BELIEVE about him. You must also confess that you are a sinner and that you need to be saved. You must ask The Father for forgiveness in Yeshua's Name and be willing to change. You must invite Yahweh into your heart to be your Savior

Fourth, you must **SERVE**. The proof is in the pudding! If you really are Born Again, then you will allow Yeshua to be not only your Savior, but also your LORD. That means that you commit to let Him have control over your life from now on. It does not mean that you will never make a mistake, but you must live each day to serve Him from now on.

So, are you ready to get Born Again? Great! Then just say your own prayer to Yahweh God as I told you to do in the ACCEPT step – what you know about Him; what you believe about Him; the forgiveness that need from Him; what you need Him to do in your life and heart. He'll give you the words to pray. Congratulations on becoming a part of the greatest clique on earth – The Body of Christ. Find a good church to go to and get baptized. Read your Bible and pray every day. I pray for you right now for the baptism of the Holy Spirit, with the evidence of speaking in tongues. Below are some scriptures to get you started!

"[3]*Jesus answered him, I assure you, most solemnly I tell you, that unless a person is born again (anew, from above), he cannot ever see (know, be acquainted with, and experience) the Kingdom of God. (John 3:3, AMP)"*

[14]*And just as Moses lifted up the serpent in the desert [on a pole], so must [so it is necessary that] the Son of Man be lifted up [on the cross],* [15]*In order that everyone who believes in Him (Yeshua) [who cleaves to Him, trusts Him, and relies on Him] may not perish, but have eternal life and [actually] live forever!* [16]*For God so greatly loved and dearly prized the world that He [even] gave up His only begotten (unique) Son, so that whoever believes in (trusts in, clings to, relies on) Him shall not perish (come to destruction, be lost) but have eternal (everlasting) life.*

"¹⁷For God did not send the Son into the world in order to judge (to reject, to condemn, to pass sentence on) the world, but that the world might find salvation and be made safe and sound through Him. (John 3:14-17, AMP)"

"Therefore He is able also to save to the uttermost (completely, perfectly, finally, and for all time and eternity) those who come to God through Him, since He is always living to make petition to God and intercede with Him and intervene for them. (Heb 7:25, AMP)"

"For it is by believing in your heart that you are made right with God, and it is by confessing with your mouth that you are saved. (Rom 10:10)"

"But if we confess our sins to Him, He is faithful and just to forgive us and to cleanse us from every wrong. (1 John 1:9)"

"And so, dear brothers and sisters, I plead with you to give your bodies to God. Let them be a living and Holy sacrifice – the kind he will accept. When you think of what he has done for you, is this too much to ask? (Rom 12:1)"

"If you [really] love Me, you will keep (obey) My commands. (John 14:15, AMP)"

"¹⁵And then he told them, "Go into all the world and preach the Good News to everyone, everywhere. ¹⁶Anyone who believes and is baptized will be saved. But anyone who refuses to believe will be condemned. (Mark 16:15-16)"

"John baptized with water, but in just a few days you will be baptized with the Holy Spirit. (Acts 1:5)"

"Peter replied, 'Each of you must turn from your sins and turn to God, and be baptized in the name of Jesus Christ for the forgiveness of your sins. Then you will receive the gift of the Holy Spirit.' (Acts 2:38)"

"⁹But you are not controlled by your sinful nature. 'You are controlled by the Spirit if you have the Spirit of Jesus living in you. (And remember that those who don't have the Spirit of Christ living in them are not Christians at all.)' (Rom 8:9)"

Please leave a comment on my website "guest book" or e-mail me to let me know that you have become BORN AGAIN! All of my contact info can be found on my website <u>www.drintimacy.com</u>!

Personal Notes

"STDs: Sexually Transmitted Demons", gives a raw and gritty account of the damaging spiritual side effects of illicit sexual behavior. It is quick and fun but – POWERFUL! A must read for every teenager and every adult that has a teenager or has ever been one! **THIS WILL CHANGE HOW YOU THINK ABOUT SEX FOREVER!** Get STDs for only $10 – A special just for reading this book – at *www.drintimacy.com/STDs_TY_Special.html*!

I Am Victoriously Free!

After being abused
I was lost and confused
But I am Victoriously Free!

My heart badly trampled
My life was in shambles
But I am Victoriously Free!

Though in hopeless despair
Did nobody care
But I am Victoriously Free!

Because of betrayal and lies
I learned to despise
But I am Victoriously Free!

I became wayward and wild
In my – inner child
But I am Victoriously Free!

My choices were wrong
And my suffering was long
But I am Victoriously Free!

In darkness I cried
In spirit I died
But Yeshua replied
And restored me inside
So I am Victoriously Free!

Because Yah reached His Hand
In Light I now stand
And I am Victoriously Free!

I'd love to connect with you!
Please visit my website!

Find all of my social media links and donation infomration on the site. Thanks for your support. ***www.drintimacy.com***

www.ingramcontent.com/pod-product-compliance
Lightning Source LLC
Chambersburg PA
CBHW070750230426
43665CB00017B/2324